FEARLESS CRITIC

SEATTLE
RESTAURANT
GUIDE

WWW.FEARLESSCRITIC.COM/SEATTLE

Also from **Fearless Critic**

The Wine Trials 2011: 175 wines under $15 that beat out
$50-150 bottles in brown-bag blind tastings

The Beer Trials: the essential guide to
the world's most popular beers

Fearless Critic San Antonio Restaurant Guide

Fearless Critic Portland Restaurant Guide

Fearless Critic Washington DC Restaurant Guide

Fearless Critic Houston Restaurant Guide

Fearless Critic Austin Restaurant Guide

Fearless Critic New Haven Restaurant Guide

On **fearlesscritic.com**

For everyone: sortable lists and ratings, what's open now,
new reviews, daily rotating reviews, and more

For subscribers: the entire text of Fearless Critic

First edition, 2011

Printed in the United States of America

10 9 8 7 6 5 4 3 2 1

ISBN 978-1-60816-019-8

Contents

Fearless Critics

Robin Goldstein, Editor-in-Chief
Alexis Herschkowitsch, Associate Publisher
Kent Wang, Chief Technology Officer
Erin McReynolds, Editor
Justin Yu, Executive Chef
Tim Palin, Graphic Designer
Evan O'Neil, Graphic Designer

Contributing editors

Andrea Armeni, Barry Goldstein, Jacob Katz, David Menschel, Clare
Murumba, Susan Stubbs, Hal Stubbs, Lu Stubbs

Special thanks

Fearless Critic would like to thank Ed Cavazos, Leslie Doherty, Julian
Faulkner, Andrea Fleck-Nisbet, Andrew Gajkowski, Barry Goldstein,
Rosie Goldstein, Shannon Kelly, Kurtis Lowe, Jenny Mandel, David Matt,
Clare Murumba, Colleen Owens, Jill Owens, Steven Pace, Judy Peck,
Michael Powell, Marci Saunders, April Savard, Walter Schmamp,
Giuliano Stiglitz, Hal Stubbs, Lu Stubbs, Susan Stubbs, Frank Tasty,
Heather Tietgens, Chris Tudor, Katie Tudor, Mike Vago, Sara Vielma-Bay,
Tyce Walters, Walter Weintz, Peter Workman, the Yale Entrepreneurial
Society, and the staff at Workman Publishing.

About the managing editorial team

Robin Goldstein is the founder and editor-in-chief of the *Fearless Critic* series, a contributing writer to the *New York Times* Freakonomics blog, and a visiting scholar in behavioral economics at the University of California, Berkeley, where he studies food and wine perception. He has authored six books of restaurant reviews and has written for more than 30 *Fodor's* travel guides, from Italy to Thailand, Argentina to Hong Kong. Robin is a graduate of Harvard University and the Yale Law School. He has a certificate in cooking from the French Culinary Institute in New York and a WSET advanced wine and spirits certificate.

Alexis Herschkowitsch has written for *The Wine Trials,* five *Fearless Critic* guides, and five *Fodor's* travel guides, from El Salvador to Thailand. Alexis is a graduate of the University of Texas at Austin and has a WSET advanced wine and spirits certificate.

About the Seattle editors

Carissa Bluestone has edited and contributed to dozens of travel guides. She's written about Seattle for *Fodor's*, Concierge.com, and TravelandLeisure.com. She co-edited and contributed to *Worldchanging: A User's Guide for the 21st Century* and has written about sustainable tourism and food systems for Worldchanging.com.

Jay Friedman combines food writing with his other life as a sex educator: he writes a regular "Hot Plate" column about sex and food for *Edible Seattle* and a weekly "Sexy Feast" column for *Seattle Weekly*'s Voracious blog, which gives a lesson in love learned from a restaurant dish. He is also the food editor at TheSunbreak.com, a blogger (Gastrolust.com) and an avid cook who likes to make kimchi, xiao long bao, or anything with offal.

About the panel of Seattle critics

Patricia & John Eddy run CookLocal.com, where they cook with local and seasonal ingredients from Seattle's farmers' markets. Their hope is that one day cooking local won't be just a trend, but a common way of life.

Ed Essey, dubbed a "professional diner," learns languages for their culinary utility (e.g. Cantonese), visits the aquarium to work up an appetite for a sushi meal, spent a summer as a competitive wine taster, and is as equally happy with a delicious bowl of street noodles as with a molecular gastonomist's 10-course degustation.

Morgan Greenseth has become deeply involved in the local food community since landing in Seattle. When not designing commercial interiors for Dynamik Space, she's cooking for her business Mini Empire Bakery or volunteering with community-enrichment projects like the People's Parking Lot and urban farming collective Alleycat Acres.

Scott Heimendinger is a Microsoftee by day and DIY molecular gastronomist by night. He believes in making modernist cooking techniques available to home cooks without having to spend thousands on pricy equipment.

Heidi Leigh Johansen is a Seattle native, editor, and travel writer whose clients include *Fodor's* travel guides. Her travels have allowed her to sample cuisines across the globe, from camarones a la diabla near Zihuatanejo to chili-pepper crawfish on Beijing's Ghost Street.

Kanako Koizumi is a personal chef who teaches classes on Japanese home cooking for PCC Cooks. She is also a food writer and restaurant reviewer for *YouMaga* magazine.

Brandon Krebs has worked for a local wine distributor/importer for eight years and has eaten at most of the restaurants in the city. He spends a lot of his free time cooking at home, drawing on his travels and years spent living in France.

Chelsea Lin is the current editor for Citysearch Seattle, and enjoys writing about, eating in, and sharing all aspects of her new Pacific Northwest city.

Michael Natkin is a Seattle-based cook with experience in some of the city's best restaurants. His blog, Herbivoracious.com, is a destination for high-quality vegetarian recipes and food photography.

The Surly Gourmand quickly obtained food-blogging notoriety when he started Surlygourmand.blogspot.com to complain about the best restaurants in Seattle. Despite his reputation as a rascal, he's since landed gigs writing for more reputable publications such as *Seattle Weekly* and *Seattle Metropolitan* Magazine.

Michael Tamayo has an extensive knowledge of bad food: he's an elementary school teacher in the Central District. When not consuming square pizzas and tater tots, he searches the city for Filipino home cooking and the perfect sandwich.

Lorna Yee is the co-author of *The Newlywed Kitchen: Delicious Meals for Couples Cooking Together*, and a food writer at Seattle Magazine. She blogs at CookingThroughChina.com, which details her at-home culinary adventures, from dumplings to Taiwanese beef noodle soup.

Rocky Yeh is a bon vivant who goes around eating and drinking everything that sounds good, and trying to make a living at it—or at least not go into his eyeballs in debt.

Ratings and reviews represent a council consensus; no council member is individually responsible for the rating or review of any single restaurant. Differences of opinion are resolved by the editors, and are not necessarily endorsed by individual council members. Fearless Critics and Council members are not allowed to participate in the reviews, ratings, or evaluations of restaurants with which they are or ever have been associated or have any personal ties

The Fearless Critic system

If you're not familiar with the Fearless Critic style and philosophy, then welcome to a new kind of restaurant guide. Within these pages are 250 relentlessly opinionated full-page reviews of places to eat in the greater Seattle area. We do not accept advertising from dining establishments, chefs, or restaurateurs.

We evaluate restaurants incognito, and we pay for our own meals. Most reviews are informed by years of repeat visits by our Fearless Critic panel, a team of local food nerds, chefs, critics, and writers who have been dining intensively in Seattle for years.

In order to qualify for inclusion in this book, an establishment must serve food and be relevant to readers, whether for positive or negative reasons. Some restaurants that didn't make the cut for this book will have online reviews posted at www.fearlesscritic.com/seattle. We encourage you to let us know about places we might have missed by emailing us at fearless@fearlesscritic.com, so that they might be included in the next edition.

Brutally honest

As you might guess from the name of the book, Fearless Critic is brutally honest. We tell you exactly what we'd tell a good friend if she called us up and asked what we really thought of a place. Although some have called us "scathing," it is not our goal to stir controversy or insult restaurants.

We do believe, however, that in a world of advertorials and user-generated review websites, restaurant consumers deserve a hard-nosed advocate that can deliver the unapologetic, unvarnished truth. We hope to help you decide where to eat, and also where not to eat.

Therein, we believe, lies much of the usefulness of food criticism. For how is one to choose between two places if both are portrayed in dizzying, worshipful prose? Or if you don't know if the review you're reading is written by a real critic, or by the restaurant owner's brother?

And how frustrating is it when you spend a lot of your hard-earned money on a restaurant for a special occasion or date on the strength of what turns out to have been a sugar-coated review?

We aim for a punchy evaluation of a restaurant's strengths and weaknesses that ends with a clear judgment and recommendation. We hope that the money you've spent on this book will save you from wasting hundreds of dollars on boring meals. In short, our duty is to our readers, not to the restaurants. We don't expect you to agree with everything we say, but we do hope that you will give us the chance to earn your trust over the course of its 250 reviews. Whether you concur or dissent, we would love to hear from you. Engaging feedback makes our jobs worthwhile. Visit us at fearlesscritic.com to post your own opinions, or your thoughts on ours.

The rating scale

Two or more numerical ratings are assigned to most establishments. Ratings are not assigned to bakeries, groceries, markets, sweets shops, or other establishments that don't serve full meals.

Food rating (1 to 10 in increments of 0.5): This is a measure of the pure deliciousness of the food on offer. We close our eyes to reputation, price, and puffery when we taste, so don't be surprised to find a greasy spoon outscoring a historic, upscale, sit-down establishment, for one simple reason: the food just tastes better. Ambition and creativity are rewarded, but only if they also translate to deliciousness. A food score above 8 constitutes a recommendation; a 9 or above is a high recommendation. Don't expect grade inflation here.

Feel rating (1 to 10 in increments of 0.5): Rather than counting the number of pieces of silverware on the table or the number of minutes and seconds before the food arrives, we ask ourselves a simple question: does being here make us happy? Does the staff make us feel good? The most emphatic "yes" inspires the highest rating. We don't give out points for tablecloths or tuxedos. We reward warm lighting, comfortable seating, a finely realized theme, a strong sense of place or tradition, and a staff that's welcoming, professional, and contagiously enthusiastic about the food they're serving.

Wine rating (1 to 10 in increments of 0.5): Breadth, care of selection, and price are included in these ratings. More points are not necessarily awarded for the sheer number of wines served. The criteria used for these ratings are explained more fully in the "lists" section, where our rankings appear.

Neighborhoods

We have divided the city of Seattle into the neighborhoods delineated below. Outside the city limits, the municipality name (e.g. Issaquah, Bellevue, Edmonds) is listed in lieu of the neighborhood name.

Ballard: From Shilshole Bay to 8th Avenue NW and from N. 45th Street to NW 80th Street. Encompasses sub-neighborhoods Sunset Hill, Loyal Heights, and Whittier Heights.

Beacon Hill: Stretches east from I–5 to Rainier Avenue S/MLK Jr. Way S. and north from S. Norfolk Street to S. Dearborn Street. Part of the larger area known as South Seattle.

Belltown: Adjacent to Downtown, north from Virginia Street to Denny Way, east from the waterfront to Boren Avenue.

Capitol Hill: Directly east of I–5 from Downtown, stretching east to 23rd Avenue. North from Madison Street to the Volunteer Park area. The commercial core of the neighborhood is referred to the Pike–Pine Corridor or just Pike–Pine.

Central District (C.D.): Stretches east from 14th Avenue to Martin Luther King Jr. Way (MLK) and north from E. Yesler Way to E. Union St. This encompasses First Hill, an area south of Madison Street and east of I-5 around Swedish and Harborview medical centers and the Seattle University campus.

Downtown: Stretching north from Yesler Way to Virginia Street, east from the waterfront to Boren Avenue.

Eastlake: The eastern shore of Lake Union north of Aloha Street.

Eastside: The official name for Seattle's eastern 'burbs, this encompasses the towns of Kirkland, Redmond, Issaquah, and Woodinville. Kirkland is on the eastern shore of Lake Washington, with Redmond next door and Woodinville to the north. Issaquah is the farthest town from Seattle, off of I-90. The city of Bellevue, while technically part of the Eastside, has a large enough dining scene to warrant its own category.

Fremont: Directly north of the Lake Washington Ship Canal on the western side of Aurora Avenue (Rte. 99). Stretches west to Leary Way NW and north to N. 45th Street. Includes the area around Leary Way between Fremont and Ballard known as "Free-lard."

Georgetown: Industrial neighborhood starting south of the West Seattle Bridge and stretching to Boeing Airfield. Stretches east from E. Marginal Way to I–5.

Green Lake: Area directly around Green Lake. Southern border is N. 50th Street, northern border is N. 80th Street.

International District (I.D.): South from Yesler Way to Dearborn Street, east from 4th Avenue to roughly 12th Avenue. The historic core of this area used to be called Chinatown. The area encompasses Little Saigon, which lies mostly on the eastern side of I–5.

Madison Park: The eastern and southern border is Lake Washington Boulevard E. The western border is Lake Washington and the northern border is Union Bay.

Madrona: Stretches east from Martin Luther King Jr. Way to Lake Washington and north from Cherry Street to E. Denny Way.

North Seattle: Hodgepodge of neighborhoods north of 85th Street. Includes Northgate, Shoreline, Mountlake Terrace, Lynnwood, among others.

Phinney Ridge: Above Fremont, stretching east from 8th Avenue NW to Aurora Avenue N. (99) and north from N. 46th Street to N. 80th Street. This encompasses the lower part of Greenwood, which stretches north from N. 80th Street to N. 105th Street.

Pioneer Square: North from S. King Street to Cherry Street, east from Alaskan Way to 2nd Avenue.

Queen Anne: Stretches north from Denny Way to Nickerson Street and east from 15th Avenue W. to Aurora Avenue N. (99). Includes the Seattle Center (i.e., the place with the Space Needle). Divided into Lower Queen Anne and Upper Queen Anne, with Galer Street the dividing line. This area also encompasses Magnolia and Interbay, adjacent neighborhoods that make up the peninsula west of 15th Avenue W.

Ravenna: Stretches east from 15th Avenue W. to 35th Avenue NE and north from NE Ravenna Boulevard/NE 55th Street to NE 75th Street.

South Lake Union: From the south end of Lake Union to Denny Way and west to east from Dexter Avenue North to Eastlake Avenue. May include some pieces of the Cascade neighborhood.

South Seattle: Hodgepodge of neighborhoods south of I–90 that encompasses the Rainier Valley (Mt. Baker, Beacon Hill, Columbia City, Rainier Beach, Seward Park).

University District: Directly east of I–5 from Wallingford. Stretches east to 35th Avenue NE and north from Portage Bay to NE Ravenna Blvd.

Wallingford: Stretches east from Aurora Avenue N. (99) to I–5 and north from the ship canal to N. 50th Street.

West Seattle: The northern half of the peninsula reached via the West Seattle Bridge. The southern boundary is roughly SW Barton Street. Encompasses many different sub-neighborhoods, including Alki and Junction.

The other stuff on the page

Average dinner price: This dollar value is a guide to how much, on average, you should expect to spend per person on a full dinner at the restaurant, including one alcoholic beverage and a 20% tip (for table-service establishments; we encourage you to tip at coffeeshops and take-out joints too, but we don't figure it into the meal price). At simple take-out places, this might be just a sandwich and a soda; at more elaborate sit-down restaurants, we usually figure in the cost of an appetizer (one for every person) and dessert (one for every two people). If the restaurant pushes bottled water or side dishes on you, we figure that in, too. For alcoholic drinks, too, we are guided by what people generally tend to order—from a beer to a third of a bottle of low-to-midpriced wine. Only restaurants that serve full meals and have ratings are eligible for price estimates.

Genre: Every establishment in the *Fearless Critic* book is associated with one or more culinary genres. Our "Lists" section includes a cross-referenced guide to all restaurants by genre. Most genres—e.g. **Indian** or **pizza**—are self-explanatory, but some require clarification: **American** covers traditional meat-and-potatoes fare, bar food, breakfast food, comfort food, burgers, greasy spoons, and so on. **Steakhouses** have their own category, as does **Southern** cuisine, which includes soul food, fried chicken, Cajun, and Louisiana Creole cooking. We use the word **Modern** (not "New American") to describe the new wave of upmarket cuisine that draws upon diverse world ingredients and technique. This includes the market-to-table and haute nostalgic restaurants (Adam Platt might call them "haute barnyard") that have become fashionable lately. **Vegefusion** is world fusion cuisine aimed mainly at vegetarian and vegans. **Breads** is used to denote a place known for its bread. **Coffee**, of course, doesn't apply to any restaurant serving coffee—almost all of them do—but rather to an establishment where that's a particular focus.

Establishment type: We have divided eating establishments into several categories. The largest category is **casual restaurant**, which means a place with waiter service at tables but a generally laid-back atmosphere without much fuss. An **upmarket restaurant** is a place with more elegant, trendy, or special-occasion ambitions. The **counter service** category includes cafeterias, self-service places, and also establishments where you place an order at a counter but it is then brought out to your table. We see a **bar** as an establishment that's fundamentally about serving drinks at heart, but it must serve food to be included (although the kitchen often closes before the doors). **Café**

means a place whose primary business is the provision of coffee or tea, but it must serve food of some sort to be included in the book.

Address: We have included addresses and neighborhood designations for up to three locations, and where feasible, we have indexed additional locations in the Lists section of the book. For chains with more than three locations, consult www.fearlesscritic.com/seattle for a listing of the others.

Special features: These appear in the middle column of information. By **date-friendly**, we mean establishments that we find particularly romantic in some way—and that doesn't necessarily mean tuxedoed waiters or high prices. We look for warm lighting, good vibes, and a sense of easy fun. **Kid-friendly** doesn't just mean a couple of high chairs in the corner; it means a place where the little ones will actually be happy, whether for culinary reasons or for the availability of special activities or play areas. The **live music** designation includes establishments that have it only on certain days or nights, so call ahead if it's atmospherically important to you. **Outdoor dining** can mean anything from a couple of sidewalk tables to a sprawling beer garden. **Wi-Fi** has to be free to qualify—this is the 21st century, after all. We are particularly careful when choosing which establishments to flag as **veg-friendly**. The designation is not limited to vegetarian-only places, but we look for menus where vegetarians will not just be accommodated—they'll actually have an ample selection.

Fearless feedback

The heart and soul of this endeavor is our belief that the world of restaurant reviewing can be improved by opening outspoken channels of communication between restaurants and their customers. If you have a bad meal, or a great one, tell the restaurant what was right and what was wrong. It can only help. And tell us too; we've set up comments at www.fearlesscritic.com/seattle so that readers can express agreement or dissent. It doesn't require registration, and you can post anonymously. Our panelists will do their best to respond periodically.

The fine print

This entire book is a work of opinion, and should be understood as such. Any and all judgments rendered upon restaurants within these pages, regardless of tense, are intended as statements of pure opinion. Facts have been thoroughly checked with the restaurants in person, via telephone, and on the restaurants' websites; we have gone to the utmost lengths to ensure that every fact is correct, and that every ingredient in every dish is properly referenced. Any factual errors that nonetheless remain are purely unintentional. That said, menus and plates (not to mention hours of operation) change so frequently at restaurants that any printed book, however new, cannot help but be a bit behind the times. Check in at www.fearlesscritic.com/seattle for new reviews, updates, discussion boards, and more.

About Fearless Critic Media

Fearless Critic Media is a lean, fiercely independent publishing house founded by Robin Goldstein in 2006 and dedicated to providing useful information in an engaging format. In conjunction with its partner, Workman Publishing Company, Fearless Critic Media publishes relentlessly opinionated, irreverent food and wine books. Look for *The Wine Trials 2011*, *The Beer Trials*, and our restaurant guides to cities including Austin, Houston, Washington DC, Portland, San Antonio, and more, in bookstores, gift stores, and food and wine shops nationwide and on powells.com, barnesandnoble.com, and amazon.com. For more information, see **www.fearlesscritic.com**. Fearless Critic books are distributed by **Workman Publishing Company (workman.com)**.

If you're a wine drinker, check out **the world's bestselling guide to wines under $15** from the Fearless Critic editors. Now on sale online and at stores.

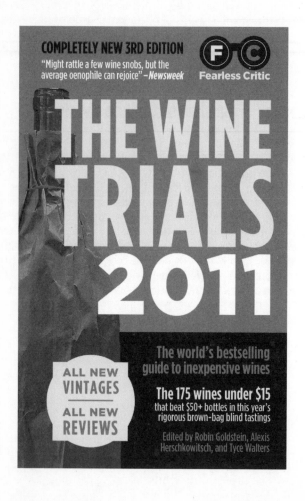

On sale online and in bookstores

Preface

Although Portland's endearingly DIY food scene seems to get all the ink these days, it was arguably Seattle that first introduced Pacific Northwest cooking to the rest of the nation. In the 1990s, before the region became a regular in national food media style sections, Seattle chefs like Tom Douglas and Jerry Traunfeld were already being profiled for their "quirky" commitment to local seafood, produce, and wine.

Northwest cooking—or at least the upscale restaurant version of it—was a lot less difficult to define in the '90s: salmon, soy glaze, superfluous daikon and wasabi. Okay, there was a little more to it than that, but in Seattle there was a time when it was nearly indistinguishable from pan-Asian. Nowadays, Italian or "rustic" European influences are predominant, as is the so-called "nose-to-tail" genre (food writers enjoy speculating on when exactly marrow bones will go out of fashion), and most chefs emphasize game, pork, and grass-fed beef. "Pacific Northwest" has become a pretty fluid descriptor, the culinary equivalent of a Photoshop filter that can make any picture sepia-toned. Add a few key ingredients—foraged mushrooms, local seafood, late-summer wild berries—and anything from ironic 1950s comfort food to French-Korean fusion to molecular gastronomy becomes part of the Northwest lexicon.

If that sounds like a cynical observation, I assure you that it's not. Years of New York City dining and travel writing taught me plenty about cuisines, but I didn't really understand ingredients until I moved to Seattle. The Northwest's bounty is absurd, and the intense focus on this raw material is a defining and beautiful part of the Seattle food scene. Being a foodie in this town is not just about restaurant openings. It's about CSA subscriptions and sous vide experiments and home canning. It's about growing hops in your backyard and about seeing a vegan potluck as a glorious challenge, not a punchline. It's about carbonating your own seltzer, because, well, why wouldn't you?

Despite its role in leading the charge, Seattle now occupies a strange place in the West Coast food landscape. It's the classic middle child, perhaps: not yet as cosmopolitan as the Bay Area, but no longer as gritty and risk-taking as Portland. For a while, it seemed that this in-between position was yield great benefits, especially when it manifested as ongoing resistance to Hollywood hype and placebo-effect bullshit, and a continuing focus, instead, on steady self-improvement.

But Seattle is now in the midst of some culinary growing pains. Although the city certainly didn't ride out the first two years of the recession unfazed, money from tech industries and a promised biotech boom now seem to have everyone forever feeling that Seattle is poised at the brink of realizing a much higher international profile. Jagged infusions of capital, lofty ambitions, and representation on shows like Top Chef have begun to bring some of the politics, mudslinging, and celebrity chef ass-kissing usually associated with bigger-city scenes.

But none of this quite fits here yet. The buzzworthy places are still pulling from a relatively small pool of talent, and sometimes everyone seems to be cribbing from the same test: the city already has two bona fide empires (Tom Douglas and Ethan Stowell with six and four restaurants respectively), and popular concepts (fancy cupcakes, fancy ice cream) seem to become chains overnight. If one place has success with a particular brand of bacon, it will be on 10 other menus within weeks. Especially at higher price points, restaurateurs seem to be engaged in an endless hedging of bets, trying to cater to the whims of every possible diner: ruining a painstakingly created European bistro vibe with flat-screen TVs; turning premium cuts of meat into sliders for happy-hour crowds; setting up outdoor seating in front of a faux-speakeasy. Too many restaurateurs don't seem to know what their restaurants should be. Some of the most hyped high-end spots are simultaneously cults of personality and irritatingly unfocused.

But maybe these are just the complaints of those who have time to become regulars at places long enough to be ritually disappointed. Except for the San Diegans who seem obsessed with denigrate Seattle's Mexican food, and a few Portland hipsters who signed addendums to their leases promising not to like anything that didn't originate in Portland, most out-of-towners and recent transplants think the Seattle dining scene rocks. The visitors I talk to rave about the high quality of the ingredients, the affordability (Seattleites may feel their city getting more expensive by the day, but a lot of the top-tier restaurants here are charging what would be considered mid-range prices in places like New York or L.A.), and even the most "famous" restaurants are accessible (to this day, within the city limits there is only one restaurant that requires men to wear jackets, and that policy is joyfully ridiculed in this book). More importantly, participating in the local, organic hubbub no longer requires being either hippie or hipster. You can find it in chain hotels, random pubs, and trendy ultralounges. And while it's easy to ridicule some of those instantiations, too, let us rejoice in the fact that the gospel of local ingredients has finally become mainstream.

Although in the past year there has been a flurry of notable openings and closings all over town, Capitol Hill is the city's current hotspot. A few years ago it wasn't much more than coffee houses, hipster burrito joints, and the odd upscale spot like Lark, but rampant condo-building has created a lot of new restaurant space; the upper-range places and gastropubs threaten to outnumber the pho joints and dive bars. A lot has been happening north of the Lake Washington Ship Canal, too. Ballard always seems poised to eclipse Capitol Hill, and at press time it was getting two new highly anticipated spots, including the latest Ethan Stowell venture. Wallingford's formerly humble 45th Street now has three top restaurants: Tilth, Joule, and Sutra. Outside the city, Bellevue and its surrounding Eastside 'burbs are experiencing a mini restaurant boom, but let's not forget the authentic Asian joints amidst some new places that stress style over substance.

Lest you think the only thing cooking in Seattle kitchens are chanterelles and garlic scapes, the city does have other cuisines. The immigrant communities, from the Swedes to the Chinese, have been steadily moving outward as the city densifies and gentrifies. The best Chinese food is in Bellevue. The best Thai food, Issaquah. The best Norwegian goodies? Possibly as far as Poulsbo, on the Kitsap Peninsula. And thankfully for urbanites, Seattle's Chinese, Japanese, and Southeast Asian populations, all of whom played a great role in shaping the young city, are still represented in the International District, which is all about cheap noodle soups, dim sum, barbecued duck, and bahn mi.

And some of the cuisines that seem to be disappearing from the city core are now easier to reconnect with thanks to the Central Link light rail, which started operating in 2009. It travels from Sea-Tac airport to Downtown, and in the process it passes through a host of neighborhoods with a lot of undiscovered restaurants—the next edition might be all about Ethiopian in Columbia City, or Vietnamese, Thai, and Laotian off the Othello and Rainier Beach stops.

A few changes percolating at City Hall could lead to some very welcome changes. Because of outdated zoning restrictions, Seattle has very few street vendors beyond a few taco trucks, a few high-concept food trucks, and a few dirty-water-dog carts that set up shop in its nightlife districts. But a pilot program, which would include code revisions to bring more food carts to Broadway in Capitol Hill, is already in the works. (Write your local politician and support it!) The City Council also recently relaxed restrictions on urban farming and tending backyard chickens. If this urban farming movement continues to grow, the "local" food touted by restaurants could take on a new meaning.

One thing's for sure: the food scene here isn't stagnating anytime soon. These 250 reviews, which represent the joint opinion of a panel of experienced food nerds, constitute just a fraction of the restaurants in town. Our goal was not to maximize page count, but rather to maximize utility: to review the restaurants that we believe should be most relevant to your food experience in the city. This means not just pointing the way to the unknown gems, but also warning you away from some overrated, overpriced big names. This is an imperfect science, but I hope that you find our work to be useful, and that this book helps you broaden your perspective and narrow your search.

-Carissa Bluestone and the Editorial Team

Most delicious

These are Seattle's **top 100 kitchens** judged from a **pure food** perspective. Ties are ordered by feel rating.

Rank		Food	Cuisine	Location	Type	Price
1	Café Juanita	9.5	Italian	Eastside	Upmarket	$80
2	Joule	9.5	Modern	Wallingford	Upmarket	$50
3	Crush	9.5	Modern	Madison Park	Upmarket	$75
4	Le Pichet	9.0	French	Downtown	Upmarket	$50
5	Sitka & Spruce	9.0	Modern	Capitol Hill	Casual	$50
6	Spinasse	9.0	Italian	Capitol Hill	Upmarket	$60
7	Art of the Table	9.0	Modern	Wallingford	Upmarket	$55
8	Restaurant Zoë	9.0	Modern	Belltown	Upmarket	$65
9	Lark	9.0	Modern	Capitol Hill	Upmarket	$55
10	Anchovies & Olives	9.0	Seafood	Capitol Hill	Upmarket	$55
11	Canlis	9.0	Modern	Queen Anne	Upmarket	$110
12	Trellis	9.0	Modern	Eastside	Upmarket	$60
13	Kisaku	9.0	Japanese	Green Lake	Casual	$45
14	Noodle Boat	9.0	Thai	Eastside	Casual	$25
15	Shiro's	9.0	Japanese	Belltown	Upmarket	$55
16	Paseo	9.0	Sandwiches	Multiple locations	Counter	$15
17	Olivar	8.5	Spanish	Capitol Hill	Upmarket	$55
18	Boat Street Café	8.5	French	Queen Anne	Upmarket	$50
19	Café Presse	8.5	French	Capitol Hill	Casual	$40
20	Corson Building	8.5	Modern	Georgetown	Upmarket	$80
21	Dinette	8.5	Modern	Capitol Hill	Upmarket	$45
22	El Mestizo	8.5	Mexican	C.D.	Casual	$30
23	Eva Restaurant	8.5	Modern	Green Lake	Upmarket	$45
24	Tilikum Place Café	8.5	Modern	Queen Anne	Casual	$50
25	Matt's in the Market	8.5	Modern	Downtown	Upmarket	$70
26	Tavolàta	8.5	Italian	Belltown	Upmarket	$50
27	Campagne	8.5	French	Downtown	Upmarket	$60
28	Cantinetta	8.5	Italian	Multiple locations	Upmarket	$50
29	JaK's Grill	8.5	Steakhouse	Multiple locations	Upmarket	$75
30	Poppy	8.5	Modern, Indian	Capitol Hill	Upmarket	$55
31	Spur	8.5	Modern	Belltown	Upmarket	$55
32	Green Leaf	8.5	Vietnamese	I.D.	Casual	$30
33	Salumi	8.5	Italian	Pioneer Square	Counter	$15
34	Señor Moose	8.5	Mexican	Ballard	Casual	$35
35	Serious Pie	8.5	Pizza	Belltown	Casual	$35
36	Bamboo Garden	8.5	Chinese	Bellevue	Casual	$20
37	Chiso	8.5	Japanese	Fremont	Upmarket	$45
38	Harvest Vine	8.5	Spanish	Madison Park	Upmarket	$65
39	Metropolitan Grill	8.5	Steakhouse	Downtown	Upmarket	$110
40	Meskel	8.5	Ethiopian	C.D.	Casual	$20
41	Mr. Gyros	8.5	Middle Eastern	Phinney	Counter	$15
42	Travelers Tea Co.	8.5	Indian	Capitol Hill	Café	$10
43	Shiki	8.5	Japanese	Queen Anne	Casual	$45
44	Mirak	8.5	Korean	South Seattle	Casual	$25
45	Viengthong	8.5	Thai, Laotian	Beacon Hill	Casual	$25
46	Fonté	8.0	Modern	Downtown	Café	$25

47	Herbfarm	8.0	Modern	Eastside	Upmarket	$250
48	Mulleady's	8.0	Irish	Queen Anne	Casual	$30
49	Palace Kitchen	8.0	Modern	Belltown	Upmarket	$55
50	Smith	8.0	Modern	Capitol Hill	Casual	$30
51	How to Cook a Wolf	8.0	Italian	Queen Anne	Upmarket	$50
52	May Thai	8.0	Thai	Wallingford	Casual	$35
53	Monsoon	8.0	Vietnamese	Multiple locations	Upmarket	$55
54	Plum	8.0	Vegefusion	Capitol Hill	Casual	$40
55	Stumbling Goat	8.0	Modern	Phinney	Upmarket	$50
56	Tavern Law	8.0	Modern	Capitol Hill	Bar	$50
57	Toulouse Petit	8.0	Southern	Queen Anne	Upmarket	$50
58	Branzino	8.0	Italian	Belltown	Upmarket	$50
59	June	8.0	French	Madrona	Upmarket	$50
60	La Isla	8.0	Puerto Rican	Ballard	Casual	$35
61	Rover's	8.0	French	Madison Park	Upmarket	$150
62	Sutra	8.0	Vegefusion	Wallingford	Upmarket	$50
63	TASTE	8.0	Modern	Downtown	Upmarket	$55
64	Annapurna	8.0	Indian	Capitol Hill	Casual	$20
65	La Medusa	8.0	Italian	Columbia City	Casual	$50
66	Spring Hill	8.0	Modern	West Seattle	Upmarket	$60
67	Tamarind Tree	8.0	Vietnamese	I.D.	Casual	$35
68	Via Tribunali	8.0	Pizza	Multiple locations	Casual	$35
69	Guanaco's Tacos Pupusería	8.0	Salvadoran	Multiple locations	Casual	$10
70	Henry's Taiwan	8.0	Chinese	Multiple locations	Casual	$15
71	Mashiko	8.0	Japanese	West Seattle	Casual	$50
72	Pike Street Fish Fry	8.0	Seafood	Capitol Hill	Counter	$10
73	Spiced	8.0	Chinese	Bellevue	Casual	$20
74	Tutta Bella	8.0	Pizza	Multiple locations	Casual	$35
75	La Carta de Oaxaca	8.0	Mexican	Ballard	Casual	$40
76	Taste of India	8.0	Indian	U District	Casual	$30
77	Tsukushinbo	8.0	Japanese	I.D.	Casual	$25
78	Facing East	8.0	Chinese	Bellevue	Casual	$25
79	Pho Bac	8.0	Vietnamese	Multiple locations	Casual	$10
80	BCD Tofu House	8.0	Korean	Multiple locations	Counter	$20
81	Skillet	8.0	American	South Lake Union	Food cart	$15
82	Hosoonyi	8.0	Korean	Edmonds	Casual	$25
83	Inay's	8.0	Filipino	Beacon Hill	Counter	$15
84	Mesob	8.0	Ethiopian	C.D.	Casual	$20
85	Bastille	7.5	French	Ballard	Upmarket	$50
86	The Saint	7.5	Mexican	Capitol Hill	Upmarket	$35
87	Sambar	7.5	French	Ballard	Bar	$40
88	Tilth	7.5	Modern	Wallingford	Upmarket	$60
89	Brad's Swingside Café	7.5	Italian	Fremont	Upmarket	$40
90	Chez Shea	7.5	French	Downtown	Upmarket	$65
91	Marrakesh	7.5	Moroccan	Belltown	Casual	$35
92	Pair	7.5	Modern	Ravenna	Upmarket	$50
93	Pan Africa	7.5	Pan-African	Downtown	Casual	$30
94	611 Supreme	7.5	French	Capitol Hill	Casual	$30
95	A Caprice Kitchen	7.5	Modern	Ballard	Upmarket	$55
96	B&O Espresso	7.5	Coffee, Sweets	Capitol Hill	Café	$15
97	Buddha Ruksa	7.5	Thai	West Seattle	Casual	$30
98	Café Campagne	7.5	French	Downtown	Casual	$40
99	Collins Pub	7.5	American	Pioneer Square	Casual	$40
100	Copper Gate	7.5	Scandinavian	Ballard	Casual	$30

Good vibes

Fearless Critic's feel rating measures the enjoyment we get from the atmosphere and people. Here are the **top 45.** Ties are ordered by food rating.

Rank		Feel	Cuisine	Location	Type	Price
1	Le Pichet	9.5	French	Downtown	Upmarket	$50
2	Sitka & Spruce	9.5	Modern	Capitol Hill	Casual	$50
3	Spinasse	9.5	Italian	Capitol Hill	Upmarket	$60
4	Olivar	9.5	Spanish	Capitol Hill	Upmarket	$55
5	Café Juanita	9.0	Italian	Eastside	Upmarket	$80
6	Joule	9.0	Modern	Wallingford	Upmarket	$50
7	Art of the Table	9.0	Modern	Wallingford	Upmarket	$55
8	Restaurant Zoë	9.0	Modern	Belltown	Upmarket	$65
9	Boat Street Café	9.0	French	Queen Anne	Upmarket	$50
10	Café Presse	9.0	French	Capitol Hill	Casual	$40
11	Corson Building	9.0	Modern	Georgetown	Upmarket	$80
12	Dinette	9.0	Modern	Capitol Hill	Upmarket	$45
13	El Mestizo	9.0	Mexican	C.D.	Casual	$30
14	Eva Restaurant	9.0	Modern	Green Lake	Upmarket	$45
15	Tilikum Place Café	9.0	Modern	Queen Anne	Casual	$50
16	Bastille	9.0	French	Ballard	Upmarket	$50
17	The Saint	9.0	Mexican	Capitol Hill	Upmarket	$35
18	Sambar	9.0	French	Ballard	Bar	$40
19	Tilth	9.0	Modern	Wallingford	Upmarket	$60
20	Pink Door	9.0	Italian	Downtown	Casual	$50
21	Quinn's Pub	9.0	Modern	Capitol Hill	Casual	$35
22	Knee High Stocking Co.	9.0	American	Capitol Hill	Bar	$30
23	Oddfellows	9.0	American	Capitol Hill	Casual	$40
24	Wild Ginger	9.0	Pan-Asian	Multiple locations	Upmarket	$55
25	The Zig Zag Café	9.0	Modern	Downtown	Bar	$35
26	Lark	8.5	Modern	Capitol Hill	Upmarket	$55
27	Matt's in the Market	8.5	Modern	Downtown	Upmarket	$70
28	Tavolàta	8.5	Italian	Belltown	Upmarket	$50
29	Fonté	8.5	Modern	Downtown	Café	$25
30	Herbfarm	8.5	Modern	Eastside	Upmarket	$250
31	Mulleady's	8.5	Irish	Queen Anne	Casual	$30
32	Palace Kitchen	8.5	Modern	Belltown	Upmarket	$55
33	Smith	8.5	Modern	Capitol Hill	Casual	$30
34	Brad's Swingside Café	8.5	Italian	Fremont	Upmarket	$40
35	Chez Shea	8.5	French	Downtown	Upmarket	$65
36	Marrakesh	8.5	Moroccan	Belltown	Casual	$35
37	Pair	8.5	Modern	Ravenna	Upmarket	$50
38	Pan Africa	8.5	Pan-African	Downtown	Casual	$30
39	611 Supreme	8.5	French	Capitol Hill	Casual	$30
40	Barking Frog	8.5	Modern	Eastside	Upmarket	$75
41	Barrio	8.5	Mexican	Multiple locations	Upmarket	$40
42	Black Bottle	8.5	Modern	Belltown	Bar	$35
43	Ocho	8.5	Spanish	Ballard	Casual	$30
44	Salty's	8.5	Seafood	West Seattle	Upmarket	$70
45	13 Coins	8.5	American	Multiple locations	Upmarket	$55

Wine

Fearless Critic's wine ratings, which include sake, consider quality, creativity, value, and depth—in that order. A small but interesting list that is carefully paired with the food might rank higher than a thick, overpriced volume of prestigious producers. We do, however, award extra points for older vintages. Establishments only receive a wine rating if we judge their wine programs to be ambitious or significant. Ties are ordered first by feel rating, then by food rating.

	Name	Cuisine	Location	Type	Price
9.5	Wild Ginger	Pan-Asian	Multiple locations	Upmarket	$55
9.5	Canlis	Modern	Queen Anne	Upmarket	$110
9.5	Rover's	French	Madison Park	Upmarket	$150
9.5	Daniel's Broiler	Steakhouse	Multiple locations	Upmarket	$95
9.0	Spinasse	Italian	Capitol Hill	Upmarket	$60
9.0	Café Juanita	Italian	Eastside	Upmarket	$80
9.0	Boat Street Café	French	Queen Anne	Upmarket	$50
9.0	Herbfarm	Modern	Eastside	Upmarket	$250
9.0	Barking Frog	Modern	Eastside	Upmarket	$75
9.0	Volunteer Park Café	Modern, American	Capitol Hill	Casual	$50
9.0	El Gaucho	Steakhouse	Multiple locations	Upmarket	$110
9.0	Waterfront Grill	Seafood	Downtown	Upmarket	$85
9.0	Serafina	Italian	Eastlake	Upmarket	$55
9.0	Crush	Modern	Madison Park	Upmarket	$75
9.0	Metropolitan Grill	Steakhouse	Downtown	Upmarket	$110
9.0	Barolo	Italian	Belltown	Upmarket	$65
8.5	Sitka & Spruce	Modern	Capitol Hill	Casual	$50
8.5	Restaurant Zoë	Modern	Belltown	Upmarket	$65
8.5	Corson Building	Modern	Georgetown	Upmarket	$80
8.5	Eva Restaurant	Modern	Green Lake	Upmarket	$45
8.5	Tavolàta	Italian	Belltown	Upmarket	$50
8.5	Le Gourmand	French	Ballard	Upmarket	$85
8.5	La Medusa	Italian	Columbia City	Casual	$50
8.5	Vios	Greek	Multiple locations	Casual	$35
8.0	Le Pichet	French	Downtown	Upmarket	$50
8.0	Olivar	Spanish, French	Capitol Hill	Upmarket	$55
8.0	Café Presse	French	Capitol Hill	Casual	$40
8.0	Dinette	Modern	Capitol Hill	Upmarket	$45
8.0	Tilth	Modern	Wallingford	Upmarket	$60
8.0	Pink Door	Italian	Downtown	Casual	$50
8.0	Lark	Modern	Capitol Hill	Upmarket	$55
8.0	Matt's in the Market	Modern	Downtown	Upmarket	$70
8.0	Fonté	Modern, Coffee	Downtown	Café	$25
8.0	Brad's Swingside Café	Italian	Fremont	Upmarket	$40
8.0	Chez Shea	French	Downtown	Upmarket	$65
8.0	Pair	Modern	Ravenna	Upmarket	$50
8.0	Anchovies & Olives	Seafood, Italian	Capitol Hill	Upmarket	$55
8.0	Poppy	Modern, Indian	Capitol Hill	Upmarket	$55
8.0	How to Cook a Wolf	Italian	Queen Anne	Upmarket	$50
8.0	Toulouse Petit	Southern	Queen Anne	Upmarket	$50
8.0	The Tin Table	Modern	Capitol Hill	Upmarket	$50

8.0	ART Restaurant & Lounge	Modern	Downtown	Upmarket	$60
8.0	John Howie Steak	Steakhouse	Bellevue	Upmarket	$110
8.0	Volterra	Italian	Ballard	Upmarket	$55
8.0	BOKA	Modern	Downtown	Upmarket	$65
8.0	Harvest Vine	Spanish	Madison Park	Upmarket	$65
8.0	Via Tribunali	Pizza	Multiple locations	Casual	$35
8.0	Blueacre Seafood	Seafood	Belltown	Upmarket	$50
8.0	Steelhead Diner	Modern	Downtown	Upmarket	$50
8.0	Betty	American	Queen Anne	Casual	$45
7.5	Campagne	French	Downtown	Upmarket	$60
7.5	Cantinetta	Italian	Multiple locations	Upmarket	$50
7.5	JaK's Grill	Steakhouse	Multiple locations	Upmarket	$75
7.5	Buddha Ruksa	Thai	West Seattle	Casual	$30
7.5	Earth & Ocean	Modern	Downtown	Upmarket	$60
7.5	Carmelita	Vegefusion	Phinney	Upmarket	$50
7.5	Serious Pie	Pizza	Belltown	Casual	$35
7.5	Branzino	Italian	Belltown	Upmarket	$50
7.5	Dahlia Lounge	Modern	Belltown	Upmarket	$70
7.5	Cicchetti	Italian	Eastlake	Upmarket	$40
7.5	Delancey	Pizza	Ballard	Casual	$40
7.5	Red Fin	Pan-Asian	Belltown	Upmarket	$50
7.0	Art of the Table	Modern	Wallingford	Upmarket	$55
7.0	Black Bottle	Modern	Belltown	Bar	$35
7.0	Monsoon	Vietnamese	Multiple locations	Upmarket	$55
7.0	Plum	Vegefusion	Capitol Hill	Casual	$40
7.0	A Caprice Kitchen	Modern	Ballard	Upmarket	$55
7.0	Lola	Greek, Moroccan	Belltown	Casual	$60
7.0	Crow	Modern	Queen Anne	Upmarket	$45
7.0	Bisato	Modern	Belltown	Upmarket	$60
7.0	Sutra	Vegefusion	Wallingford	Upmarket	$50
7.0	emmer&rye	Modern	Queen Anne	Casual	$45
7.0	Ristorante Machiavelli	Italian	Capitol Hill	Casual	$40
7.0	Tidbit	Spanish, Italian	Capitol Hill	Casual	$40
7.0	Mashiko	Japanese	West Seattle	Casual	$50
7.0	Tutta Bella	Pizza	Multiple locations	Casual	$35
7.0	Picnic	Sandwiches	Phinney	Café	$15
6.5	Palace Kitchen	Modern	Belltown	Upmarket	$55
6.5	611 Supreme	French	Capitol Hill	Casual	$30
6.5	Elliott's Oyster House	Seafood	Downtown	Casual	$60
6.5	35th Street Bistro	French	Fremont	Upmarket	$50
6.5	Ventana	Modern	Belltown	Upmarket	$45
6.0	Bastille	French	Ballard	Upmarket	$50
6.0	Ocho	Spanish	Ballard	Casual	$30
6.0	Citizen	French, Sandwiches	Queen Anne	Café	$20
6.0	Bizzarro	Italian	Wallingford	Casual	$40
6.0	Chiso	Japanese	Fremont	Upmarket	$45
5.0	Café Flora	Vegefusion	Madison Park	Upmarket	$40
5.0	Cedars	Indian	U District	Casual	$30

By genre

Places to eat **listed by culinary concept, ranked by food rating**. Establishments that don't serve full meals (e.g. cafés, bakeries, grocery stores) appear as "NR" at the bottom of the list.

American *includes traditional American food, bar food, burgers, greasy-spoon fare, and breakfast food. For creative American or market-to-table cuisine, see "Modern." For steakhouses, Southern cuisine, sandwiches, or breads, see those genres.*

8.0	Skillet	South Lake Union	Food cart	$15
7.5	B&O Espresso	Capitol Hill	Café	$15
7.5	Collins Pub	Pioneer Square	Casual	$40
7.5	St. Cloud's	Madrona	Casual	$45
7.5	Red Mill	Multiple locations	Counter	$10
7.5	Dante's Inferno Dogs	Multiple locations	Food cart	$5
7.0	Agua Verde	U District	Casual	$20
7.0	FareStart	Downtown	Casual	$20
7.0	Volunteer Park Café	Capitol Hill	Casual	$50
7.0	Dish	Fremont	Casual	$15
7.0	Po Dog	Capitol Hill	Counter	$10
7.0	Table 219	Capitol Hill	Upmarket	$40
7.0	Lunchbox Laboratory	Ballard	Counter	$20
6.5	Knee High Stocking Co.	Capitol Hill	Bar	$30
6.5	Dick's Drive-In	Multiple locations	Counter	$5
6.5	Betty	Queen Anne	Casual	$45
6.5	Glo's	Capitol Hill	Casual	$15
6.0	Oddfellows	Capitol Hill	Casual	$40
4.0	Beth's	Green Lake	Casual	$15
3.0	13 Coins	Multiple locations	Upmarket	$55

Belgian

6.5	Brouwer's	Fremont	Casual	$40

Breads

NR	Bakery Nouveau	West Seattle	Counter	
NR	Café Besalu	Ballard	Café	
NR	Volunteer Park Café	Capitol Hill	Casual	

Chinese

8.5	Bamboo Garden	Bellevue	Casual	$20
8.0	Henry's Taiwan	Multiple locations	Casual	$15
8.0	Spiced	Bellevue	Casual	$20
8.0	Facing East	Bellevue	Casual	$25
7.5	Boiling Point	Bellevue	Casual	$25
7.5	Ton Kiang	I.D.	Casual	$10
7.5	Café Ori	Bellevue	Casual	$15
7.5	Fu Man Dumpling House	North Seattle	Casual	$15
7.5	Sichuanese Cuisine	I.D.	Casual	$15
7.0	Chiang's Gourmet	Ravenna	Casual	$30
7.0	Harbor City	I.D.	Casual	$15

Chinese *continued*

7.0	Canton Noodle House	I.D.	Casual	$10
6.5	Szechuan Chef	Bellevue	Casual	$20
6.5	Kau Kau	I.D.	Casual	$10
6.5	King's BBQ	I.D.	Counter	$10
6.5	Hing Loon	I.D.	Casual	$20
4.0	Seven Stars Pepper	I.D.	Casual	$20
3.0	Jade Garden	I.D.	Casual	$20

Coffee

NR	B&O Espresso	Capitol Hill	Café
NR	Bakery Nouveau	West Seattle	Counter
NR	Café Besalu	Ballard	Café
NR	Caffé Vita	Multiple locations	Café
NR	Cupcake Royale	Multiple locations	Counter
NR	Espresso Vivace	Multiple locations	Café
NR	Fonté	Downtown	Café
NR	Honoré	Ballard	Counter
NR	Thai Curry Simple	I.D.	Casual
NR	Zoka	Multiple locations	Café

Ethiopian

8.5	Meskel	C.D.	Casual	$20
8.0	Mesob	C.D.	Casual	$20
7.5	Tagla Café	Columbia City	Casual	$20

Filipino

8.0	Inay's	Beacon Hill	Counter	$15

French

9.0	Le Pichet	Downtown	Upmarket	$50
8.5	Olivar	Capitol Hill	Upmarket	$55
8.5	Boat Street Café	Queen Anne	Upmarket	$50
8.5	Café Presse	Capitol Hill	Casual	$40
8.5	Campagne	Downtown	Upmarket	$60
8.0	June	Madrona	Upmarket	$50
8.0	Rover's	Madison Park	Upmarket	$150
7.5	Bastille	Ballard	Upmarket	$50
7.5	Sambar	Ballard	Bar	$40
7.5	611 Supreme	Capitol Hill	Casual	$30
7.5	Chez Shea	Downtown	Upmarket	$65
7.5	35th Street Bistro	Fremont	Upmarket	$50
7.5	Café Campagne	Downtown	Casual	$40
7.5	Le Gourmand	Ballard	Upmarket	$85
7.5	Madison Park Café	Madison Park	Upmarket	$60
7.0	Luc	Capitol Hill	Casual	$45
7.0	Anita's Crêpes	Ballard	Casual	$30
6.0	Citizen	Queen Anne	Café	$20

Greek

7.5	Lola	Belltown	Casual	$60
7.5	Vios	Multiple locations	Casual	$35

Hawaiian

6.5	Marination Mobile	South Lake Union	Food cart	$5

Ice Cream

NR	Full Tilt	Multiple locations	Counter	
NR	Molly Moon's	Multiple locations	Counter	

Indian

8.5	Poppy	Capitol Hill	Upmarket	$55
8.5	Travelers Tea Co.	Capitol Hill	Café	$10
8.0	Annapurna	Capitol Hill	Casual	$20
8.0	Taste of India	U District	Casual	$30
7.5	Mayuri	Bellevue	Casual	$25
7.0	Cedars	U District	Casual	$30
7.0	Bengal Tiger	U District	Casual	$25

Indonesian

7.0	Julia's Indonesian Kitchen	Ravenna	Casual	$25

Irish

8.0	Mulleady's	Queen Anne	Casual	$30

Italian

9.5	Café Juanita	Eastside	Upmarket	$80
9.0	Spinasse	Capitol Hill	Upmarket	$60
9.0	Anchovies & Olives	Capitol Hill	Upmarket	$55
8.5	Tavolàta	Belltown	Upmarket	$50
8.5	Cantinetta	Multiple locations	Upmarket	$50
8.5	Salumi	Pioneer Square	Counter	$15
8.0	How to Cook a Wolf	Queen Anne	Upmarket	$50
8.0	Branzino	Belltown	Upmarket	$50
8.0	La Medusa	Columbia City	Casual	$50
7.5	Brad's Swingside Café	Fremont	Upmarket	$40
7.0	Pink Door	Downtown	Casual	$50
7.0	Bizzarro	Wallingford	Casual	$40
7.0	Osteria La Spiga	Capitol Hill	Upmarket	$50
7.0	Ristorante Machiavelli	Capitol Hill	Casual	$40
7.0	Tidbit	Capitol Hill	Casual	$40
7.0	Volterra	Ballard	Upmarket	$55
6.5	La Rustica	West Seattle	Upmarket	$55
6.5	Cicchetti	Eastlake	Upmarket	$40
6.0	Barolo	Belltown	Upmarket	$65
5.0	Serafina	Eastlake	Upmarket	$55

Japanese

9.0	Kisaku	Green Lake	Casual	$45
9.0	Shiro's	Belltown	Upmarket	$55
8.5	Chiso	Fremont	Upmarket	$45
8.5	Shiki	Queen Anne	Casual	$45
8.0	Mashiko	West Seattle	Casual	$50
8.0	Tsukushinbo	I.D.	Casual	$25
7.5	Maneki	I.D.	Casual	$30

Japanese *continued*

7.5	Moshi Moshi	Ballard	Upmarket	$40
7.0	Kushibar	Belltown	Casual	$35
7.0	Boom Noodle	Multiple locations	Upmarket	$35
7.0	Red Fin	Belltown	Upmarket	$50
7.0	Samurai Noodle	Multiple locations	Counter	$10
7.0	Nishino	Madison Park	Upmarket	$70
6.5	Wabi Sabi	Beacon Hill	Casual	$45
6.0	I Love Sushi	Multiple locations	Casual	$60
6.0	Umi	Belltown	Upmarket	$50
6.0	Genki Sushi	Multiple locations	Casual	$15
5.0	Blue C	Multiple locations	Counter	$20

Korean

8.5	Mirak	South Seattle	Casual	$25
8.0	BCD Tofu House	Multiple locations	Counter	$20
8.0	Hosoonyi	Edmonds	Casual	$25
7.5	Ka Won	North Seattle	Casual	$25
7.0	Kimchi Bistro	Capitol Hill	Casual	$25
6.5	Marination Mobile	South Lake Union	Food cart	$5

Laotian

8.5	Viengthong	Beacon Hill	Casual	$25

Malaysian

6.5	Malay Satay Hut	Multiple locations	Casual	$25

Mexican

8.5	El Mestizo	C.D.	Casual	$30
8.5	Señor Moose	Ballard	Casual	$35
8.0	La Carta de Oaxaca	Ballard	Casual	$40
7.5	The Saint	Capitol Hill	Upmarket	$35
7.5	Barracuda Taquería	Belltown	Counter	$10
7.5	El Puerco Llorón	Downtown	Counter	$10
7.0	Barrio	Multiple locations	Upmarket	$40
7.0	Agua Verde	U District	Casual	$20
7.0	Tacos El Asadero	South Seattle	Food cart	$5
6.5	Marination Mobile	South Lake Union	Food cart	$5
6.5	Taco Gringos	Capitol Hill	Counter	$10

Middle Eastern

8.5	Mr. Gyros	Phinney	Counter	$15
7.5	Lola	Belltown	Casual	$60
7.0	Cedars	U District	Casual	$30
6.5	Cicchetti	Eastlake	Upmarket	$40

Modern

9.5	Joule	Wallingford	Upmarket	$50
9.5	Crush	Madison Park	Upmarket	$75
9.0	Sitka & Spruce	Capitol Hill	Casual	$50
9.0	Art of the Table	Wallingford	Upmarket	$55
9.0	Restaurant Zoë	Belltown	Upmarket	$65

Modern *continued*

9.0	Lark	Capitol Hill	Upmarket	$55
9.0	Canlis	Queen Anne	Upmarket	$110
9.0	Trellis	Eastside	Upmarket	$60
8.5	Corson Building	Georgetown	Upmarket	$80
8.5	Dinette	Capitol Hill	Upmarket	$45
8.5	Eva Restaurant	Green Lake	Upmarket	$45
8.5	Tilikum Place Café	Queen Anne	Casual	$50
8.5	Matt's in the Market	Downtown	Upmarket	$70
8.5	Poppy	Capitol Hill	Upmarket	$55
8.5	Spur	Belltown	Upmarket	$55
8.0	Fonté	Downtown	Café	$25
8.0	Herbfarm	Eastside	Upmarket	$250
8.0	Palace Kitchen	Belltown	Upmarket	$55
8.0	Smith	Capitol Hill	Casual	$30
8.0	Stumbling Goat	Phinney	Upmarket	$50
8.0	Tavern Law	Capitol Hill	Bar	$50
8.0	TASTE	Downtown	Upmarket	$55
8.0	Spring Hill	West Seattle	Upmarket	$60
7.5	Tilth	Wallingford	Upmarket	$60
7.5	Pair	Ravenna	Upmarket	$50
7.5	A Caprice Kitchen	Ballard	Upmarket	$55
7.5	Earth & Ocean	Downtown	Upmarket	$60
7.5	emmer&rye	Queen Anne	Casual	$45
7.5	Mistral Kitchen	Belltown	Upmarket	$65
7.5	Nettletown	Eastlake	Casual	$20
7.0	Quinn's Pub	Capitol Hill	Casual	$35
7.0	Barking Frog	Eastside	Upmarket	$75
7.0	Crow	Queen Anne	Upmarket	$45
7.0	The Tin Table	Capitol Hill	Upmarket	$50
7.0	Volunteer Park Café	Capitol Hill	Casual	$50
7.0	Dahlia Lounge	Belltown	Upmarket	$70
7.0	Marjorie	Capitol Hill	Upmarket	$55
7.0	Fresh Bistro	West Seattle	Upmarket	$50
7.0	Steelhead Diner	Downtown	Upmarket	$50
7.0	Pearl	Bellevue	Upmarket	$60
6.5	Black Bottle	Belltown	Bar	$35
6.5	ART Restaurant & Lounge	Downtown	Upmarket	$60
6.5	BOKA	Downtown	Upmarket	$65
6.0	The Zig Zag Café	Downtown	Bar	$35
6.0	Bisato	Belltown	Upmarket	$60
4.0	Ventana	Belltown	Upmarket	$45

Moroccan

7.5	Marrakesh	Belltown	Casual	$35
7.5	Lola	Belltown	Casual	$60

Pan-African

7.5	Pan Africa	Downtown	Casual	$30

Pan-Asian

7.0	Red Fin	Belltown	Upmarket	$50
6.0	Wild Ginger	Multiple locations	Upmarket	$55
5.0	Thai Curry Simple	I.D.	Casual	$10

Puerto Rican

8.0	La Isla	Ballard	Casual	$35

Russian

7.5	Piroshky Piroshky	Downtown	Counter	$10

Salvadoran

8.0	Guanaco's Tacos Pupusería	Multiple locations	Casual	$10

Sandwiches

9.0	Paseo	Multiple locations	Counter	$15
8.5	Salumi	Pioneer Square	Counter	$15
7.5	Picnic	Phinney	Café	$15
7.5	Tat's	Pioneer Square	Counter	$15
7.5	Saigon Deli	I.D.	Counter	$5
7.2	I Love New York	Multiple locations	Counter	$15
7.0	Homegrown	Multiple locations	Counter	$15
7.0	Baguette Box	Multiple locations	Counter	$15
7.0	Other Coast Café	Ballard	Counter	$10
6.5	Thoa's	Downtown	Casual	$40
6.0	Citizen	Queen Anne	Café	$20
5.0	Delicatus	Pioneer Square	Casual	$15

Scandinavian

7.5	Copper Gate	Ballard	Casual	$30

Seafood

9.0	Anchovies & Olives	Capitol Hill	Upmarket	$55
8.0	Pike Street Fish Fry	Capitol Hill	Counter	$10
7.5	Elliott's Oyster House	Downtown	Casual	$60
7.5	Blueacre Seafood	Belltown	Upmarket	$50
7.5	Flying Fish	South Lake Union	Upmarket	$60
6.5	Etta's	Downtown	Upmarket	$65
6.5	Pike Place Chowder	Multiple locations	Counter	$10
6.0	Salty's	West Seattle	Upmarket	$70
6.0	Waterfront Grill	Downtown	Upmarket	$85
4.0	Ray's Boathouse	Ballard	Upmarket	$65

Southern *includes soul food, Cajun, Creole*

8.0	Toulouse Petit	Queen Anne	Upmarket	$50
7.5	Ezell's	Multiple locations	Counter	$10
7.0	Captain Black's	Capitol Hill	Casual	$25
6.0	Kingfish Café	Capitol Hill	Casual	$45
5.0	Brickyard BBQ	West Seattle	Casual	$25
5.0	Maximus/Minimus	Downtown	Food cart	$10

Spanish

8.5	Olivar	Capitol Hill	Upmarket	$55
8.5	Harvest Vine	Madison Park	Upmarket	$65
7.0	Tidbit	Capitol Hill	Casual	$40
6.0	Ocho	Ballard	Casual	$30
5.0	Tango	Capitol Hill	Upmarket	$50

Steakhouse

8.5	JaK's Grill	Multiple locations	Upmarket	$75
8.5	Metropolitan Grill	Downtown	Upmarket	$110
7.5	John Howie Steak	Bellevue	Upmarket	$110
7.0	Daniel's Broiler	Multiple locations	Upmarket	$95
6.5	El Gaucho	Multiple locations	Upmarket	$110

Sweets

NR	Anita's Crêpes	Ballard	Casual
NR	B&O Espresso	Capitol Hill	Café
NR	Bakery Nouveau	West Seattle	Counter
NR	Café Besalu	Ballard	Café
NR	Citizen	Queen Anne	Café
NR	Cupcake Royale	Multiple locations	Counter
NR	D'Ambrosio Gelato	Ballard	Counter
NR	Espresso Vivace	Multiple locations	Café
NR	Full Tilt	Multiple locations	Counter
NR	Hiroki	Green Lake	Counter
NR	Honoré	Ballard	Counter
NR	Molly Moon's	Multiple locations	Counter
NR	Trophy Cupcakes	Multiple locations	Counter
NR	Zoka	Multiple locations	Café

Thai

9.0	Noodle Boat	Eastside	Casual	$25
8.5	Viengthong	Beacon Hill	Casual	$25
8.0	May Thai	Wallingford	Casual	$35
7.5	Buddha Ruksa	West Seattle	Casual	$30
6.5	Thai Tom	U District	Casual	$15

Vegefusion

8.0	Plum	Capitol Hill	Casual	$40
8.0	Sutra	Wallingford	Upmarket	$50
7.5	Georgetown Liquor Co.	Georgetown	Bar	$25
7.0	Café Flora	Madison Park	Upmarket	$40
7.0	Carmelita	Phinney	Upmarket	$50
7.0	Silence Heart Nest	Fremont	Casual	$15
6.5	In the Bowl	Capitol Hill	Casual	$25

Vietnamese

8.5	Green Leaf	I.D.	Casual	$30
8.0	Monsoon	Multiple locations	Upmarket	$55
8.0	Tamarind Tree	I.D.	Casual	$35
8.0	Pho Bac	Multiple locations	Casual	$10
7.5	Monkey Bridge	Ballard	Casual	$25
7.5	Saigon Deli	I.D.	Counter	$5
7.5	Vietnam Restaurant	Multiple locations	Casual	$10
7.0	Long Provincial	Belltown	Upmarket	$30
7.0	Baguette Box	Multiple locations	Counter	$15
6.5	Thoa's	Downtown	Casual	$40
6.5	Pho Than Brothers	Multiple locations	Casual	$10

By location

Places to eat **listed by neighborhood, suburb, or town, ranked by food rating**. Establishments that don't serve full meals (e.g. cafés, bakeries, grocery stores) appear as "NR" at the bottom of the list.

Ballard

		Cuisine	Type	Price
9.0	Paseo	Sandwiches	Counter	$15
8.5	Señor Moose	Mexican	Casual	$35
8.0	La Isla	Puerto Rican	Casual	$35
8.0	La Carta de Oaxaca	Mexican	Casual	$40
7.5	Bastille	French	Upmarket	$50
7.5	Sambar	French	Bar	$40
7.5	A Caprice Kitchen	Modern	Upmarket	$55
7.5	Copper Gate	Scandinavian	Casual	$30
7.5	Le Gourmand	French	Upmarket	$85
7.5	Monkey Bridge	Vietnamese	Casual	$25
7.5	Delancey	Pizza	Casual	$40
7.5	Moshi Moshi	Japanese	Upmarket	$40
7.5	Veraci Pizza	Pizza	Counter	$25
7.5	Dante's Inferno Dogs	American	Food cart	$5
7.5	Vietnam Restaurant	Vietnamese	Casual	$10
7.0	Volterra	Italian	Upmarket	$55
7.0	Anita's Crêpes	French, Sweets	Casual	$30
7.0	Lunchbox Laboratory	American	Counter	$20
7.0	Other Coast Café	Sandwiches	Counter	$10
6.5	Pho Than Brothers	Vietnamese	Casual	$10
6.0	Ocho	Spanish	Casual	$30
4.0	Ray's Boathouse	Seafood	Upmarket	$65
NR	Café Besalu	Breads, Sweets, Coffee	Café	
NR	Cupcake Royale	Sweets, Coffee	Counter	
NR	D'Ambrosio Gelato	Sweets	Counter	
NR	Honoré	Sweets, Coffee	Counter	

Beacon Hill

		Cuisine	Type	Price
8.5	Viengthong	Thai, Laotian	Casual	$25
8.0	Pho Bac	Vietnamese	Casual	$10
8.0	Inay's	Filipino	Counter	$15
6.5	Wabi Sabi	Japanese	Casual	$45

Bellevue

		Cuisine	Type	Price
8.5	Cantinetta	Italian	Upmarket	$50
8.5	Bamboo Garden	Chinese	Casual	$20
8.0	Monsoon	Vietnamese	Upmarket	$55
8.0	Henry's Taiwan	Chinese	Casual	$15
8.0	Spiced	Chinese	Casual	$20
8.0	Facing East	Chinese	Casual	$25
7.5	John Howie Steak	Steakhouse	Upmarket	$110
7.5	Boiling Point	Chinese	Casual	$25
7.5	Mayuri	Indian	Casual	$25
7.5	Café Ori	Chinese	Casual	$15

Bellevue *continued*

7.0	Barrio	Mexican	Upmarket	$40
7.0	Boom Noodle	Japanese	Upmarket	$35
7.0	Daniel's Broiler	Steakhouse	Upmarket	$95
7.0	Pearl	Modern	Upmarket	$60
6.5	El Gaucho	Steakhouse	Upmarket	$110
6.5	Szechuan Chef	Chinese	Casual	$20
6.0	Wild Ginger	Pan-Asian	Upmarket	$55
6.0	I Love Sushi	Japanese	Casual	$60
NR	Trophy Cupcakes	Sweets	Counter	

Belltown

9.0	Restaurant Zoë	Modern	Upmarket	$65
9.0	Shiro's	Japanese	Upmarket	$55
8.5	Tavolàta	Italian	Upmarket	$50
8.5	Spur	Modern	Upmarket	$55
8.5	Serious Pie	Pizza	Casual	$35
8.0	Palace Kitchen	Modern	Upmarket	$55
8.0	Branzino	Italian	Upmarket	$50
8.0	Via Tribunali	Pizza	Casual	$35
7.5	Marrakesh	Moroccan	Casual	$35
7.5	Lola	Greek, Moroccan	Casual	$60
7.5	Mistral Kitchen	Modern	Upmarket	$65
7.5	Barracuda Taquería	Mexican	Counter	$10
7.5	Blueacre Seafood	Seafood	Upmarket	$50
7.0	Kushibar	Japanese	Casual	$35
7.0	Dahlia Lounge	Modern	Upmarket	$70
7.0	Long Provincial	Vietnamese	Upmarket	$30
7.0	Red Fin	Pan-Asian, Japanese	Upmarket	$50
6.5	Black Bottle	Modern	Bar	$35
6.5	El Gaucho	Steakhouse	Upmarket	$110
6.0	Bisato	Modern	Upmarket	$60
6.0	Umi	Japanese	Upmarket	$50
6.0	Barolo	Italian	Upmarket	$65
4.0	Ventana	Modern	Upmarket	$45

Capitol Hill

9.0	Sitka & Spruce	Modern	Casual	$50
9.0	Spinasse	Italian	Upmarket	$60
9.0	Lark	Modern	Upmarket	$55
9.0	Anchovies & Olives	Seafood, Italian	Upmarket	$55
8.5	Olivar	Spanish, French	Upmarket	$55
8.5	Café Presse	French	Casual	$40
8.5	Dinette	Modern	Upmarket	$45
8.5	Poppy	Modern, Indian	Upmarket	$55
8.5	Travelers Tea Co.	Indian	Café	$10
8.0	Smith	Modern	Casual	$30
8.0	Monsoon	Vietnamese	Upmarket	$55
8.0	Plum	Vegefusion	Casual	$40
8.0	Tavern Law	Modern	Bar	$50
8.0	Annapurna	Indian	Casual	$20
8.0	Via Tribunali	Pizza	Casual	$35
8.0	Guanaco's Tacos Pupusería	Salvadoran	Casual	$10
8.0	Pike Street Fish Fry	Seafood	Counter	$10

Capitol Hill *continued*

7.5	The Saint	Mexican	Upmarket	$35
7.5	611 Supreme	French	Casual	$30
7.5	B&O Espresso	Coffee, Sweets, American	Café	$15
7.5	Vios	Greek	Casual	$35
7.0	Quinn's Pub	Modern	Casual	$35
7.0	Barrio	Mexican	Upmarket	$40
7.0	The Tin Table	Modern	Upmarket	$50
7.0	Volunteer Park Café	Modern, American, Breads	Casual	$50
7.0	Captain Black's	Southern	Casual	$25
7.0	Marjorie	Modern	Upmarket	$55
7.0	Osteria La Spiga	Italian	Upmarket	$50
7.0	Ristorante Machiavelli	Italian	Casual	$40
7.0	Tidbit	Spanish, Italian	Casual	$40
7.0	Boom Noodle	Japanese	Upmarket	$35
7.0	Luc	French	Casual	$45
7.0	Po Dog	American	Counter	$10
7.0	Table 219	American	Upmarket	$40
7.0	Kimchi Bistro	Korean	Casual	$25
7.0	Homegrown	Sandwiches	Counter	$15
7.0	Baguette Box	Sandwiches, Vietnamese	Counter	$15
6.5	Knee High Stocking Co.	American	Bar	$30
6.5	Dick's Drive-In	American	Counter	$5
6.5	In the Bowl	Vegefusion	Casual	$25
6.5	Pho Than Brothers	Vietnamese	Casual	$10
6.5	Glo's	American	Casual	$15
6.5	Taco Gringos	Mexican	Counter	$10
6.0	Oddfellows	American	Casual	$40
6.0	Kingfish Café	Southern	Casual	$45
6.0	Genki Sushi	Japanese	Casual	$15
5.0	Tango	Spanish	Upmarket	$50
NR	Caffé Vita	Coffee	Café	
NR	Cupcake Royale	Sweets, Coffee	Counter	
NR	Espresso Vivace	Coffee, Sweets	Café	
NR	Molly Moon's	Sweets, Ice Cream	Counter	

Central District

8.5	El Mestizo	Mexican	Casual	$30
8.5	Meskel	Ethiopian	Casual	$20
8.0	Mesob	Ethiopian	Casual	$20
7.5	Ezell's	Southern	Counter	$10

Columbia City

8.0	La Medusa	Italian	Casual	$50
8.0	Tutta Bella	Pizza	Casual	$35
7.5	Flying Squirrel	Pizza	Casual	$30
7.5	Tagla Café	Ethiopian	Casual	$20
NR	Full Tilt	Sweets, Ice Cream	Counter	

Downtown

9.0	Le Pichet	French	Upmarket	$50
8.5	Matt's in the Market	Modern	Upmarket	$70
8.5	Campagne	French	Upmarket	$60
8.5	Metropolitan Grill	Steakhouse	Upmarket	$110

Downtown *continued*

8.0	Fonté	Modern, Coffee	Café	$25
8.0	TASTE	Modern	Upmarket	$55
8.0	Pho Bac	Vietnamese	Casual	$10
7.5	Chez Shea	French	Upmarket	$65
7.5	Pan Africa	Pan-African	Casual	$30
7.5	Café Campagne	French	Casual	$40
7.5	Earth & Ocean	Modern	Upmarket	$60
7.5	Elliott's Oyster House	Seafood	Casual	$60
7.5	El Puerco Llorón	Mexican	Counter	$10
7.5	Piroshky Piroshky	Russian	Counter	$10
7.2	I Love New York	Sandwiches	Counter	$15
7.0	Pink Door	Italian	Casual	$50
7.0	FareStart	American	Casual	$20
7.0	Steelhead Diner	Modern	Upmarket	$50
6.5	ART Restaurant & Lounge	Modern	Upmarket	$60
6.5	BOKA	Modern	Upmarket	$65
6.5	Thoa's	Vietnamese, Sandwiches	Casual	$40
6.5	Etta's	Seafood	Upmarket	$65
6.5	Pike Place Chowder	Seafood	Counter	$10
6.0	Wild Ginger	Pan-Asian	Upmarket	$55
6.0	The Zig Zag Café	Modern	Bar	$35
6.0	Waterfront Grill	Seafood	Upmarket	$85
5.0	Maximus/Minimus	Southern	Food cart	$10
5.0	Blue C	Japanese	Counter	$20

Eastlake

7.5	Nettletown	Modern	Casual	$20
6.5	Cicchetti	Italian, Middle Eastern	Upmarket	$40
6.0	I Love Sushi	Japanese	Casual	$60
5.0	Serafina	Italian	Upmarket	$55
NR	Espresso Vivace	Coffee, Sweets	Café	

Eastside

9.5	Café Juanita	Italian	Upmarket	$80
9.0	Trellis	Modern	Upmarket	$60
9.0	Noodle Boat	Thai	Casual	$25
8.0	Herbfarm	Modern	Upmarket	$250
8.0	Tutta Bella	Pizza	Casual	$35
7.0	Barking Frog	Modern	Upmarket	$75
6.5	Malay Satay Hut	Malaysian	Casual	$25
NR	Zoka	Coffee, Sweets	Café	

Edmonds

8.0	BCD Tofu House	Korean	Counter	$20
8.0	Hosoonyi	Korean	Casual	$25

Fremont

9.0	Paseo	Sandwiches	Counter	$15
8.5	Chiso	Japanese	Upmarket	$45
8.0	Via Tribunali	Pizza	Casual	$35
7.5	Brad's Swingside Café	Italian	Upmarket	$40
7.5	35th Street Bistro	French	Upmarket	$50

Fremont *continued*

7.0	Dish	American	Casual	$15
7.0	Silence Heart Nest	Vegefusion	Casual	$15
7.0	Homegrown	Sandwiches	Counter	$15
7.0	Baguette Box	Sandwiches, Vietnamese	Counter	$15
6.5	Brouwer's	Belgian	Casual	$40
5.0	Blue C	Japanese	Counter	$20
NR	Caffé Vita	Coffee	Café	

Georgetown

8.5	Corson Building	Modern	Upmarket	$80
8.0	Via Tribunali	Pizza	Casual	$35
7.5	Georgetown Liquor Co.	Vegefusion	Bar	$25

Green Lake

9.0	Kisaku	Japanese	Casual	$45
8.5	Eva Restaurant	Modern	Upmarket	$45
6.5	Pho Than Brothers	Vietnamese	Casual	$10
4.0	Beth's	American	Casual	$15
NR	Hiroki	Sweets	Counter	
NR	Zoka	Coffee, Sweets	Café	

International District

8.5	Green Leaf	Vietnamese	Casual	$30
8.0	Tamarind Tree	Vietnamese	Casual	$35
8.0	Henry's Taiwan	Chinese	Casual	$15
8.0	Tsukushinbo	Japanese	Casual	$25
8.0	Pho Bac	Vietnamese	Casual	$10
7.5	Maneki	Japanese	Casual	$30
7.5	Ton Kiang	Chinese	Casual	$10
7.5	Saigon Deli	Vietnamese, Sandwiches	Counter	$5
7.5	Sichuanese Cuisine	Chinese	Casual	$15
7.0	Samurai Noodle	Japanese	Counter	$10
7.0	Harbor City	Chinese	Casual	$15
7.0	Canton Noodle House	Chinese	Casual	$10
6.5	Kau Kau	Chinese	Casual	$10
6.5	Malay Satay Hut	Malaysian	Casual	$25
6.5	King's BBQ	Chinese	Counter	$10
6.5	Hing Loon	Chinese	Casual	$20
5.0	Thai Curry Simple	Pan-Asian, Coffee	Casual	$10
4.0	Seven Stars Pepper	Chinese	Casual	$20
3.0	Jade Garden	Chinese	Casual	$20

Madison Park

9.5	Crush	Modern	Upmarket	$75
8.5	Harvest Vine	Spanish	Upmarket	$65
8.0	Rover's	French	Upmarket	$150
7.5	Madison Park Café	French	Upmarket	$60
7.0	Café Flora	Vegefusion	Upmarket	$40
7.0	Nishino	Japanese	Upmarket	$70

Madrona

8.0	June	French	Upmarket	$50
7.5	St. Cloud's	American	Casual	$45
7.0	Daniel's Broiler	Steakhouse	Upmarket	$95
NR	Cupcake Royale	Sweets, Coffee	Counter	

North Seattle

8.0	BCD Tofu House	Korean	Counter	$20
7.5	Ka Won	Korean	Casual	$25
7.5	Ezell's	Southern	Counter	$10
7.5	Fu Man Dumpling House	Chinese	Casual	$15
6.5	Dick's Drive-In	American	Counter	$5

Phinney Ridge

8.5	Mr. Gyros	Middle Eastern	Counter	$15
8.0	Stumbling Goat	Modern	Upmarket	$50
7.5	Red Mill	American	Counter	$10
7.5	Picnic	Sandwiches	Café	$15
7.0	Carmelita	Vegefusion	Upmarket	$50

Pioneer Square

8.5	Salumi	Italian, Sandwiches	Counter	$15
7.5	Collins Pub	American	Casual	$40
7.5	Tat's	Sandwiches	Counter	$15
5.0	Delicatus	Sandwiches	Casual	$15
NR	Caffé Vita	Coffee	Café	

Queen Anne

9.0	Canlis	Modern	Upmarket	$110
8.5	Boat Street Café	French	Upmarket	$50
8.5	Tilikum Place Café	Modern	Casual	$50
8.5	Shiki	Japanese	Casual	$45
8.0	Mulleady's	Irish	Casual	$30
8.0	How to Cook a Wolf	Italian	Upmarket	$50
8.0	Toulouse Petit	Southern	Upmarket	$50
8.0	Via Tribunali	Pizza	Casual	$35
7.5	emmer&rye	Modern	Casual	$45
7.0	Crow	Modern	Upmarket	$45
6.5	Dick's Drive-In	American	Counter	$5
6.5	Betty	American	Casual	$45
6.0	Citizen	French, Sandwiches	Café	$20
6.0	Genki Sushi	Japanese	Casual	$15
NR	Caffé Vita	Coffee	Café	

Ravenna

7.5	Pair	Modern	Upmarket	$50
7.5	Vios	Greek	Casual	$35
7.0	Julia's Indonesian Kitchen	Indonesian	Casual	$25
7.0	Chiang's Gourmet	Chinese	Casual	$30

South Lake Union

8.0	Tutta Bella	Pizza	Casual	$35
8.0	Skillet	American	Food cart	$15
7.5	Flying Fish	Seafood	Upmarket	$60
7.0	Daniel's Broiler	Steakhouse	Upmarket	$95
6.5	Marination Mobile	Korean, Hawaiian	Food cart	$5
3.0	13 Coins	American	Upmarket	$55
NR	Espresso Vivace	Coffee, Sweets	Café	

South Seattle

8.5	Mirak	Korean	Casual	$25
7.5	Ezell's	Southern	Counter	$10
7.0	Tacos El Asadero	Mexican	Food cart	$5
3.0	13 Coins	American	Upmarket	$55
NR	Full Tilt	Sweets, Ice Cream	Counter	

University District

8.5	JaK's Grill	Steakhouse	Upmarket	$75
8.0	Guanaco's Tacos Pupusería	Salvadoran	Casual	$10
8.0	Taste of India	Indian	Casual	$30
7.5	Dante's Inferno Dogs	American	Food cart	$5
7.5	Vietnam Restaurant	Vietnamese	Casual	$10
7.2	I Love New York	Sandwiches	Counter	$15
7.0	Agua Verde	Mexican, American	Casual	$20
7.0	Boom Noodle	Japanese	Upmarket	$35
7.0	Cedars	Indian, Middle Eastern	Casual	$30
7.0	Samurai Noodle	Japanese	Counter	$10
7.0	Bengal Tiger	Indian	Casual	$25
6.5	Pho Than Brothers	Vietnamese	Casual	$10
6.5	Thai Tom	Thai	Casual	$15
5.0	Blue C	Japanese	Counter	$20
NR	Full Tilt	Sweets, Ice Cream	Counter	
NR	Trophy Cupcakes	Sweets	Counter	
NR	Zoka	Coffee, Sweets	Café	

Wallingford

9.5	Joule	Modern	Upmarket	$50
9.0	Art of the Table	Modern	Upmarket	$55
8.5	Cantinetta	Italian	Upmarket	$50
8.0	May Thai	Thai	Casual	$35
8.0	Sutra	Vegefusion	Upmarket	$50
8.0	Tutta Bella	Pizza	Casual	$35
7.5	Tilth	Modern	Upmarket	$60
7.0	Bizzarro	Italian	Casual	$40
6.5	Dick's Drive-In	American	Counter	$5
NR	Molly Moon's	Sweets, Ice Cream	Counter	
NR	Trophy Cupcakes	Sweets	Counter	

West Seattle

8.5	JaK's Grill	Steakhouse	Upmarket	$75
8.0	Spring Hill	Modern	Upmarket	$60
8.0	Mashiko	Japanese	Casual	$50
7.5	Buddha Ruksa	Thai	Casual	$30

West Seattle *continued*

7.0	Fresh Bistro	Modern	Upmarket	$50
6.5	La Rustica	Italian	Upmarket	$55
6.5	Pho Than Brothers	Vietnamese	Casual	$10
6.0	Salty's	Seafood	Upmarket	$70
5.0	Brickyard BBQ	Southern	Casual	$25
NR	Bakery Nouveau	Breads, Sweets, Coffee	Counter	
NR	Cupcake Royale	Sweets, Coffee	Counter	

By special feature

Ranked by food rating. Establishments that don't serve full meals (e.g. cafés, bakeries, grocery stores) appear as "NR" at the bottom of the list.

	Breakfast	Cuisine	Location	Type	Price
9.0	Le Pichet	French	Downtown	Upmarket	$50
9.0	Trellis	Modern	Eastside	Upmarket	$60
8.5	Café Presse	French	Capitol Hill	Casual	$40
8.5	Señor Moose	Mexican	Ballard	Casual	$35
8.0	Fonté	Modern, Coffee	Downtown	Café	$25
8.0	Plum	Vegefusion	Capitol Hill	Casual	$40
8.0	Toulouse Petit	Southern	Queen Anne	Upmarket	$50
8.0	Pho Bac	Vietnamese	Multiple locations	Casual	$10
8.0	BCD Tofu House	Korean	Multiple locations	Counter	$20
8.0	Inay's	Filipino	Beacon Hill	Counter	$15
7.5	B&O Espresso	Coffee, Sweets	Capitol Hill	Café	$15
7.5	Earth & Ocean	Modern	Downtown	Upmarket	$60
7.5	Lola	Greek, Moroccan	Belltown	Casual	$60
7.5	Barracuda Taquería	Mexican	Belltown	Counter	$10
7.5	Tagla Café	Ethiopian	Columbia City	Casual	$20
7.5	Vios	Greek	Multiple locations	Casual	$35
7.5	Tat's	Sandwiches	Pioneer Square	Counter	$15
7.5	Ton Kiang	Chinese	I.D.	Casual	$10
7.5	Piroshky Piroshky	Russian	Downtown	Counter	$10
7.5	Saigon Deli	Vietnamese	I.D.	Counter	$5
7.2	I Love New York	Sandwiches	Multiple locations	Counter	$15
7.0	Barking Frog	Modern	Eastside	Upmarket	$75
7.0	Agua Verde	Mexican, American	U District	Casual	$20
7.0	Café Flora	Vegefusion	Madison Park	Upmarket	$40
7.0	Volunteer Park Café	Modern, American	Capitol Hill	Casual	$50
7.0	Dish	American	Fremont	Casual	$15
7.0	Red Fin	Pan-Asian	Belltown	Upmarket	$50
7.0	Silence Heart Nest	Vegefusion	Fremont	Casual	$15
7.0	Anita's Crêpes	French, Sweets	Ballard	Casual	$30
7.0	Harbor City	Chinese	I.D.	Casual	$15
7.0	Homegrown	Sandwiches	Multiple locations	Counter	$15
6.5	ART Restaurant & Lounge	Modern	Downtown	Upmarket	$60
6.5	BOKA	Modern	Downtown	Upmarket	$65
6.5	Glo's	American	Capitol Hill	Casual	$15
6.0	Oddfellows	American	Capitol Hill	Casual	$40
6.0	Citizen	French, Sandwiches	Queen Anne	Café	$20
5.0	Thai Curry Simple	Pan-Asian, Coffee	I.D.	Casual	$10
4.0	Beth's	American	Green Lake	Casual	$15
3.0	13 Coins	American	Multiple locations	Upmarket	$55
3.0	Jade Garden	Chinese	I.D.	Casual	$20
NR	Bakery Nouveau	Breads, Sweets	West Seattle	Counter	

Breakfast *continued*

NR	Café Besalu	Breads, Sweets	Ballard	Café
NR	Caffé Vita	Coffee	Multiple locations	Café
NR	Cupcake Royale	Sweets, Coffee	Multiple locations	Counter
NR	Espresso Vivace	Coffee, Sweets	Multiple locations	Café
NR	Hiroki	Sweets	Green Lake	Counter
NR	Honoré	Sweets, Coffee	Ballard	Counter
NR	Trophy Cupcakes	Sweets	Multiple locations	Counter
NR	Zoka	Coffee, Sweets	Multiple locations	Café

Brunch

9.0	Sitka & Spruce	Modern	Capitol Hill	Casual	$50
9.0	Trellis	Modern	Eastside	Upmarket	$60
8.5	Olivar	Spanish, French	Capitol Hill	Upmarket	$55
8.5	Boat Street Café	French	Queen Anne	Upmarket	$50
8.5	Corson Building	Modern	Georgetown	Upmarket	$80
8.5	El Mestizo	Mexican	C.D.	Casual	$30
8.5	Tilikum Place Café	Modern	Queen Anne	Casual	$50
8.5	Señor Moose	Mexican	Ballard	Casual	$35
8.5	Harvest Vine	Spanish	Madison Park	Upmarket	$65
8.0	Mulleady's	Irish	Queen Anne	Casual	$30
8.0	Smith	Modern	Capitol Hill	Casual	$30
8.0	Monsoon	Vietnamese	Multiple locations	Upmarket	$55
8.0	Plum	Vegefusion	Capitol Hill	Casual	$40
8.0	June	French	Madrona	Upmarket	$50
8.0	TASTE	Modern	Downtown	Upmarket	$55
8.0	Spring Hill	Modern	West Seattle	Upmarket	$60
7.5	Bastille	French	Ballard	Upmarket	$50
7.5	Tilth	Modern	Wallingford	Upmarket	$60
7.5	Pan Africa	Pan-African	Downtown	Casual	$30
7.5	611 Supreme	French	Capitol Hill	Casual	$30
7.5	A Caprice Kitchen	Modern	Ballard	Upmarket	$55
7.5	B&O Espresso	Coffee, Sweets	Capitol Hill	Café	$15
7.5	Café Campagne	French	Downtown	Casual	$40
7.5	Earth & Ocean	Modern	Downtown	Upmarket	$60
7.5	St. Cloud's	American	Madrona	Casual	$45
7.5	35th Street Bistro	French	Fremont	Upmarket	$50
7.5	emmer&rye	Modern	Queen Anne	Casual	$45
7.5	Mistral Kitchen	Modern	Belltown	Upmarket	$65
7.5	Nettletown	Modern	Eastlake	Casual	$20
7.5	Vios	Greek	Multiple locations	Casual	$35
7.5	Madison Park Café	French	Madison Park	Upmarket	$60
7.5	Georgetown Liquor Co.	Vegefusion	Georgetown	Bar	$25
7.0	Barking Frog	Modern	Eastside	Upmarket	$75
7.0	Barrio	Mexican	Multiple locations	Upmarket	$40
7.0	Café Flora	Vegefusion	Madison Park	Upmarket	$40
7.0	Dahlia Lounge	Modern	Belltown	Upmarket	$70
7.0	Volterra	Italian	Ballard	Upmarket	$55
7.0	Fresh Bistro	Modern	West Seattle	Upmarket	$50
7.0	Red Fin	Pan-Asian	Belltown	Upmarket	$50
7.0	Table 219	American	Capitol Hill	Upmarket	$40
7.0	Chiang's Gourmet	Chinese	Ravenna	Casual	$30
7.0	Harbor City	Chinese	I.D.	Casual	$15
6.5	ART Restaurant & Lounge	Modern	Downtown	Upmarket	$60
6.5	Etta's	Seafood	Downtown	Upmarket	$65

Brunch *continued*

6.0	Wild Ginger	Pan-Asian	Multiple locations	Upmarket	$55
6.0	Salty's	Seafood	West Seattle	Upmarket	$70
6.0	Kingfish Café	Southern	Capitol Hill	Casual	$45
5.0	Serafina	Italian	Eastlake	Upmarket	$55
3.0	Jade Garden	Chinese	I.D.	Casual	$20

BYO *We consider any restaurant with a corkage fee of $10 or under to be BYO. If there is a wine program, however, it is polite to tip on what you would have spent had you not brought your own. Offering a taste is optional.*

8.5	Café Presse	French	Capitol Hill	Casual	$40
8.5	Metropolitan Grill	Steakhouse	Downtown	Upmarket	$110
8.0	Smith	Modern	Capitol Hill	Casual	$30
8.0	TASTE	Modern	Downtown	Upmarket	$55
8.0	Guanaco's Tacos Pupusería	Salvadoran	Multiple locations	Casual	$10
8.0	Mashiko	Japanese	West Seattle	Casual	$50
8.0	Tutta Bella	Pizza	Multiple locations	Casual	$35
8.0	La Carta de Oaxaca	Mexican	Ballard	Casual	$40
7.5	Pan Africa	Pan-African	Downtown	Casual	$30
7.5	Le Gourmand	French	Ballard	Upmarket	$85
7.5	Mayuri	Indian	Bellevue	Casual	$25
7.5	Café Ori	Chinese	Bellevue	Casual	$15
7.0	Barrio	Mexican	Multiple locations	Upmarket	$40
7.0	Kushibar	Japanese	Belltown	Casual	$35
7.0	Julia's Indonesian Kitchen	Indonesian	Ravenna	Casual	$25
7.0	Osteria La Spiga	Italian	Capitol Hill	Upmarket	$50
7.0	Table 219	American	Capitol Hill	Upmarket	$40
7.0	Cedars	Indian	U District	Casual	$30
7.0	Chiang's Gourmet	Chinese	Ravenna	Casual	$30
7.0	Bengal Tiger	Indian	U District	Casual	$25
6.5	Thoa's	Vietnamese	Downtown	Casual	$40
6.5	Wabi Sabi	Japanese	Beacon Hill	Casual	$45
6.0	Kingfish Café	Southern	Capitol Hill	Casual	$45
5.0	Tango	Spanish	Capitol Hill	Upmarket	$50
5.0	Delicatus	Sandwiches	Pioneer Square	Casual	$15

Date-friendly

9.5	Café Juanita	Italian	Eastside	Upmarket	$80
9.5	Joule	Modern	Wallingford	Upmarket	$50
9.5	Crush	Modern	Madison Park	Upmarket	$75
9.0	Le Pichet	French	Downtown	Upmarket	$50
9.0	Sitka & Spruce	Modern	Capitol Hill	Casual	$50
9.0	Spinasse	Italian	Capitol Hill	Upmarket	$60
9.0	Restaurant Zoë	Modern	Belltown	Upmarket	$65
9.0	Lark	Modern	Capitol Hill	Upmarket	$55
9.0	Anchovies & Olives	Seafood, Italian	Capitol Hill	Upmarket	$55
9.0	Canlis	Modern	Queen Anne	Upmarket	$110
9.0	Trellis	Modern	Eastside	Upmarket	$60
8.5	Olivar	Spanish, French	Capitol Hill	Upmarket	$55
8.5	Boat Street Café	French	Queen Anne	Upmarket	$50
8.5	Café Presse	French	Capitol Hill	Casual	$40
8.5	Dinette	Modern	Capitol Hill	Upmarket	$45
8.5	Eva Restaurant	Modern	Green Lake	Upmarket	$45
8.5	Tilikum Place Café	Modern	Queen Anne	Casual	$50

Date-friendly *continued*

8.5	Matt's in the Market	Modern	Downtown	Upmarket	$70
8.5	Tavolàta	Italian	Belltown	Upmarket	$50
8.5	Campagne	French	Downtown	Upmarket	$60
8.5	JaK's Grill	Steakhouse	Multiple locations	Upmarket	$75
8.5	Poppy	Modern, Indian	Capitol Hill	Upmarket	$55
8.5	Spur	Modern	Belltown	Upmarket	$55
8.5	Harvest Vine	Spanish	Madison Park	Upmarket	$65
8.5	Metropolitan Grill	Steakhouse	Downtown	Upmarket	$110
8.0	Herbfarm	Modern	Eastside	Upmarket	$250
8.0	Palace Kitchen	Modern	Belltown	Upmarket	$55
8.0	Smith	Modern	Capitol Hill	Casual	$30
8.0	How to Cook a Wolf	Italian	Queen Anne	Upmarket	$50
8.0	May Thai	Thai	Wallingford	Casual	$35
8.0	Monsoon	Vietnamese	Multiple locations	Upmarket	$55
8.0	Plum	Vegefusion	Capitol Hill	Casual	$40
8.0	Stumbling Goat	Modern	Phinney	Upmarket	$50
8.0	Tavern Law	Modern	Capitol Hill	Bar	$50
8.0	June	French	Madrona	Upmarket	$50
8.0	Rover's	French	Madison Park	Upmarket	$150
8.0	Sutra	Vegefusion	Wallingford	Upmarket	$50
8.0	TASTE	Modern	Downtown	Upmarket	$55
8.0	La Medusa	Italian	Columbia City	Casual	$50
7.5	Bastille	French	Ballard	Upmarket	$50
7.5	Tilth	Modern	Wallingford	Upmarket	$60
7.5	Chez Shea	French	Downtown	Upmarket	$65
7.5	Pair	Modern	Ravenna	Upmarket	$50
7.5	B&O Espresso	Coffee, Sweets	Capitol Hill	Café	$15
7.5	Buddha Ruksa	Thai	West Seattle	Casual	$30
7.5	Earth & Ocean	Modern	Downtown	Upmarket	$60
7.5	Le Gourmand	French	Ballard	Upmarket	$85
7.5	Lola	Greek, Moroccan	Belltown	Casual	$60
7.5	Monkey Bridge	Vietnamese	Ballard	Casual	$25
7.5	John Howie Steak	Steakhouse	Bellevue	Upmarket	$110
7.5	Mistral Kitchen	Modern	Belltown	Upmarket	$65
7.5	Blueacre Seafood	Seafood	Belltown	Upmarket	$50
7.5	Madison Park Café	French	Madison Park	Upmarket	$60
7.5	Flying Fish	Seafood	South Lake Union	Upmarket	$60
7.0	Pink Door	Italian	Downtown	Casual	$50
7.0	Barking Frog	Modern	Eastside	Upmarket	$75
7.0	Café Flora	Vegefusion	Madison Park	Upmarket	$40
7.0	Carmelita	Vegefusion	Phinney	Upmarket	$50
7.0	Kushibar	Japanese	Belltown	Casual	$35
7.0	Dahlia Lounge	Modern	Belltown	Upmarket	$70
7.0	Marjorie	Modern	Capitol Hill	Upmarket	$55
7.0	Osteria La Spiga	Italian	Capitol Hill	Upmarket	$50
7.0	Ristorante Machiavelli	Italian	Capitol Hill	Casual	$40
7.0	Tidbit	Spanish, Italian	Capitol Hill	Casual	$40
7.0	Volterra	Italian	Ballard	Upmarket	$55
7.0	Daniel's Broiler	Steakhouse	Multiple locations	Upmarket	$95
7.0	Fresh Bistro	Modern	West Seattle	Upmarket	$50
7.0	Luc	French	Capitol Hill	Casual	$45
7.0	Pearl	Modern	Bellevue	Upmarket	$60
6.5	Black Bottle	Modern	Belltown	Bar	$35
6.5	ART Restaurant & Lounge	Modern	Downtown	Upmarket	$60

Date-friendly *continued*

6.5	El Gaucho	Steakhouse	Multiple locations	Upmarket	$110
6.5	La Rustica	Italian	West Seattle	Upmarket	$55
6.5	BOKA	Modern	Downtown	Upmarket	$65
6.5	Etta's	Seafood	Downtown	Upmarket	$65
6.0	Wild Ginger	Pan-Asian	Multiple locations	Upmarket	$55
6.0	The Zig Zag Café	Modern	Downtown	Bar	$35
6.0	Bisato	Modern	Belltown	Upmarket	$60
6.0	Waterfront Grill	Seafood	Downtown	Upmarket	$85
6.0	Kingfish Café	Southern	Capitol Hill	Casual	$45
6.0	Genki Sushi	Japanese	Multiple locations	Casual	$15
5.0	Serafina	Italian	Eastlake	Upmarket	$55
5.0	Tango	Spanish	Capitol Hill	Upmarket	$50
4.0	Ventana	Modern	Belltown	Upmarket	$45
3.0	13 Coins	American	Multiple locations	Upmarket	$55

Kid-friendly

8.5	Señor Moose	Mexican	Ballard	Casual	$35
8.5	Bamboo Garden	Chinese	Bellevue	Casual	$20
8.5	Meskel	Ethiopian	C.D.	Casual	$20
8.5	Mr. Gyros	Middle Eastern	Phinney	Counter	$15
8.5	Mirak	Korean	South Seattle	Casual	$25
8.0	Mulleady's	Irish	Queen Anne	Casual	$30
8.0	Smith	Modern	Capitol Hill	Casual	$30
8.0	June	French	Madrona	Upmarket	$50
8.0	La Medusa	Italian	Columbia City	Casual	$50
8.0	Tamarind Tree	Vietnamese	I.D.	Casual	$35
8.0	Guanaco's Tacos Pupusería	Salvadoran	Multiple locations	Casual	$10
8.0	Tutta Bella	Pizza	Multiple locations	Casual	$35
8.0	Taste of India	Indian	U District	Casual	$30
8.0	Facing East	Chinese	Bellevue	Casual	$25
8.0	Pho Bac	Vietnamese	Multiple locations	Casual	$10
8.0	BCD Tofu House	Korean	Multiple locations	Counter	$20
8.0	Hosoonyi	Korean	Edmonds	Casual	$25
8.0	Inay's	Filipino	Beacon Hill	Counter	$15
8.0	Mesob	Ethiopian	C.D.	Casual	$20
7.5	St. Cloud's	American	Madrona	Casual	$45
7.5	Flying Squirrel	Pizza	Columbia City	Casual	$30
7.5	Barracuda Taquería	Mexican	Belltown	Counter	$10
7.5	Boiling Point	Chinese	Bellevue	Casual	$25
7.5	Tagla Café	Ethiopian	Columbia City	Casual	$20
7.5	Vios	Greek	Multiple locations	Casual	$35
7.5	Mayuri	Indian	Bellevue	Casual	$25
7.5	Red Mill	American	Multiple locations	Counter	$10
7.5	Picnic	Sandwiches	Phinney	Café	$15
7.5	Tat's	Sandwiches	Pioneer Square	Counter	$15
7.5	Veraci Pizza	Pizza	Ballard	Counter	$25
7.5	Ka Won	Korean	North Seattle	Casual	$25
7.5	Dante's Inferno Dogs	American	Multiple locations	Food cart	$5
7.5	Piroshky Piroshky	Russian	Downtown	Counter	$10
7.5	Café Ori	Chinese	Bellevue	Casual	$15
7.2	I Love New York	Sandwiches	Multiple locations	Counter	$15
7.0	Agua Verde	Mexican, American	U District	Casual	$20
7.0	Café Flora	Vegefusion	Madison Park	Upmarket	$40
7.0	Volunteer Park Café	Modern, American	Capitol Hill	Casual	$50

Kid-friendly *continued*

7.0	Julia's Indonesian Kitchen	Indonesian	Ravenna	Casual	$25
7.0	Dish	American	Fremont	Casual	$15
7.0	Po Dog	American	Capitol Hill	Counter	$10
7.0	Silence Heart Nest	Vegefusion	Fremont	Casual	$15
7.0	Anita's Crêpes	French, Sweets	Ballard	Casual	$30
7.0	Cedars	Indian	U District	Casual	$30
7.0	Chiang's Gourmet	Chinese	Ravenna	Casual	$30
7.0	Samurai Noodle	Japanese	Multiple locations	Counter	$10
7.0	Baguette Box	Sandwiches	Multiple locations	Counter	$15
7.0	Bengal Tiger	Indian	U District	Casual	$25
7.0	Lunchbox Laboratory	American	Ballard	Counter	$20
7.0	Other Coast Café	Sandwiches	Ballard	Counter	$10
6.5	Dick's Drive-In	American	Multiple locations	Counter	$5
6.5	Szechuan Chef	Chinese	Bellevue	Casual	$20
6.5	Malay Satay Hut	Malaysian	Multiple locations	Casual	$25
6.5	Hing Loon	Chinese	I.D.	Casual	$20
6.5	Pho Than Brothers	Vietnamese	Multiple locations	Casual	$10
6.5	Pike Place Chowder	Seafood	Multiple locations	Counter	$10
6.5	Glo's	American	Capitol Hill	Casual	$15
6.0	Salty's	Seafood	West Seattle	Upmarket	$70
5.0	Blue C	Japanese	Multiple locations	Counter	$20
4.0	Ray's Boathouse	Seafood	Ballard	Upmarket	$65
4.0	Beth's	American	Green Lake	Casual	$15
3.0	Jade Garden	Chinese	I.D.	Casual	$20
NR	Bakery Nouveau	Breads, Sweets	West Seattle	Counter	
NR	Café Besalu	Breads, Sweets	Ballard	Café	
NR	Cupcake Royale	Sweets, Coffee	Multiple locations	Counter	
NR	D'Ambrosio Gelato	Sweets	Ballard	Counter	
NR	Full Tilt	Sweets, Ice Cream	Multiple locations	Counter	
NR	Honoré	Sweets, Coffee	Ballard	Counter	
NR	Molly Moon's	Sweets, Ice Cream	Multiple locations	Counter	
NR	Trophy Cupcakes	Sweets	Multiple locations	Counter	
NR	Zoka	Coffee, Sweets	Multiple locations	Café	

Live music *of any kind, from jazz piano to rock, even occasionally*

9.0	Le Pichet	French	Downtown	Upmarket	$50
8.0	May Thai	Thai	Wallingford	Casual	$35
8.0	Tutta Bella	Pizza	Multiple locations	Casual	$35
7.5	Sambar	French	Ballard	Bar	$40
7.5	Marrakesh	Moroccan	Belltown	Casual	$35
7.5	611 Supreme	French	Capitol Hill	Casual	$30
7.5	St. Cloud's	American	Madrona	Casual	$45
7.0	Pink Door	Italian	Downtown	Casual	$50
7.0	Agua Verde	Mexican, American	U District	Casual	$20
7.0	Osteria La Spiga	Italian	Capitol Hill	Upmarket	$50
7.0	Daniel's Broiler	Steakhouse	Multiple locations	Upmarket	$95
6.5	El Gaucho	Steakhouse	Multiple locations	Upmarket	$110
6.0	Waterfront Grill	Seafood	Downtown	Upmarket	$85
5.0	Serafina	Italian	Eastlake	Upmarket	$55
3.0	13 Coins	American	Multiple locations	Upmarket	$55
NR	Full Tilt	Sweets, Ice Cream	Multiple locations	Counter	

Outdoor dining *of any kind, from sidewalk tables to a big backyard patio*

9.0	Le Pichet	French	Downtown	Upmarket	$50
9.0	Trellis	Modern	Eastside	Upmarket	$60
8.5	Boat Street Café	French	Queen Anne	Upmarket	$50
8.5	Café Presse	French	Capitol Hill	Casual	$40
8.5	Campagne	French	Downtown	Upmarket	$60
8.0	Mulleady's	Irish	Queen Anne	Casual	$30
8.0	May Thai	Thai	Wallingford	Casual	$35
8.0	Monsoon	Vietnamese	Multiple locations	Upmarket	$55
8.0	Stumbling Goat	Modern	Phinney	Upmarket	$50
8.0	Tavern Law	Modern	Capitol Hill	Bar	$50
8.0	La Isla	Puerto Rican	Ballard	Casual	$35
8.0	Tamarind Tree	Vietnamese	I.D.	Casual	$35
8.0	Tutta Bella	Pizza	Multiple locations	Casual	$35
7.5	Bastille	French	Ballard	Upmarket	$50
7.5	Sambar	French	Ballard	Bar	$40
7.5	Tilth	Modern	Wallingford	Upmarket	$60
7.5	Brad's Swingside Café	Italian	Fremont	Upmarket	$40
7.5	Pan Africa	Pan-African	Downtown	Casual	$30
7.5	A Caprice Kitchen	Modern	Ballard	Upmarket	$55
7.5	B&O Espresso	Coffee, Sweets	Capitol Hill	Café	$15
7.5	Collins Pub	American	Pioneer Square	Casual	$40
7.5	Copper Gate	Scandinavian	Ballard	Casual	$30
7.5	St. Cloud's	American	Madrona	Casual	$45
7.5	35th Street Bistro	French	Fremont	Upmarket	$50
7.5	emmer&rye	Modern	Queen Anne	Casual	$45
7.5	Flying Squirrel	Pizza	Columbia City	Casual	$30
7.5	Madison Park Café	French	Madison Park	Upmarket	$60
7.5	Red Mill	American	Multiple locations	Counter	$10
7.5	Flying Fish	Seafood	South Lake Union	Upmarket	$60
7.5	Picnic	Sandwiches	Phinney	Café	$15
7.5	Tat's	Sandwiches	Pioneer Square	Counter	$15
7.5	Dante's Inferno Dogs	American	Multiple locations	Food cart	$5
7.0	Pink Door	Italian	Downtown	Casual	$50
7.0	Agua Verde	Mexican, American	U District	Casual	$20
7.0	Carmelita	Vegefusion	Phinney	Upmarket	$50
7.0	Kushibar	Japanese	Belltown	Casual	$35
7.0	Volunteer Park Café	Modern, American	Capitol Hill	Casual	$50
7.0	Captain Black's	Southern	Capitol Hill	Casual	$25
7.0	Marjorie	Modern	Capitol Hill	Upmarket	$55
7.0	Osteria La Spiga	Italian	Capitol Hill	Upmarket	$50
7.0	Volterra	Italian	Ballard	Upmarket	$55
7.0	Daniel's Broiler	Steakhouse	Multiple locations	Upmarket	$95
7.0	Dish	American	Fremont	Casual	$15
7.0	Fresh Bistro	Modern	West Seattle	Upmarket	$50
7.0	Red Fin	Pan-Asian	Belltown	Upmarket	$50
7.0	Steelhead Diner	Modern	Downtown	Upmarket	$50
7.0	Anita's Crêpes	French, Sweets	Ballard	Casual	$30
7.0	Cedars	Indian	U District	Casual	$30
7.0	Homegrown	Sandwiches	Multiple locations	Counter	$15
7.0	Tacos El Asadero	Mexican	South Seattle	Food cart	$5
7.0	Lunchbox Laboratory	American	Ballard	Counter	$20
6.5	Black Bottle	Modern	Belltown	Bar	$35
6.5	Brouwer's	Belgian	Fremont	Casual	$40
6.5	La Rustica	Italian	West Seattle	Upmarket	$55

Outdoor dining *continued*

6.5	Marination Mobile	Korean, Hawaiian	South Lake Union	Food cart	$5
6.5	Cicchetti	Italian	Eastlake	Upmarket	$40
6.5	Thoa's	Vietnamese	Downtown	Casual	$40
6.5	Pike Place Chowder	Seafood	Multiple locations	Counter	$10
6.0	Oddfellows	American	Capitol Hill	Casual	$40
6.0	The Zig Zag Café	Modern	Downtown	Bar	$35
6.0	Salty's	Seafood	West Seattle	Upmarket	$70
6.0	Citizen	French, Sandwiches	Queen Anne	Café	$20
6.0	I Love Sushi	Japanese	Multiple locations	Casual	$60
6.0	Waterfront Grill	Seafood	Downtown	Upmarket	$85
5.0	Brickyard BBQ	Southern	West Seattle	Casual	$25
5.0	Serafina	Italian	Eastlake	Upmarket	$55
4.0	Ray's Boathouse	Seafood	Ballard	Upmarket	$65
NR	Bakery Nouveau	Breads, Sweets	West Seattle	Counter	
NR	Café Besalu	Breads, Sweets	Ballard	Café	
NR	Caffé Vita	Coffee	Multiple locations	Café	
NR	Espresso Vivace	Coffee, Sweets	Multiple locations	Café	
NR	Trophy Cupcakes	Sweets	Multiple locations	Counter	
NR	Zoka	Coffee, Sweets	Multiple locations	Café	

Wi-Fi

8.5	Café Presse	French	Capitol Hill	Casual	$40
8.5	Tilikum Place Café	Modern	Queen Anne	Casual	$50
8.0	Fonté	Modern, Coffee	Downtown	Café	$25
8.0	Plum	Vegefusion	Capitol Hill	Casual	$40
7.5	B&O Espresso	Coffee, Sweets	Capitol Hill	Café	$15
7.0	Captain Black's	Southern	Capitol Hill	Casual	$25
7.0	Boom Noodle	Japanese	Multiple locations	Upmarket	$35
6.0	Oddfellows	American	Capitol Hill	Casual	$40
6.0	Citizen	French, Sandwiches	Queen Anne	Café	$20
5.0	Brickyard BBQ	Southern	West Seattle	Casual	$25
NR	Caffé Vita	Coffee	Multiple locations	Café	
NR	Cupcake Royale	Sweets, Coffee	Multiple locations	Counter	
NR	Espresso Vivace	Coffee, Sweets	Multiple locations	Café	
NR	Zoka	Coffee, Sweets	Multiple locations	Café	

Vegetarian-friendly guide

Places to eat that are **unusually strong in vegetarian options.** This doesn't just mean that there are salads or veggie pastas available; it means that vegetarians will really be happy with the selection at these places. Ranked by **food rating** unless otherwise noted. Establishments that don't serve full meals (e.g. cafés, bakeries, grocery stores) appear as "NR" at the bottom of the list.

All vegetarian-friendly establishments

9.5	Café Juanita	Italian	Eastside	Upmarket	$80
9.0	Sitka & Spruce	Modern	Capitol Hill	Casual	$50
9.0	Spinasse	Italian	Capitol Hill	Upmarket	$60
9.0	Restaurant Zoë	Modern	Belltown	Upmarket	$65
9.0	Lark	Modern	Capitol Hill	Upmarket	$55
9.0	Anchovies & Olives	Seafood, Italian	Capitol Hill	Upmarket	$55
9.0	Noodle Boat	Thai	Eastside	Casual	$25
9.0	Paseo	Sandwiches	Multiple locations	Counter	$15
8.5	Olivar	Spanish, French	Capitol Hill	Upmarket	$55
8.5	Café Presse	French	Capitol Hill	Casual	$40
8.5	Dinette	Modern	Capitol Hill	Upmarket	$45
8.5	Tilikum Place Café	Modern	Queen Anne	Casual	$50
8.5	Tavolàta	Italian	Belltown	Upmarket	$50
8.5	Cantinetta	Italian	Multiple locations	Upmarket	$50
8.5	Poppy	Modern, Indian	Capitol Hill	Upmarket	$55
8.5	Green Leaf	Vietnamese	I.D.	Casual	$30
8.5	Serious Pie	Pizza	Belltown	Casual	$35
8.5	Meskel	Ethiopian	C.D.	Casual	$20
8.5	Mr. Gyros	Middle Eastern	Phinney	Counter	$15
8.5	Travelers Tea Co.	Indian	Capitol Hill	Café	$10
8.0	Fonté	Modern, Coffee	Downtown	Café	$25
8.0	May Thai	Thai	Wallingford	Casual	$35
8.0	Plum	Vegefusion	Capitol Hill	Casual	$40
8.0	Sutra	Vegefusion	Wallingford	Upmarket	$50
8.0	TASTE	Modern	Downtown	Upmarket	$55
8.0	Annapurna	Indian	Capitol Hill	Casual	$20
8.0	La Medusa	Italian	Columbia City	Casual	$50
8.0	Tamarind Tree	Vietnamese	I.D.	Casual	$35
8.0	Via Tribunali	Pizza	Multiple locations	Casual	$35
8.0	Spiced	Chinese	Bellevue	Casual	$20
8.0	Tutta Bella	Pizza	Multiple locations	Casual	$35
8.0	Taste of India	Indian	U District	Casual	$30
8.0	BCD Tofu House	Korean	Multiple locations	Counter	$20
8.0	Mesob	Ethiopian	C.D.	Casual	$20
7.5	Tilth	Modern	Wallingford	Upmarket	$60
7.5	Brad's Swingside Café	Italian	Fremont	Upmarket	$40
7.5	Marrakesh	Moroccan	Belltown	Casual	$35
7.5	Pan Africa	Pan-African	Downtown	Casual	$30

All vegetarian-friendly establishments *continued*

7.5	611 Supreme	French	Capitol Hill	Casual	$30
7.5	A Caprice Kitchen	Modern	Ballard	Upmarket	$55
7.5	Monkey Bridge	Vietnamese	Ballard	Casual	$25
7.5	Flying Squirrel	Pizza	Columbia City	Casual	$30
7.5	Nettletown	Modern	Eastlake	Casual	$20
7.5	Tagla Café	Ethiopian	Columbia City	Casual	$20
7.5	Vios	Greek	Multiple locations	Casual	$35
7.5	Delancey	Pizza	Ballard	Casual	$40
7.5	Maneki	Japanese	I.D.	Casual	$30
7.5	Mayuri	Indian	Bellevue	Casual	$25
7.5	Georgetown Liquor Co.	Vegefusion	Georgetown	Bar	$25
7.5	Veraci Pizza	Pizza	Ballard	Counter	$25
7.5	Piroshky Piroshky	Russian	Downtown	Counter	$10
7.5	Saigon Deli	Vietnamese	I.D.	Counter	$5
7.0	Pink Door	Italian	Downtown	Casual	$50
7.0	Agua Verde	Mexican, American	U District	Casual	$20
7.0	Café Flora	Vegefusion	Madison Park	Upmarket	$40
7.0	Carmelita	Vegefusion	Phinney	Upmarket	$50
7.0	The Tin Table	Modern	Capitol Hill	Upmarket	$50
7.0	Bizzarro	Italian	Wallingford	Casual	$40
7.0	Julia's Indonesian Kitchen	Indonesian	Ravenna	Casual	$25
7.0	Long Provincial	Vietnamese	Belltown	Upmarket	$30
7.0	Osteria La Spiga	Italian	Capitol Hill	Upmarket	$50
7.0	Ristorante Machiavelli	Italian	Capitol Hill	Casual	$40
7.0	Tidbit	Spanish, Italian	Capitol Hill	Casual	$40
7.0	Volterra	Italian	Ballard	Upmarket	$55
7.0	Dish	American	Fremont	Casual	$15
7.0	Fresh Bistro	Modern	West Seattle	Upmarket	$50
7.0	Silence Heart Nest	Vegefusion	Fremont	Casual	$15
7.0	Anita's Crêpes	French, Sweets	Ballard	Casual	$30
7.0	Cedars	Indian	U District	Casual	$30
7.0	Kimchi Bistro	Korean	Capitol Hill	Casual	$25
7.0	Bengal Tiger	Indian	U District	Casual	$25
6.5	Black Bottle	Modern	Belltown	Bar	$35
6.5	La Rustica	Italian	West Seattle	Upmarket	$55
6.5	Szechuan Chef	Chinese	Bellevue	Casual	$20
6.5	In the Bowl	Vegefusion	Capitol Hill	Casual	$25
6.5	Glo's	American	Capitol Hill	Casual	$15
6.0	Citizen	French, Sandwiches	Queen Anne	Café	$20
6.0	Genki Sushi	Japanese	Multiple locations	Casual	$15
6.0	Barolo	Italian	Belltown	Upmarket	$65
5.0	Serafina	Italian	Eastlake	Upmarket	$55
5.0	Maximus/Minimus	Southern	Downtown	Food cart	$10
4.0	Seven Stars Pepper	Chinese	I.D.	Casual	$20

Vegetarian-friendly with top feel ratings

9.5	Sitka & Spruce	Modern	Capitol Hill	Casual	$50
9.5	Spinasse	Italian	Capitol Hill	Upmarket	$60
9.5	Olivar	Spanish, French	Capitol Hill	Upmarket	$55
9.0	Café Juanita	Italian	Eastside	Upmarket	$80
9.0	Restaurant Zoë	Modern	Belltown	Upmarket	$65
9.0	Café Presse	French	Capitol Hill	Casual	$40
9.0	Dinette	Modern	Capitol Hill	Upmarket	$45
9.0	Tilikum Place Café	Modern	Queen Anne	Casual	$50

Vegetarian-friendly with top feel ratings _continued_

9.0	Tilth	Modern	Wallingford	Upmarket	$60
9.0	Pink Door	Italian	Downtown	Casual	$50
8.5	Lark	Modern	Capitol Hill	Upmarket	$55
8.5	Tavolàta	Italian	Belltown	Upmarket	$50
8.5	Fonté	Modern, Coffee	Downtown	Café	$25
8.5	Brad's Swingside Café	Italian	Fremont	Upmarket	$40
8.5	Marrakesh	Moroccan	Belltown	Casual	$35
8.5	Pan Africa	Pan-African	Downtown	Casual	$30
8.5	611 Supreme	French	Capitol Hill	Casual	$30
8.5	Black Bottle	Modern	Belltown	Bar	$35
8.0	Anchovies & Olives	Seafood, Italian	Capitol Hill	Upmarket	$55
8.0	Cantinetta	Italian	Multiple locations	Upmarket	$50
8.0	Poppy	Modern, Indian	Capitol Hill	Upmarket	$55
8.0	May Thai	Thai	Wallingford	Casual	$35
8.0	Plum	Vegefusion	Capitol Hill	Casual	$40
8.0	A Caprice Kitchen	Modern	Ballard	Upmarket	$55
8.0	Monkey Bridge	Vietnamese	Ballard	Casual	$25
8.0	Agua Verde	Mexican, American	U District	Casual	$20
8.0	Café Flora	Vegefusion	Madison Park	Upmarket	$40
8.0	Carmelita	Vegefusion	Phinney	Upmarket	$50
8.0	The Tin Table	Modern	Capitol Hill	Upmarket	$50
8.0	La Rustica	Italian	West Seattle	Upmarket	$55
8.0	Citizen	French, Sandwiches	Queen Anne	Café	$20
8.0	Serafina	Italian	Eastlake	Upmarket	$55
7.5	Green Leaf	Vietnamese	I.D.	Casual	$30
7.5	Serious Pie	Pizza	Belltown	Casual	$35
7.5	Sutra	Vegefusion	Wallingford	Upmarket	$50
7.5	TASTE	Modern	Downtown	Upmarket	$55
7.5	Flying Squirrel	Pizza	Columbia City	Casual	$30
7.5	Bizzarro	Italian	Wallingford	Casual	$40
7.5	Julia's Indonesian Kitchen	Indonesian	Ravenna	Casual	$25
7.5	Long Provincial	Vietnamese	Belltown	Upmarket	$30
7.5	Osteria La Spiga	Italian	Capitol Hill	Upmarket	$50
7.5	Ristorante Machiavelli	Italian	Capitol Hill	Casual	$40
7.5	Tidbit	Spanish, Italian	Capitol Hill	Casual	$40
7.5	Volterra	Italian	Ballard	Upmarket	$55
7.5	Szechuan Chef	Chinese	Bellevue	Casual	$20
7.0	Noodle Boat	Thai	Eastside	Casual	$25
7.0	Annapurna	Indian	Capitol Hill	Casual	$20
7.0	La Medusa	Italian	Columbia City	Casual	$50
7.0	Tamarind Tree	Vietnamese	I.D.	Casual	$35
7.0	Via Tribunali	Pizza	Multiple locations	Casual	$35
7.0	Nettletown	Modern	Eastlake	Casual	$20
7.0	Tagla Café	Ethiopian	Columbia City	Casual	$20
7.0	Vios	Greek	Multiple locations	Casual	$35

Vegetarian-friendly and date-friendly

9.5	Café Juanita	Italian	Eastside	Upmarket	$80
9.0	Sitka & Spruce	Modern	Capitol Hill	Casual	$50
9.0	Spinasse	Italian	Capitol Hill	Upmarket	$60
9.0	Restaurant Zoë	Modern	Belltown	Upmarket	$65
9.0	Lark	Modern	Capitol Hill	Upmarket	$55
9.0	Anchovies & Olives	Seafood, Italian	Capitol Hill	Upmarket	$55
8.5	Olivar	Spanish, French	Capitol Hill	Upmarket	$55

Vegetarian-friendly and date-friendly *continued*

8.5	Café Presse	French	Capitol Hill	Casual	$40
8.5	Dinette	Modern	Capitol Hill	Upmarket	$45
8.5	Tilikum Place Café	Modern	Queen Anne	Casual	$50
8.5	Tavolàta	Italian	Belltown	Upmarket	$50
8.5	Poppy	Modern, Indian	Capitol Hill	Upmarket	$55
8.0	May Thai	Thai	Wallingford	Casual	$35
8.0	Plum	Vegefusion	Capitol Hill	Casual	$40
8.0	Sutra	Vegefusion	Wallingford	Upmarket	$50
8.0	TASTE	Modern	Downtown	Upmarket	$55
8.0	La Medusa	Italian	Columbia City	Casual	$50
7.5	Tilth	Modern	Wallingford	Upmarket	$60
7.5	Monkey Bridge	Vietnamese	Ballard	Casual	$25
7.0	Pink Door	Italian	Downtown	Casual	$50
7.0	Café Flora	Vegefusion	Madison Park	Upmarket	$40
7.0	Carmelita	Vegefusion	Phinney	Upmarket	$50
7.0	Osteria La Spiga	Italian	Capitol Hill	Upmarket	$50
7.0	Ristorante Machiavelli	Italian	Capitol Hill	Casual	$40
7.0	Tidbit	Spanish, Italian	Capitol Hill	Casual	$40
7.0	Volterra	Italian	Ballard	Upmarket	$55
7.0	Fresh Bistro	Modern	West Seattle	Upmarket	$50
6.5	Black Bottle	Modern	Belltown	Bar	$35
6.5	La Rustica	Italian	West Seattle	Upmarket	$50
6.0	Genki Sushi	Japanese	Multiple locations	Casual	$15
5.0	Serafina	Italian	Eastlake	Upmarket	$55

Vegetarian-friendly and kid-friendly

8.5	Meskel	Ethiopian	C.D.	Casual	$20
8.5	Mr. Gyros	Middle Eastern	Phinney	Counter	$15
8.0	La Medusa	Italian	Columbia City	Casual	$50
8.0	Tamarind Tree	Vietnamese	I.D.	Casual	$35
8.0	Tutta Bella	Pizza	Multiple locations	Casual	$35
8.0	Taste of India	Indian	U District	Casual	$30
8.0	BCD Tofu House	Korean	Multiple locations	Counter	$20
8.0	Mesob	Ethiopian	C.D.	Casual	$20
7.5	Flying Squirrel	Pizza	Columbia City	Casual	$30
7.5	Tagla Café	Ethiopian	Columbia City	Casual	$20
7.5	Vios	Greek	Multiple locations	Casual	$35
7.5	Mayuri	Indian	Bellevue	Casual	$25
7.5	Veraci Pizza	Pizza	Ballard	Counter	$25
7.5	Piroshky Piroshky	Russian	Downtown	Counter	$10
7.0	Agua Verde	Mexican, American	U District	Casual	$20
7.0	Café Flora	Vegefusion	Madison Park	Upmarket	$40
7.0	Julia's Indonesian Kitchen	Indonesian	Ravenna	Casual	$25
7.0	Dish	American	Fremont	Casual	$15
7.0	Silence Heart Nest	Vegefusion	Fremont	Casual	$15
7.0	Anita's Crêpes	French, Sweets	Ballard	Casual	$30
7.0	Cedars	Indian	U District	Casual	$30
7.0	Bengal Tiger	Indian	U District	Casual	$25
6.5	Szechuan Chef	Chinese	Bellevue	Casual	$20
6.5	Glo's	American	Capitol Hill	Casual	$15

What's still open?

This is our late-night guide to Seattle food. These places claim to stay open as follows; still, we recommend calling first, as the hours sometimes aren't honored on slow nights. Establishments that don't serve full meals (e.g. cafés, bakeries, grocery stores) appear as "NR" at the bottom of the list.

Weekday food after 10pm

9.0	Le Pichet	French	Downtown	Upmarket	$50
9.0	Sitka & Spruce	Modern	Capitol Hill	Casual	$50
9.0	Lark	Modern	Capitol Hill	Upmarket	$55
9.0	Anchovies & Olives	Seafood, Italian	Capitol Hill	Upmarket	$55
9.0	Shiro's	Japanese	Belltown	Upmarket	$55
8.5	Café Presse	French	Capitol Hill	Casual	$40
8.5	Dinette	Modern	Capitol Hill	Upmarket	$45
8.5	Tavolàta	Italian	Belltown	Upmarket	$50
8.5	Poppy	Modern, Indian	Capitol Hill	Upmarket	$55
8.5	Spur	Modern	Belltown	Upmarket	$55
8.5	Serious Pie	Pizza	Belltown	Casual	$35
8.5	Meskel	Ethiopian	C.D.	Casual	$20
8.0	Mulleady's	Irish	Queen Anne	Casual	$30
8.0	Palace Kitchen	Modern	Belltown	Upmarket	$55
8.0	Smith	Modern	Capitol Hill	Casual	$30
8.0	How to Cook a Wolf	Italian	Queen Anne	Upmarket	$50
8.0	May Thai	Thai	Wallingford	Casual	$35
8.0	Plum	Vegefusion	Capitol Hill	Casual	$40
8.0	Tavern Law	Modern	Capitol Hill	Bar	$50
8.0	Toulouse Petit	Southern	Queen Anne	Upmarket	$50
8.0	Branzino	Italian	Belltown	Upmarket	$50
8.0	La Isla	Puerto Rican	Ballard	Casual	$35
8.0	Via Tribunali	Pizza	Multiple locations	Casual	$35
8.0	Pike Street Fish Fry	Seafood	Capitol Hill	Counter	$10
8.0	La Carta de Oaxaca	Mexican	Ballard	Casual	$40
8.0	BCD Tofu House	Korean	Multiple locations	Counter	$20
8.0	Mesob	Ethiopian	C.D.	Casual	$20
7.5	Bastille	French	Ballard	Upmarket	$50
7.5	The Saint	Mexican	Capitol Hill	Upmarket	$35
7.5	Sambar	French	Ballard	Bar	$40
7.5	611 Supreme	French	Capitol Hill	Casual	$30
7.5	B&O Espresso	Coffee, Sweets	Capitol Hill	Café	$15
7.5	Collins Pub	American	Pioneer Square	Casual	$40
7.5	Copper Gate	Scandinavian	Ballard	Casual	$30
7.5	Lola	Greek, Moroccan	Belltown	Casual	$60
7.5	St. Cloud's	American	Madrona	Casual	$45
7.5	Boiling Point	Chinese	Bellevue	Casual	$25
7.5	Maneki	Japanese	I.D.	Casual	$30
7.5	Flying Fish	Seafood	South Lake Union	Upmarket	$60

Weekday food after 10pm *continued*

7.5	Ka Won	Korean	North Seattle	Casual	$25
7.0	Quinn's Pub	Modern	Capitol Hill	Casual	$35
7.0	Kushibar	Japanese	Belltown	Casual	$35
7.0	The Tin Table	Modern	Capitol Hill	Upmarket	$50
7.0	Captain Black's	Southern	Capitol Hill	Casual	$25
7.0	Long Provincial	Vietnamese	Belltown	Upmarket	$30
7.0	Osteria La Spiga	Italian	Capitol Hill	Upmarket	$50
7.0	Ristorante Machiavelli	Italian	Capitol Hill	Casual	$40
7.0	Luc	French	Capitol Hill	Casual	$45
7.0	Po Dog	American	Capitol Hill	Counter	$10
7.0	Red Fin	Pan-Asian	Belltown	Upmarket	$50
7.0	Harbor City	Chinese	I.D.	Casual	$15
6.5	Knee High Stocking Co.	American	Capitol Hill	Bar	$30
6.5	Black Bottle	Modern	Belltown	Bar	$35
6.5	El Gaucho	Steakhouse	Multiple locations	Upmarket	$110
6.5	BOKA	Modern	Downtown	Upmarket	$65
6.5	Dick's Drive-In	American	Multiple locations	Counter	$5
6.5	Cicchetti	Italian	Eastlake	Upmarket	$40
6.5	Hing Loon	Chinese	I.D.	Casual	$20
6.5	Taco Gringos	Mexican	Capitol Hill	Counter	$10
6.0	Oddfellows	American	Capitol Hill	Casual	$40
6.0	Wild Ginger	Pan-Asian	Multiple locations	Upmarket	$55
6.0	The Zig Zag Café	Modern	Downtown	Bar	$35
6.0	Ocho	Spanish	Ballard	Casual	$30
6.0	Bisato	Modern	Belltown	Upmarket	$60
6.0	Umi	Japanese	Belltown	Upmarket	$50
6.0	Waterfront Grill	Seafood	Downtown	Upmarket	$85
6.0	Barolo	Italian	Belltown	Upmarket	$65
5.0	Brickyard BBQ	Southern	West Seattle	Casual	$25
5.0	Tango	Spanish	Capitol Hill	Upmarket	$50
4.0	Ventana	Modern	Belltown	Upmarket	$45
4.0	Beth's	American	Green Lake	Casual	$15
4.0	Seven Stars Pepper	Chinese	I.D.	Casual	$20
3.0	13 Coins	American	Multiple locations	Upmarket	$55
3.0	Jade Garden	Chinese	I.D.	Casual	$20
NR	Caffé Vita	Coffee	Multiple locations	Café	
NR	Cupcake Royale	Sweets, Coffee	Multiple locations	Counter	
NR	Espresso Vivace	Coffee, Sweets	Multiple locations	Café	
NR	Molly Moon's	Sweets, Ice Cream	Multiple locations	Counter	

Weekday food after 11pm

9.0	Le Pichet	French	Downtown	Upmarket	$50
8.5	Café Presse	French	Capitol Hill	Casual	$40
8.0	Mulleady's	Irish	Queen Anne	Casual	$30
8.0	Palace Kitchen	Modern	Belltown	Upmarket	$55
8.0	Smith	Modern	Capitol Hill	Casual	$30
8.0	May Thai	Thai	Wallingford	Casual	$35
8.0	Tavern Law	Modern	Capitol Hill	Bar	$50
8.0	Toulouse Petit	Southern	Queen Anne	Upmarket	$50
8.0	Via Tribunali	Pizza	Multiple locations	Casual	$35
8.0	Pike Street Fish Fry	Seafood	Capitol Hill	Counter	$10
8.0	BCD Tofu House	Korean	Multiple locations	Counter	$20
8.0	Mesob	Ethiopian	C.D.	Casual	$20
7.5	Bastille	French	Ballard	Upmarket	$50

Weekday food after 11pm *continued*

7.5	The Saint	Mexican	Capitol Hill	Upmarket	$35
7.5	Sambar	French	Ballard	Bar	$40
7.5	Collins Pub	American	Pioneer Square	Casual	$40
7.5	Lola	Greek, Moroccan	Belltown	Casual	$60
7.0	Quinn's Pub	Modern	Capitol Hill	Casual	$35
7.0	Kushibar	Japanese	Belltown	Casual	$35
7.0	The Tin Table	Modern	Capitol Hill	Upmarket	$50
7.0	Captain Black's	Southern	Capitol Hill	Casual	$25
7.0	Long Provincial	Vietnamese	Belltown	Upmarket	$30
7.0	Luc	French	Capitol Hill	Casual	$45
7.0	Po Dog	American	Capitol Hill	Counter	$10
6.5	Knee High Stocking Co.	American	Capitol Hill	Bar	$30
6.5	Black Bottle	Modern	Belltown	Bar	$35
6.5	BOKA	Modern	Downtown	Upmarket	$65
6.5	Dick's Drive-In	American	Multiple locations	Counter	$5
6.5	Cicchetti	Italian	Eastlake	Upmarket	$40
6.5	Hing Loon	Chinese	I.D.	Casual	$20
6.5	Taco Gringos	Mexican	Capitol Hill	Counter	$10
6.0	The Zig Zag Café	Modern	Downtown	Bar	$35
6.0	Ocho	Spanish	Ballard	Casual	$30
6.0	Umi	Japanese	Belltown	Upmarket	$50
5.0	Brickyard BBQ	Southern	West Seattle	Casual	$25
4.0	Ventana	Modern	Belltown	Upmarket	$45
4.0	Beth's	American	Green Lake	Casual	$15
4.0	Seven Stars Pepper	Chinese	I.D.	Casual	$20
3.0	13 Coins	American	Multiple locations	Upmarket	$55
3.0	Jade Garden	Chinese	I.D.	Casual	$20

Weekday food after midnight

8.5	Café Presse	French	Capitol Hill	Casual	$40
8.0	Palace Kitchen	Modern	Belltown	Upmarket	$55
8.0	Smith	Modern	Capitol Hill	Casual	$30
8.0	May Thai	Thai	Wallingford	Casual	$35
8.0	Toulouse Petit	Southern	Queen Anne	Upmarket	$50
8.0	BCD Tofu House	Korean	Multiple locations	Counter	$20
7.5	Bastille	French	Ballard	Upmarket	$50
7.5	The Saint	Mexican	Capitol Hill	Upmarket	$35
7.5	Collins Pub	American	Pioneer Square	Casual	$40
7.0	Kushibar	Japanese	Belltown	Casual	$35
7.0	The Tin Table	Modern	Capitol Hill	Upmarket	$50
7.0	Captain Black's	Southern	Capitol Hill	Casual	$25
6.5	Knee High Stocking Co.	American	Capitol Hill	Bar	$30
6.5	Dick's Drive-In	American	Multiple locations	Counter	$5
6.5	Hing Loon	Chinese	I.D.	Casual	$20
6.5	Taco Gringos	Mexican	Capitol Hill	Counter	$10
6.0	The Zig Zag Café	Modern	Downtown	Bar	$35
6.0	Ocho	Spanish	Ballard	Casual	$30
6.0	Umi	Japanese	Belltown	Upmarket	$50
5.0	Brickyard BBQ	Southern	West Seattle	Casual	$25
4.0	Beth's	American	Green Lake	Casual	$15
4.0	Seven Stars Pepper	Chinese	I.D.	Casual	$20
3.0	13 Coins	American	Multiple locations	Upmarket	$55
3.0	Jade Garden	Chinese	I.D.	Casual	$20

Weekday food after 1am

8.5	Café Presse	French	Capitol Hill	Casual	$40
8.0	Smith	Modern	Capitol Hill	Casual	$30
8.0	May Thai	Thai	Wallingford	Casual	$35
8.0	BCD Tofu House	Korean	Multiple locations	Counter	$20
7.5	The Saint	Mexican	Capitol Hill	Upmarket	$35
7.5	Collins Pub	American	Pioneer Square	Casual	$40
7.0	Captain Black's	Southern	Capitol Hill	Casual	$25
6.5	Dick's Drive-In	American	Multiple locations	Counter	$5
6.5	Taco Gringos	Mexican	Capitol Hill	Counter	$10
6.0	Ocho	Spanish	Ballard	Casual	$30
5.0	Brickyard BBQ	Southern	West Seattle	Casual	$25
4.0	Beth's	American	Green Lake	Casual	$15
4.0	Seven Stars Pepper	Chinese	I.D.	Casual	$20
3.0	13 Coins	American	Multiple locations	Upmarket	$55
3.0	Jade Garden	Chinese	I.D.	Casual	$20

Weekday food after 2am

8.0	BCD Tofu House	Korean	Multiple locations	Counter	$20
6.5	Taco Gringos	Mexican	Capitol Hill	Counter	$10
4.0	Beth's	American	Green Lake	Casual	$15
4.0	Seven Stars Pepper	Chinese	I.D.	Casual	$20
3.0	13 Coins	American	Multiple locations	Upmarket	$55
3.0	Jade Garden	Chinese	I.D.	Casual	$20

Weekend food after 10pm

9.5	Joule	Modern	Wallingford	Upmarket	$50
9.0	Le Pichet	French	Downtown	Upmarket	$50
9.0	Sitka & Spruce	Modern	Capitol Hill	Casual	$50
9.0	Spinasse	Italian	Capitol Hill	Upmarket	$60
9.0	Restaurant Zoë	Modern	Belltown	Upmarket	$65
9.0	Lark	Modern	Capitol Hill	Upmarket	$55
9.0	Anchovies & Olives	Seafood, Italian	Capitol Hill	Upmarket	$55
9.0	Kisaku	Japanese	Green Lake	Casual	$45
9.0	Shiro's	Japanese	Belltown	Upmarket	$55
8.5	Olivar	Spanish, French	Capitol Hill	Upmarket	$55
8.5	Café Presse	French	Capitol Hill	Casual	$40
8.5	Corson Building	Modern	Georgetown	Upmarket	$80
8.5	Dinette	Modern	Capitol Hill	Upmarket	$45
8.5	El Mestizo	Mexican	C.D.	Casual	$30
8.5	Tavolàta	Italian	Belltown	Upmarket	$50
8.5	Cantinetta	Italian	Multiple locations	Upmarket	$50
8.5	JaK's Grill	Steakhouse	Multiple locations	Upmarket	$75
8.5	Poppy	Modern, Indian	Capitol Hill	Upmarket	$55
8.5	Spur	Modern	Belltown	Upmarket	$55
8.5	Serious Pie	Pizza	Belltown	Casual	$35
8.5	Chiso	Japanese	Fremont	Upmarket	$45
8.5	Metropolitan Grill	Steakhouse	Downtown	Upmarket	$110
8.5	Meskel	Ethiopian	C.D.	Casual	$20
8.0	Mulleady's	Irish	Queen Anne	Casual	$30
8.0	Palace Kitchen	Modern	Belltown	Upmarket	$55
8.0	Smith	Modern	Capitol Hill	Casual	$30
8.0	How to Cook a Wolf	Italian	Queen Anne	Upmarket	$50
8.0	May Thai	Thai	Wallingford	Casual	$35

Weekend food after 10pm *continued*

8.0	Plum	Vegefusion	Capitol Hill	Casual	$40
8.0	Tavern Law	Modern	Capitol Hill	Bar	$50
8.0	Toulouse Petit	Southern	Queen Anne	Upmarket	$50
8.0	Branzino	Italian	Belltown	Upmarket	$50
8.0	June	French	Madrona	Upmarket	$50
8.0	La Isla	Puerto Rican	Ballard	Casual	$35
8.0	Tamarind Tree	Vietnamese	I.D.	Casual	$35
8.0	Via Tribunali	Pizza	Multiple locations	Casual	$35
8.0	Mashiko	Japanese	West Seattle	Casual	$50
8.0	Pike Street Fish Fry	Seafood	Capitol Hill	Counter	$10
8.0	Tutta Bella	Pizza	Multiple locations	Casual	$35
8.0	La Carta de Oaxaca	Mexican	Ballard	Casual	$40
8.0	BCD Tofu House	Korean	Multiple locations	Counter	$20
8.0	Mesob	Ethiopian	C.D.	Casual	$20
7.5	Bastille	French	Ballard	Upmarket	$50
7.5	The Saint	Mexican	Capitol Hill	Upmarket	$35
7.5	Sambar	French	Ballard	Bar	$40
7.5	Tilth	Modern	Wallingford	Upmarket	$60
7.5	611 Supreme	French	Capitol Hill	Casual	$30
7.5	B&O Espresso	Coffee, Sweets	Capitol Hill	Café	$15
7.5	Café Campagne	French	Downtown	Casual	$40
7.5	Collins Pub	American	Pioneer Square	Casual	$40
7.5	Copper Gate	Scandinavian	Ballard	Casual	$30
7.5	Elliott's Oyster House	Seafood	Downtown	Casual	$60
7.5	Lola	Greek, Moroccan	Belltown	Casual	$60
7.5	St. Cloud's	American	Madrona	Casual	$45
7.5	emmer&rye	Modern	Queen Anne	Casual	$45
7.5	John Howie Steak	Steakhouse	Bellevue	Upmarket	$110
7.5	Mistral Kitchen	Modern	Belltown	Upmarket	$65
7.5	Barracuda Taquería	Mexican	Belltown	Counter	$10
7.5	Boiling Point	Chinese	Bellevue	Casual	$25
7.5	Tagla Café	Ethiopian	Columbia City	Casual	$20
7.5	Maneki	Japanese	I.D.	Casual	$30
7.5	Moshi Moshi	Japanese	Ballard	Upmarket	$40
7.5	Flying Fish	Seafood	South Lake Union	Upmarket	$60
7.5	Georgetown Liquor Co.	Vegefusion	Georgetown	Bar	$25
7.5	Ka Won	Korean	North Seattle	Casual	$25
7.5	Ezell's	Southern	Multiple locations	Counter	$10
7.0	Pink Door	Italian	Downtown	Casual	$50
7.0	Quinn's Pub	Modern	Capitol Hill	Casual	$35
7.0	Barrio	Mexican	Multiple locations	Upmarket	$40
7.0	Crow	Modern	Queen Anne	Upmarket	$45
7.0	Kushibar	Japanese	Belltown	Casual	$35
7.0	The Tin Table	Modern	Capitol Hill	Upmarket	$50
7.0	Captain Black's	Southern	Capitol Hill	Casual	$25
7.0	Dahlia Lounge	Modern	Belltown	Upmarket	$70
7.0	Long Provincial	Vietnamese	Belltown	Upmarket	$30
7.0	Marjorie	Modern	Capitol Hill	Upmarket	$55
7.0	Osteria La Spiga	Italian	Capitol Hill	Upmarket	$50
7.0	Ristorante Machiavelli	Italian	Capitol Hill	Casual	$40
7.0	Volterra	Italian	Ballard	Upmarket	$55
7.0	Boom Noodle	Japanese	Multiple locations	Upmarket	$35
7.0	Fresh Bistro	Modern	West Seattle	Upmarket	$50
7.0	Luc	French	Capitol Hill	Casual	$45

Weekend food after 10pm *continued*

7.0	Po Dog	American	Capitol Hill	Counter	$10
7.0	Red Fin	Pan-Asian	Belltown	Upmarket	$50
7.0	Chiang's Gourmet	Chinese	Ravenna	Casual	$30
7.0	Harbor City	Chinese	I.D.	Casual	$15
6.5	Knee High Stocking Co.	American	Capitol Hill	Bar	$30
6.5	Black Bottle	Modern	Belltown	Bar	$35
6.5	Brouwer's	Belgian	Fremont	Casual	$40
6.5	El Gaucho	Steakhouse	Multiple locations	Upmarket	$110
6.5	La Rustica	Italian	West Seattle	Upmarket	$55
6.5	BOKA	Modern	Downtown	Upmarket	$65
6.5	Dick's Drive-In	American	Multiple locations	Counter	$5
6.5	Cicchetti	Italian	Eastlake	Upmarket	$40
6.5	Wabi Sabi	Japanese	Beacon Hill	Casual	$45
6.5	Hing Loon	Chinese	I.D.	Casual	$20
6.5	Taco Gringos	Mexican	Capitol Hill	Counter	$10
6.0	Oddfellows	American	Capitol Hill	Casual	$40
6.0	Wild Ginger	Pan-Asian	Multiple locations	Upmarket	$55
6.0	The Zig Zag Café	Modern	Downtown	Bar	$35
6.0	Ocho	Spanish	Ballard	Casual	$30
6.0	Bisato	Modern	Belltown	Upmarket	$60
6.0	I Love Sushi	Japanese	Multiple locations	Casual	$60
6.0	Umi	Japanese	Belltown	Upmarket	$50
6.0	Waterfront Grill	Seafood	Downtown	Upmarket	$85
6.0	Kingfish Café	Southern	Capitol Hill	Casual	$45
6.0	Genki Sushi	Japanese	Multiple locations	Casual	$15
6.0	Barolo	Italian	Belltown	Upmarket	$65
5.0	Brickyard BBQ	Southern	West Seattle	Casual	$25
5.0	Serafina	Italian	Eastlake	Upmarket	$55
5.0	Tango	Spanish	Capitol Hill	Upmarket	$50
4.0	Ventana	Modern	Belltown	Upmarket	$45
4.0	Beth's	American	Green Lake	Casual	$15
4.0	Seven Stars Pepper	Chinese	I.D.	Casual	$20
3.0	13 Coins	American	Multiple locations	Upmarket	$55
3.0	Jade Garden	Chinese	I.D.	Casual	$20
NR	Caffé Vita	Coffee	Multiple locations	Café	
NR	Cupcake Royale	Sweets, Coffee	Multiple locations	Counter	
NR	D'Ambrosio Gelato	Sweets	Ballard	Counter	
NR	Espresso Vivace	Coffee, Sweets	Multiple locations	Café	
NR	Molly Moon's	Sweets, Ice Cream	Multiple locations	Counter	

Weekend food after 11pm

9.0	Le Pichet	French	Downtown	Upmarket	$50
9.0	Anchovies & Olives	Seafood, Italian	Capitol Hill	Upmarket	$55
8.5	Café Presse	French	Capitol Hill	Casual	$40
8.5	Tavolàta	Italian	Belltown	Upmarket	$50
8.5	Poppy	Modern, Indian	Capitol Hill	Upmarket	$55
8.0	Mulleady's	Irish	Queen Anne	Casual	$30
8.0	Palace Kitchen	Modern	Belltown	Upmarket	$55
8.0	Smith	Modern	Capitol Hill	Casual	$30
8.0	How to Cook a Wolf	Italian	Queen Anne	Upmarket	$50
8.0	May Thai	Thai	Wallingford	Casual	$35
8.0	Tavern Law	Modern	Capitol Hill	Bar	$50
8.0	Toulouse Petit	Southern	Queen Anne	Upmarket	$50
8.0	Branzino	Italian	Belltown	Upmarket	$50

Weekend food after 11pm *continued*

8.0	Tamarind Tree	Vietnamese	I.D.	Casual	$35
8.0	Via Tribunali	Pizza	Multiple locations	Casual	$35
8.0	Pike Street Fish Fry	Seafood	Capitol Hill	Counter	$10
8.0	La Carta de Oaxaca	Mexican	Ballard	Casual	$40
8.0	BCD Tofu House	Korean	Multiple locations	Counter	$20
8.0	Mesob	Ethiopian	C.D.	Casual	$20
7.5	Bastille	French	Ballard	Upmarket	$50
7.5	The Saint	Mexican	Capitol Hill	Upmarket	$35
7.5	Sambar	French	Ballard	Bar	$40
7.5	B&O Espresso	Coffee, Sweets	Capitol Hill	Café	$15
7.5	Collins Pub	American	Pioneer Square	Casual	$40
7.5	Lola	Greek, Moroccan	Belltown	Casual	$60
7.5	St. Cloud's	American	Madrona	Casual	$45
7.5	Mistral Kitchen	Modern	Belltown	Upmarket	$65
7.0	Quinn's Pub	Modern	Capitol Hill	Casual	$35
7.0	Kushibar	Japanese	Belltown	Casual	$35
7.0	The Tin Table	Modern	Capitol Hill	Upmarket	$50
7.0	Captain Black's	Southern	Capitol Hill	Casual	$25
7.0	Long Provincial	Vietnamese	Belltown	Upmarket	$30
7.0	Osteria La Spiga	Italian	Capitol Hill	Upmarket	$50
7.0	Boom Noodle	Japanese	Multiple locations	Upmarket	$35
7.0	Luc	French	Capitol Hill	Casual	$45
7.0	Po Dog	American	Capitol Hill	Counter	$10
6.5	Knee High Stocking Co.	American	Capitol Hill	Bar	$30
6.5	Black Bottle	Modern	Belltown	Bar	$35
6.5	El Gaucho	Steakhouse	Multiple locations	Upmarket	$110
6.5	BOKA	Modern	Downtown	Upmarket	$65
6.5	Dick's Drive-In	American	Multiple locations	Counter	$5
6.5	Cicchetti	Italian	Eastlake	Upmarket	$40
6.5	Hing Loon	Chinese	I.D.	Casual	$20
6.5	Taco Gringos	Mexican	Capitol Hill	Counter	$10
6.0	Oddfellows	American	Capitol Hill	Casual	$40
6.0	Wild Ginger	Pan-Asian	Multiple locations	Upmarket	$55
6.0	The Zig Zag Café	Modern	Downtown	Bar	$35
6.0	Ocho	Spanish	Ballard	Casual	$30
6.0	Umi	Japanese	Belltown	Upmarket	$50
5.0	Brickyard BBQ	Southern	West Seattle	Casual	$25
5.0	Tango	Spanish	Capitol Hill	Upmarket	$50
4.0	Ventana	Modern	Belltown	Upmarket	$45
4.0	Beth's	American	Green Lake	Casual	$15
4.0	Seven Stars Pepper	Chinese	I.D.	Casual	$20
3.0	13 Coins	American	Multiple locations	Upmarket	$55
3.0	Jade Garden	Chinese	I.D.	Casual	$20
NR	D'Ambrosio Gelato	Sweets	Ballard	Counter	

Weekend food after midnight

8.5	Café Presse	French	Capitol Hill	Casual	$40
8.0	Palace Kitchen	Modern	Belltown	Upmarket	$55
8.0	Smith	Modern	Capitol Hill	Casual	$30
8.0	May Thai	Thai	Wallingford	Casual	$35
8.0	Toulouse Petit	Southern	Queen Anne	Upmarket	$50
8.0	Via Tribunali	Pizza	Multiple locations	Casual	$35
8.0	Pike Street Fish Fry	Seafood	Capitol Hill	Counter	$10
8.0	BCD Tofu House	Korean	Multiple locations	Counter	$20

Weekend food after midnight *continued*

8.0	Mesob	Ethiopian	C.D.	Casual	$20
7.5	Bastille	French	Ballard	Upmarket	$50
7.5	The Saint	Mexican	Capitol Hill	Upmarket	$35
7.5	Sambar	French	Ballard	Bar	$40
7.5	B&O Espresso	Coffee, Sweets	Capitol Hill	Café	$15
7.5	Collins Pub	American	Pioneer Square	Casual	$40
7.0	Quinn's Pub	Modern	Capitol Hill	Casual	$35
7.0	Kushibar	Japanese	Belltown	Casual	$35
7.0	The Tin Table	Modern	Capitol Hill	Upmarket	$50
7.0	Captain Black's	Southern	Capitol Hill	Casual	$25
7.0	Long Provincial	Vietnamese	Belltown	Upmarket	$30
7.0	Po Dog	American	Capitol Hill	Counter	$10
6.5	Knee High Stocking Co.	American	Capitol Hill	Bar	$30
6.5	El Gaucho	Steakhouse	Multiple locations	Upmarket	$110
6.5	Dick's Drive-In	American	Multiple locations	Counter	$5
6.5	Cicchetti	Italian	Eastlake	Upmarket	$40
6.5	Hing Loon	Chinese	I.D.	Casual	$20
6.5	Taco Gringos	Mexican	Capitol Hill	Counter	$10
6.0	Oddfellows	American	Capitol Hill	Casual	$40
6.0	The Zig Zag Café	Modern	Downtown	Bar	$35
6.0	Ocho	Spanish	Ballard	Casual	$30
6.0	Umi	Japanese	Belltown	Upmarket	$50
5.0	Brickyard BBQ	Southern	West Seattle	Casual	$25
4.0	Beth's	American	Green Lake	Casual	$15
4.0	Seven Stars Pepper	Chinese	I.D.	Casual	$20
3.0	13 Coins	American	Multiple locations	Upmarket	$55
3.0	Jade Garden	Chinese	I.D.	Casual	$20

Weekend food after 1am

8.5	Café Presse	French	Capitol Hill	Casual	$40
8.0	Smith	Modern	Capitol Hill	Casual	$30
8.0	May Thai	Thai	Wallingford	Casual	$35
8.0	Pike Street Fish Fry	Seafood	Capitol Hill	Counter	$10
8.0	BCD Tofu House	Korean	Multiple locations	Counter	$20
8.0	Mesob	Ethiopian	C.D.	Casual	$20
7.5	The Saint	Mexican	Capitol Hill	Upmarket	$35
7.5	Sambar	French	Ballard	Bar	$40
7.5	Collins Pub	American	Pioneer Square	Casual	$40
7.0	Captain Black's	Southern	Capitol Hill	Casual	$25
7.0	Long Provincial	Vietnamese	Belltown	Upmarket	$30
7.0	Po Dog	American	Capitol Hill	Counter	$10
6.5	Knee High Stocking Co.	American	Capitol Hill	Bar	$30
6.5	Dick's Drive-In	American	Multiple locations	Counter	$5
6.5	Hing Loon	Chinese	I.D.	Casual	$20
6.5	Taco Gringos	Mexican	Capitol Hill	Counter	$10
6.0	Ocho	Spanish	Ballard	Casual	$30
5.0	Brickyard BBQ	Southern	West Seattle	Casual	$25
4.0	Beth's	American	Green Lake	Casual	$15
4.0	Seven Stars Pepper	Chinese	I.D.	Casual	$20
3.0	13 Coins	American	Multiple locations	Upmarket	$55
3.0	Jade Garden	Chinese	I.D.	Casual	$20

Weekend food after 2am

8.0	Pike Street Fish Fry	Seafood	Capitol Hill	Counter	$10
8.0	BCD Tofu House	Korean	Multiple locations	Counter	$20
7.0	Po Dog	American	Capitol Hill	Counter	$10
6.5	Taco Gringos	Mexican	Capitol Hill	Counter	$10
4.0	Beth's	American	Green Lake	Casual	$15
4.0	Seven Stars Pepper	Chinese	I.D.	Casual	$20
3.0	13 Coins	American	Multiple locations	Upmarket	$55
3.0	Jade Garden	Chinese	I.D.	Casual	$20

Top tastes

Anything on the crudo list, Anchovies & Olives
Aunt Voula's taramosalata with grilled pita bread, Eva Restaurant
Baby clams rice cracker, Tamarind Tree
Chocolat chaud, Le Pichet
Churros, Barrio
Cochinita pibil, El Mestizo
Croissant, Café Besalu
Cuban roast sandwich (or just about any other sandwich), Paseo
Dutch baby pancakes, Tilikum Place Café
Foie gras mousse (with seasonal adornments), Mistral Kitchen
Fried Beecher's cheese curds, Steelhead Diner
Fried chicken dinner for four (Monday nights, by reservation only), Spring Hill
Fried smelt, in season, Pike Street Fish Fry
Hamachi crudo, Crush
Happy hour beef slider, ART Restaurant & Lounge
Happy hour oysters, Elliott's Oyster House
Hotate konbu jime, Kisaku
Lemon sugar crêpe, Anita's Crêpes
Lotus root salad, Green Leaf
Medley de plátanos, La Isla
Mieng kum, Noodle Boat
Miss Marjorie's plaintain chips, Marjorie
Morcilla, Harvest Vine
Oaxaca tacos, Café Flora
Oeufs en meurette, Café Campagne
Oeufs plats, Café Presse
Offal, Café Juanita
Peter Canlis prawns with a Canlis salad, Canlis
Pickles, Boat Street Café
Pork belly sliders, Spur Gastropub
Raspberry macaroon, Honoré Artisan Bakery
Soufflé potato crisps with dipping sauce, Luc
Spicy beef soup with warm baguette and nori butter, Joule
Tajarin, however it's served, Spinasse
The Other Parts of the Pig, Bamboo Garden
Triple coconut cream pie, Dahlia Lounge
Wild boar sloppy joe, Quinn's Pub
Zeppole, Tavolàta

Fearless Critic

Reviews

A Caprice Kitchen

7.5 Food
8.0 Feel

$55 Price
7.0 Wine

Heartfelt veg-friendly farm-to-table, with
an excellent brunch menu

www.capricekitchen.com

A Caprice Kitchen, whose menu is dictated by
weekly finds at the farmer's markets, fits snugly
into the "aw, shucks" territory of romanticized
country bistros. The specials are scrawled on
blackboards, and the tables are dressed up with
white cloths—only to be dressed down again
with glass tops and individual oversized flowers.
If this farm-to-table interpretation is beginning
to feel a little rote, A Caprice Kitchen does it
well, with an almost entirely vegetarian menu; it
blends in nicely with the down-to-earth vibe of
70th Street's burgeoning restaurant row.

Brunch is unequivocally good, in that
multicultural-urban-forager sort of way: French
toast, for instance, is made with challah and
served with hazelnut butter; an omelette might
come stuffed with nettle pesto and goat cheese.
At dinner, mains might be as classic as succulent
roast chicken, or they might instead reflect the
haphazardness that can mark farmer's-market
shopping, as in a hearty risotto-like concoction
of triticale (a hybrid of wheat and rye grains),
white beans, thyme, spring garlic, spinach, and
Valentina cheese that's topped with two
poached eggs.

In keeping with the local theme, the wine list
here is very specific to a few Washington State
cellars—Domanico and Parejas are two of the
regularly featured producers. This may be a
drawback if you're not enamored with Yakima
Valley bottles, but even so, you may occasionally
discover a lesser-known gem.

Modern
Upmarket restaurant

Ballard
1418 NW 70th St.
(206) 371-2886

Hours
Wed–Fri
5:30pm–9:00pm
Sat
9:00am–2:00pm
5:30pm–9:00pm
Sun
9:00am–2:00pm

Bar
Beer, wine

Credit cards
Visa, MC

Reservations
Accepted

Features
Brunch
Outdoor dining
Veg-friendly

Agua Verde

Not worth a midwinter trek, but food for
the outdoor soul when the sun is shining

www.aguaverde.com

**Mexican
American**
Casual restaurant

University District
1303 NE Boat St.
(206) 545-8570

Hours
Mon–Fri
7:30am–9:00pm
Sat–Sun
11:00am–3:30pm
4:00pm–6:00pm

Bar
Beer, wine, liquor

Credit cards
Visa, MC, AmEx

Reservations
Not accepted

Features
Kid-friendly
Live music
Outdoor dining
Veg-friendly

Agua Verde rents kayaks to anyone who wants
to paddle around Portage Bay, which means its
café would do a swift business even if all it
served were day-old Tostitos and pre-mixed
margaritas. So, kudos to Agua Verde for using
fresh ingredients and giving a fig about
sustainable sourcing, which certainly helps
elevate the fish tacos (the best thing on the
menu) and some of the daily specials (carne
asada in particular) above fast food. Yams and
spinach are employed to add some depth to
standard bean burritos, and the mangodilla
(quesadilla with mango, poblano chilies, and
scallions), though very, very wrong in principle,
is a tasty alternative to a limp grilled cheese
smothered in salsa and guac.

The problem is, no matter how hard it tries,
Agua Verde can never get its food far enough
above fast-casual levels. Points are also
deducted for long lines, practically nonexistent
service, and an interior that has little charm,
despite some loud artwork and paint.

Points are generously redistributed, however,
for the deck, which is simply a great place to sit
by the water on a beautiful day. And the
margaritas are also pretty kick-ass, especially the
toronja (grapefruit) variety.

Anchovies & Olives

The antidote to the city's Fancy Seafood
Fatigue Syndrome

www.anchoviesandolives.com

9.0	8.0
Food	Feel

$55	8.0
Price	Wine

Anchovies & Olives has all of restaurateur Ethan
Stowell's signatures: fresh seafood and pasta in
small portions; a friendly, borderline precious,
staff; excellent Italian wines and seafood
pairings; and a casually sophisticated room that
draws a hip (but not hipster) monied crowd and
gangs of foodies. Anchovies & Olives serves the
city's most exciting and consistently delicious
seafood menu.

Stowell's strength is innovation within
reason—dishes are always well balanced. And
although the menu can reach as far out as fluke
carpaccio in a pickled watermelon broth topped
with a quenelle of avocado and sumptuously
rich sea urchin tagliarini, most pleasures are
much simpler than that (for example, tuna
tartare with arugula and green apple). The
Italian influence shows up often: mussels folded
in with homemade pasta in a spicy red sauce;
thin octopus with grilled Brussels sprouts and
pesto. The all-Italian wine list is lovely, with only
a few by-the-glass selections (as it should be).

Anchovies & Olives isn't particularly fancy, but
as one panelist put it, it's a very "adult" room.
Mood lighting softens the expanse of concrete
(both in pillar and floor form). An overused
design trick, the open kitchen, actually works
well here as a focal point—especially since the
large windows look out onto one of the Hill's
most uninspiring corners. That said, the pay
parking lot across the street must yield some
good people-watching.

Seafood
Italian
Upmarket restaurant

Capitol Hill
1550 15th Ave.
(206) 838-8080

Hours
Sun–Thu
5:00pm–11:00pm
Fri–Sat
5:00pm–midnight

Bar
Beer, wine, liquor

Credit cards
Visa, MC, AmEx

Reservations
Accepted

Features
Date-friendly
Veg-friendly

7.0 | 6.0
Food | Feel

$30
Price

Anita's Crêpes

The creativity-comfort nexus makes this the best crêperie in the northern 'hoods

www.anitascrepes.com

French Sweets
Casual restaurant

Ballard
4350 Leary Way NW
(206) 838-9997

Hours
Mon
9:00am–10:00pm
Wed–Fri
9:00am–10:00pm
Sat–Sun
8:00am–10:00pm

Bar
Beer, wine, liquor

Credit cards
Visa, MC, AmEx

Reservations
Accepted

Features
Kid-friendly
Outdoor dining
Veg-friendly

Anita Ross paid her dues (and honed her skills) slinging crêpes at farmers' markets. And although you can still find mobile versions of her crêperie at markets and events, Ross now maintains a simple sit-down café with an expanded menu.

Unsurprisingly, crêpes are the best thing coming out of this kitchen, and the best among these are the sweet varieties, like an ethereal lemon sugar crêpe. But this kitchen is also competent with other comfort-food dishes like complex and robust soups, including a French onion with lots of stringy Comté. And like most Northwest chefs, Ross knows how to give French standards a little seasonal flare: seared duck breast might come with a local cherry compote.

There's nothing too daring or revelatory about Anita's, and there's better French to be had downtown and in Capitol Hill, but this is definitely the best crêpe north of the canal. Anita's is in the not-so-charming part of Fremont/Ballard, along depressing Leary Way, in a newer commercial building of the kind that looks like a chiropractor's office no matter what you do with it. But the interior is well dressed, with wood floors, butcher's-block tables, and somewhat incongruous (but comfy) brown leather chairs.

Annapurna Café

8.0 Food   **7.0** Feel

$20 Price

Strong specialty dishes from Nepal and
Tibet complement reliable Indian fare

www.annapurnacafe.com

This basement space has an incredibly
uninspiring entrance, past a depressing teriyaki
joint and down a carpeted stairwell. The dining
room, however, is more charming than most
restaurants in the same price category: Tibetan
prayer flags decorate orange and yellow walls,
and at dinner, when the lights are dimmed, the
place has a pleasant glow.

With six types of curry, multiple saag and
masala selections, and Nepalese and Tibetan
dishes, Annapurna's menu is a little
overwhelming. Take-out is sometimes a bit
inconsistent—merely good, that is, instead of
really good—but those of us who are regulars
here can honestly say we've never had a bad
meal.

Tandoori and masala options are aromatic
and pleasantly spicy (Annapurna uses the
standard ethnic-restaurant star system for
selecting spiciness, but each level is a little
hotter than you'd expect.) Naan is great in all its
permutations, and don't forget to ask for some
mint chutney.

Standout dishes usually come from the list of
house specialties and dinner specials: for
example, Lhasa curry (a Tibetan mix of spices
and herbs in a creamy tomato sauce), mango
mazza (mango, paneer, and vegetables in a
spicy curry sauce), and anything in ko masu
curry (a Nepalese variety with spices, ginger, and
onions). There's an interesting selection of
imported bottled beers, including Lhasa, a hard-
to-find Tibetan brew.

Indian
Casual restaurant

Capitol Hill
1833 Broadway
(206) 320-7770

Hours
Mon–Thu
noon–9:30pm
Fri
noon–10:00pm
Sat
2:30pm–10:00pm
Sun
4:00pm–9:00pm

Bar
Beer, wine, liquor

Credit cards
Visa, MC, AmEx

Reservations
Accepted

Features
Good beers
Veg-friendly

Art of the Table

The last word on locavore supper clubs, at a price that's pretty easy on the wallet

www.artofthetable.net

Modern
Upmarket restaurant

Wallingford
1054 N. 39th St.
(206) 282–0942

Hours
Mon
5:00pm–10:00pm
Thu–Sat
7:00pm–7:15pm

Bar
Beer, wine, liquor

Credit cards
Visa, MC

Reservations
Essential

Features
Good beers

Chef-owner Dustin Ronspies cares so much about food that we almost worry about him—we can imagine him as the earnest hero of a graphic novel, affably living to serve while slowly being destroyed by the very thing that sustains him. Art of the Table is certainly a labor of love—despite a full schedule of set-menu suppers, the staff has topped out at four.

Each week's menu is based on trips to farmer's markets, which yield ingredients (peach, arugula) that are veritable snapshots of Washington State seasons. But Ronspies also goes outside of the Modern (Foraged) American mold, with, say, plump handmade ravioli.

On Thursday through Saturday nights, there's only one seating at 7pm—it's like a trip to Herbfarm—minus the long drive, pomp, and circumstance. ("Happy Mondays" bring à-la-carte small plates.) The wine list undershoots expectations, but there's an incredible list of international ales and lagers. The restaurant is tiny—20 seats at most, many at a communal table—and has a sweet, sunny, yellow-walled DIY vibe that is the Fremont-Wallingford hallmark. In the small kitchen, the bandana-clad chef might pause for photo ops and small talk as diners peer in over the pass-through. Each dinner is a low-key affair in which everyone is treated like family, and that's a central reason why we love it.

ART Restaurant & Lounge

This flashy hotel restaurant with a view shows potential, but style defeats substance

www.artrestaurantseattle.com

6.5	8.0
Food	Feel
$60	8.0
Price	Wine

Despite a well-pedigreed chef and a Vegas-cool interior, ART ends up replicating the same type of fancy, chilly, and ultimately empty hotel dining experience offered by many a glittering new tower. The fantastic, though obstructed, views of the Sound are nearly upstaged by the designed-to-within-an-inch-of-its-life interior, which includes lots of undulating shades of beige and brown splashed with, if you can believe it, ever-changing LED mood lighting that is at times lavender. Service is excellent, so dining here can feel special if you can ignore some of the cheesier design elements.

Creations are whimsical and clever, but sometimes to their own detriment—for example, it doesn't seem necessary to froth up a simple crab bisque into a "crab cappuccino" and put it in a coffee cup. To appreciate the talent in the kitchen, stick to the simpler, less fussy dishes like game hen with pearl-onion marmalade. During happy hour, prices go down—for instance, you can get a trio of the mini-burgers that were a big happy-hour draw at Cascadia, or an unlimited tapas buffet for less than $20.

The wine list is great any time of day—by-the-glass pours are more interesting that you often find, and the whole program is full of carefully chosen producers and a lot of local favorites. In fact, sunset drinks only might be the best way to appreciate this view—and then, when night falls, you can have dinner at a restaurant with a better value proposition.

Modern
Upmarket restaurant

Downtown
Four Seasons, 99 Union St.
(206) 749-7070

Hours
Daily
6:30am–2:00pm
5:00pm–10:00pm

Bar
Beer, wine, liquor

Credit cards
Visa, MC, AmEx

Reservations
Accepted

Features
Brunch
Date-friendly

7.5 8.0
Food | Feel

$15
Price

B&O Espresso

Desserts are so-so, coffee is better, and the
pseudo-French vibe is easy to like

www.b-oespresso.com

Coffee
Sweets
American
Café

Capitol Hill
204 Belmont Ave. E.
(206) 322-5028

Hours
Mon–Thu
11:00am–11:00pm
Fri–Sat
9:00am–1:00am
Sun
9:00am–11:00pm

Bar
Beer, wine, liquor

Credit cards
Visa, MC, AmEx

Reservations
Accepted

Features
Brunch
Date-friendly
Outdoor dining
Wi-Fi

Sure, B&O Espresso offers brunch (fluffy
omelettes, gooey chocolate pancakes, well-
seasoned fried 'taters) and dinner (so-so crab
cakes, and grilled salmon salads), but what your
average Seattleite loves most about B&O is its
dessert selection. Cases full of old-fashioned
cakes, most tooth-achingly sweet and a small
step up from the grocery store variety, makes
this local joint a popular choice for a little G-
rated hand-holding on a first date.

Despite the mediocrity of its desserts, B&O
seems to pack it in night after night. Perhaps it's
the comforting familiarity of its pseudo-French
interior, the ridiculously dim lighting (just as
effective as beer goggles!), or the fact that most
of its patrons have been coming since high
school—never discount the power of nostalgia.
Or maybe it's just because you're PMS-ragey
and really do need a 2-pound slab of the New
Orleans torte—flourless chocolate cake with
pecans and Bourbon—to chase that bottle of
Yellow Tail. (Quantity over quality in times of
distress is perfectly understandable.) True to its
name, B&O offers a whole slew of coffee drinks,
from espresso to Turkish coffee to boozy after-
dinner drinks like B52 with Baileys, Kaluha, and
Grand Marnier. Caffeine leave you too wired?
There's a full list of moderately exciting
cocktails, wines, and beers, too.

B&O Espresso has found its niche as one of
the most popular dessert spots in the city.
Anyone who values food over feel may not
know why, but one can't dispute the facts.

Baguette Box

Much pricier than real-deal banh mi, but
much more tricked-out, too

7.0 Food

5.0 Feel

$15 Price

www.baguettebox.com

From the same team that created the upscale
Vietnamese fusion at Monsoon, Baguette Box
starts with a simple idea—the banh mi
sandwich—and ends up with an eclectic menu.
The bread's a big selling point—big, chewy
baguettes do justice to the eatery's name—and
all other ingredients are of high quality: organic
mixed greens in the salads are downright perky;
beef and pork are also organic or sustainably
raised. Concoctions range in geography from
vaguely Middle Eastern (roasted leg of lamb
with cucumber yogurt and harissa) to overtly
Spanish (Serrano ham, red peppers, and
Manchego) to Vietnamese-for-beginners
(lemongrass steak with pickled daikon and
carrots).

Baguette Box's pork loin is boring, however,
and its chicken is deeply divisive. Some profess
an addiction to the crispy, garlicky drunken
chicken, but one of our panelists was reminded
of Trader Joe's orange chicken frozen dinner.

What all agree upon is that the Capitol Hill
location is far superior to the Fremont one: the
food and service are better, and instead of
being stuck between a Peet's and a Coldstone
Creamery (as in Fremont), Cap Hill's shop
occupies a classic, high-ceilinged, converted
industrial space.

**Sandwiches
Vietnamese**
Counter service

Capitol Hill
1203 Pine St.
(206) 332-0220

Fremont
626 N. 34th St.
(206) 632-1511

Hours
Daily
11:00am–8:00pm
Hours vary by location

Bar
Beer, wine

Credit cards
Visa, MC, AmEx

Features
Kid-friendly

Bakery Nouveau

The type of sinful pastry-crust eating that
defines special occasions...or Tuesdays

www.bakerynouveau.com

Breads
Sweets
Coffee
Counter service

West Seattle
4737 California Ave. SW
(206) 923-0534

Hours
Mon–Thu
6:00am–8:00pm
Fri
6:00am–10:00pm
Sat
7:00am–10:00pm
Sun
7:00am–8:00pm

Bar
None

Credit cards
Visa, MC

Reservations
Not accepted

Features
Kid-friendly
Outdoor dining

Bakery Nouveau is a near-perfect replica of a
typical Parisian bakery, and it provokes all sorts
of poetic devotion from the panel. Croissants
fragment into brittle shards when bitten, the
buttery crumbs breaking all over your sweater
like a stained glass window from a medieval
church sacked by Vikings.

Along with the croissants, confections with
designs as intricate as Victorian wallpaper, and
cakes that will make you the hero of any party,
Bakery Nouveau makes excellent quiches, the
best being the classic quiche Lorraine (fluffy
eggs dotted with chunks of crisp bacon glued
together with gruyère in a flaky pastry shell).

On weekends, expect long lines of latte-
sipping soccer moms. If you expect to sit down
in peace and quiet, the best way to experience
the bakery is midday, midweek, while skipping
work and pretending you're an unemployed
Frenchman on the dole. Don't be too hung up
on finding a suitable perch here; aside from the
seemingly miles-long pastry case, the place
looks like a pretty standard coffeehouse.

Bamboo Garden

Jellyfish, kidneys, and pig's-blood, oh my!

8.5 Food

7.0 Feel

$20 Price

www.bamboogardendining.com

We love an authentic Szechuan restaurant that doesn't tone down the spice in order to appease unadventurous diners. And we love any venue that appears to be channeling Lou Reed. So, yes, we love Bamboo Garden.

There's plenty of complexity, heat, and variety on the regular menu, but it's the section that beckons diners to "Take a Walk on the Wild Side" that excites us. Spicy dry-cooked frog, sour and spicy jellyfish, intestines from various animals—you can easily earn your trying-weird-stuff badge in one sitting. (The Wild Side also includes the area's best rendition of swimming fire fish.)

But let that not distract you from the ordinary—there's lots of "ma la" action (numbing, spicy, tingly, and fruity—all at once—from Szechuan peppercorns) in many of the dishes, especially in the fiery pot of fish pieces and the chong qing chicken. The hand-shaved noodles are another must-try.

Is it really a garden? Well, it comes closer than most of the thousands of Chinese restaurants that misuse that descriptor—there are, after all, bits of bamboo throughout the dining room. Although the place is still in the realm of casual dining, big booths, darker woods, and dimmer lighting make it look like Canlis compared to most Chinese restaurants.

Chinese
Casual restaurant

Bellevue
202 106th Pl. NE
(425) 688-7991

Hours
Mon–Thu
11:00am–3:00pm
5:00pm–9:30pm
Fri
11:00am–3:00pm
5:00pm–10:00pm
Sat–Sun
11:30am–10:00pm

Bar
Beer, wine, liquor

Credit cards
Visa, MC

Reservations
Accepted

Features
Kid-friendly

Barking Frog

Woodinville's other serious restaurant, and
a suitable end to a winery tour

www.willowslodge.com

Modern
Upmarket restaurant

Eastside
14580 NE 145th St.
(425) 424-2999

Hours
Mon–Fri
6:00am–10:30am
11:30am–2:30pm
5:00pm–10:00pm
Sat–Sun
6:00am–2:30pm
5:00pm–10:00pm

Bar
Beer, wine, liquor

Credit cards
Visa, MC, AmEx

Reservations
Accepted

Features
Brunch
Date-friendly

Nestled in the warm bosom of the fancy spa-
resort Willows Lodge, Barking Frog seems to be
doing its best impression of a Whistler après-ski
restaurant. The décor is rather dated, with an
overreliance on dark woods to create ambience,
but it does have a lovely bar circling a fire pit—
ask for a seat here or at one of the tables next
to the windows that look out onto the garden.

The food is simple contemporary Northwest
cooking—expect halibut, pea vines, foraged
mushrooms, and Dungeness crab—with a few
fun surprises (popcorn lobster with a ginger-
mirin dipping sauce, for example, or buttermilk-
fried quail, in a cute twist on chicken and
waffles). Everything's fresh and beautifully
presented, but most of it's also very heavy—
something to keep in mind on a warm summer
evening.

You could do your Woodinville wine tasting
here without leaving the grounds. All of the
best Woodinville wineries are amply
represented, as are the rest of Washington State
and Oregon. It's an overwhelmingly deep list of
regional wines, with everything from affordable
Mark Ryan and L'Ecole to $200 showpieces
from DeLille.

Barolo Ristorante

Rich food for rich people—or those wanting to play rich—at a see-and-be-seen place

6.0	5.0
Food	Feel

$65	9.0
Price	Wine

www.baroloseattle.com

Posh Barolo certainly has that fancy feeling, but there's no focus to the design. Oil paintings, the Italian marble bar, angled mirrors, and candelabra everywhere suggest (as does the menu) classic high-end Italian. But aside from some green booths and white couches in the bar area, the dominant color is black—when the lights are low, it looks like someone threw tar all over a perfectly nice restaurant.

Why would someone do such a thing?

Because this place is in Belltown. And Barolo is Belltown at its most irritating. However talented some of the people in the kitchen are, the place reeks of inauthenticity—of hipness and of not caring about the customer.

House-made pasta is the best thing here, especially when the kitchen keeps things light (gnocchi with fresh mozzarella and tomato sauce versus gnocchi al fagiano with braised pheasant, rich cheese, and foie gras).

Prices are too high, except at happy hour. The food is always at least serviceable, but the knowledge that the owners had such strong traditions in mind when opening the place makes Barolo feel like a colossal miss. But the wine list saves the day with some truly special bottles, and plenty of affordable ones, too.

Italian
Upmarket restaurant

Belltown
1940 Westlake Ave.
(206) 770-9000

Hours
Mon–Thu
11:30am–10:30pm
Fri
11:30am–11:00pm
Sat
4:30pm–11:00pm

Bar
Beer, wine, liquor

Credit cards
Visa, MC, AmEx

Reservations
Accepted

Features
Veg-friendly

Barracuda Taquería

Trendy tacos—but in a good way—that play nice with the menudo standard

www.barracudatacos.com

Mexican
Counter service

Belltown
159 Denny Way
(206) 448-2062

Hours
Mon–Thu
11:00am–10:00pm
Fri
11:00am–11:00pm
Sat
9:00am–11:00pm
Sun
9:00am–3:00pm

Bar
Beer, wine

Credit cards
Visa, MC

Reservations
Not accepted

Features
Kid-friendly

Barracuda peddles reasonably authentic Mexican street food at only slightly inflated prices (inflated by taco standards, at least—we're still talking single digits). They have tortas and sopas, but the tacos are the focus here; tangy al pastor, and luscious lengua (tongue) are amongst the highlights. Barbacoa comes as a breakfast taco, with eggs and cheese added to the slow-cooked beef.

All of these tacos are really tasty—the corn tortillas are handmade, and the fish tacos are seasonal, based on what's available at the market. Two of the less obvious offerings, the black mole and the menudo (tripe soup), are the weakest.

On the balance, this is probably the most attractive taco joint in town: an oriental rug drapes the wood floors by the counter, and although some of the hodge-podge of wooden chairs are painted white and green, there's precious little garish Mexican paraphernalia. The only attempt at art is a Mondrian-esque mural made of Dos Equis bottlecaps. Barracuda isn't too trendy, though: it's as low-key as a place with decent cheap sangría should be.

Barrio

A competent nouvelle Mexican kitchen and an even better bar

www.barriorestaurant.com

7.0 Food

8.5 Feel

$40 Price

Mexican
Upmarket restaurant

Bellevue
10650 NE 4th St.
(425) 502-5021

Capitol Hill
1420 12th Ave.
(206) 588-8105

Hours
Mon–Thu
11:30am–10:00pm
Fri
11:30am–11:00pm
Sat
10:30am–11:00pm
Sun
10:30am–10:00pm

Bar
Beer, wine, liquor, BYO

Credit cards
Visa, MC, AmEx

Reservations
Accepted

Features
Brunch
Good cocktails

It's not even worth debating Barrio's authenticity. It's exactly the type of restaurant that goes in on the ground floor of a shmancy condo development to convince the new residents that they don't stick out like a thousand popped collars. It's also owned by the Purple Café people, which isn't exactly a stunning testament to anything.

That said, some comforting words adorn Barrio's menu: al pastor, pozole, churros. There are a million ways to make not-quite-authentic Mexican food, and Barrio has chosen a reasonable path, excelling at some of the iconic dishes (chilaquiles and churros are really good), and filling in the rest of the menu with an inoffensive stew of Pacific Northwest/Nuevo Latino cooking. Witness the "border sliders": grilled wagyu beef, chorizo bacon, jack cheese, escabeche slaw, guacamole, and charred pineapple mustard.

If flavor is the most important thing, you're better off slumming it at a taco truck. If drinking heavily and reveling in the kind of immortality that only high design and the prescient flickering of hundreds of candles can deliver, Barrio won't disappoint. It's a sexy restaurant, although like most of us, it looks better in the dark; in daylight it's kind of corporate and boring. Friends, fabulous margaritas and mixed drinks, a few select nibbles, and loud conversation: there are certainly worse ways to spend an evening on the Hill.

Bastille

La controverse—conflicting opinions on the romantic, finely realized Francophilia here

www.bastilleseattle.com

French
Upmarket restaurant

Ballard
5307 Ballard Ave. NW
(206) 453-5014

Hours
Mon–Thu
4:30pm–10:00pm
Fri–Sat
4:30pm–11:00pm
Sun
10:00am–2:00pm
4:30pm–10:00pm
Daily
4:30pm–1:00am
back bar

Bar
Beer, wine, liquor

Credit cards
Visa, MC, AmEx

Reservations
Accepted

Features
Brunch
Date-friendly
Good cocktails
Outdoor dining

Bastille serves classic French brasserie dishes in a classic French environment, and lately, the results have been all over the board. At one visit, mussels may arrive plump and well balanced, but then the much-heralded lamb sliders might come out bland and dry. When your salad greens are plucked from the rooftop garden, you'll suddenly feel like you're part of something special. Midwinter, when your simple sautéed vegetables arrive overcooked, you feel like the sucker who paid $3 for bread at a French restaurant.

Fries do finally seem to be improving (sometimes), and it's about time: nearly every critic in Seattle has complained about them. Cocktails are good, and the wine list is extensive, covering France exhaustively, but the markups are insane. So why go?

Well, Bastille is beautifully designed. The main dining room has a huge zinc bar, a fire pit surrounded by bar stools, and the ideal ratio of cozy booths and café tables. The back bar, with stained glass and antique chandeliers, is like a cathedral dedicated to the patron saint of long, boozy nights with friends and lovers.

There is also the periodic, sudden food hit, such as a copper pot of super-tender braised pork cheeks, onions, and potatoes in a really dark, rich gravy.

We suggest treating Bastille either as a bar that serves food (there is real value at happy hour) or as a "we're splurging on the *experience*" expense-account spot. And who knows? You may get a great meal out of it.

BCD Tofu House

Rule of thumb: a place with "tofu" in its name is good if Korean, bad if American

8.0	5.0
Food	Feel

$20
Price

www.bcdtofu.com

Yeah, it's a chain. Yeah, the choice of locations is between Edmonds next to a Ranch 99 grocery store or in a Lynnwood H Mart food court. But BCD's Korean snacks are consistently well made, inexpensive, quick, and tasty. Nothing fancy, nothing high-end, but filling and fun.

What more can one ask from a bowl of soft tofu soup? It comes bubblingly hot to the table, along with a bounty of banchan, including a whole fried fish. Soups come with safe choices of beef or pork, or with an upgrade of ox intestines. The soups are definitely the best thing on the menu, but BCD also serves teriyaki, barbecue ribs, and bi bim bap.

Even though the Edmonds location feels much more like a real restaurant, if you have a choice, go to the North Seattle H Mart branch. H Mart is an excellent chain of Korean grocery stores, of which there aren't many in Washington State. Although it's counter-service-only in North Seattle, this is one fast-food joint where it's actually fun to watch the cooks at work while you wait for your order, half-obscured as they are by the steam rising out of the tofu bowls.

Korean
Counter service

North Seattle
3301 184th St. SW
(425) 776-8001

Edmonds
22511 Hwy. 99
(425) 670-6757

Hours
Mon–Thu
7:00am–3:00am
Fri–Sat
24 hours
Sun
7:00am–3:00am

Bar
Beer, wine

Credit cards
Visa, MC

Features
Kid-friendly
Veg-friendly

7.0 Food · 5.0 Feel

Bengal Tiger

Standard Indian that manages to stand out among the area's many lunch buffets

$25 Price

www.bengaltigerwa.com

Indian
Casual restaurant

University District
6510 Roosevelt Way NE
(206) 985-0041

Hours
Mon–Sat
11:00am–10:00pm
Sun
11:00am–9:00pm

Bar
Beer, wine, BYO

Credit cards
Visa, MC, AmEx

Reservations
Accepted

Features
Kid-friendly
Veg-friendly

UW students love their cheap Indian lunch buffets, and Bengal Tiger's is the best in the neighborhood—and one of the cheapest, too.

But this isn't just a feeding trough for broke underclassmen. It also gets high marks for dinner, when you can puzzle over a vast array of curries which could, however, benefit from a bit of editing. Butter chicken is a favorite, but after years of regular visits our panel can safely say that nothing really disappoints. A few fun extras are a good beer list, which has both the typical domestic and Pacific Northwest beers plus a nice selection of Indian beers, and better-than-average desserts (particularly anything made with mango).

The décor is a little dated—the carpet is dreadful and hopefully not reflective of the cleanliness of the kitchen—and there are too many reviews of the restaurant plastered everywhere. But the friendly staff makes dining here pleasant enough.

Beth's Café

A famous dive diner, yes, but not for the intrinsic qualities of the food

4.0 Food

5.0 Feel

$15 Price

www.bethscafe.com

A favorite of truckers, drunk college students, and people across America who once saw this local institution and its 12-egg omelette on the Food Network, Beth's Café is a nondescript hole-in-the-wall that's more about character (of which it has tons) than about the food (which sucks).

If you want biscuits that taste like they came from a can, Beth's has got them. If you crave mysterious white gravy that tastes like wallpaper paste, Beth's has got it. If the idea of a greasy 12-egg omelette so big it's served in a pizza pan, plus unlimited hash browns has you sweating and quivering with desire, then you're going to love Beth's.

The diner is more than 50 years old, and looks every bit its age. It's a Seattle landmark, but it's one that probably needs a serious facelift. You can play tunes on their junkbox, or tape your drawings up on their walls while you're waiting for your grub. They'll provide the crayons, as long as you provide the pre-game alcohol-induced artistry.

American
Casual restaurant

Green Lake
7311 Aurora Ave. N.
(206) 782-5588

Hours
24 hours

Bar
None

Credit cards
Visa, MC

Reservations
Not accepted

Features
Kid-friendly

6.5	5.0
Food	Feel

$45	8.0
Price	Wine

Betty

Reliable, if not particularly inspired, food—
and the same can be said about the décor

www.eatatbetty.com

American
Casual restaurant

Queen Anne
1507 Queen Anne Ave.
N.
(206) 352-3773

Hours
Mon–Sat
5:00pm–10:00pm
Sun
5:00pm–9:00pm

Bar
Beer, wine, liquor

Credit cards
Visa, MC, AmEx

Reservations
Accepted

The food at Betty isn't bad, but it's just not as exciting as its reputation would imply. The "Betty Burger," the only regular item on the very small menu, is juicy but bland. It's automatically served a bloody shade of rare, something of which our panel approves, but if you're squeamish about raw beef, have a conversation with your server before you order this. Reading the rest of the menu will bore you to tears if you've eaten recently at any place with a remotely Northwest agenda—the same old roast chicken with fingerling potatoes, chops of some sort with salsa freaking verde, and English peas snuggling up to everything.

Occasionally, you'll get something a little more inspired, like rabbit-and-pistachio terrine—a rustic slab of deliciousness wrapped in thick meaty slabs of bacon—or a risotto so creamy that you could use it as conditioner. But we're not convinced that's a good thing in this case. Another hit is the delicious chickpea and grilled octopus appetizer.

Betty has a pretty standard interior, with wooden booths, concrete floors, and terrible art on the walls. But if any of that is a deal-breaker, then you might be ill-suited to much of the Seattle restaurant scene.

Betty is content to follow city-wide trends. In fact, the only thing that sets it in stark contrast to its concrete-floored brethren is its awesomely affordable wine list, with good regional and European bottles.

Bisato

Expensive, hit-or-miss small plates—plan to have a second dinner afterward

6.0	8.0
Food	Feel

$60	7.0
Price	Wine

www.bisato.com

At Bisato, rectangles of polenta are served with "meat ragù" that's processed to a paste so that it can be served on its tiny gleaming plate as a quenelle. This flourish comes with an unintended consequence: the ragù has the texture of cat food.

It's probably redundant at this point to say Bisato favors style over substance. On average, 10 out of 10 small plates will look amazing; but maybe only two out of 10 will impress you. If you're in a devil-may-care mood, then you could have a lot of fun here, sipping wine and making bets with everyone at the table.

When you get a dish that actually lands—like branzino with a quenelle of black trumpet mushroom paste and asparagus risotto— everyone downs a Jello shot. In quenelle form, of course. Otherwise, you might be inspired to take your chances with the wine list: it's very interesting, with lots of unique selections, but it's also a tad overpriced.

The fancy, bright red charcuterie slicer by the bar is a cool focal point of the room, which, with its lively bar curving around the semi-open kitchen and its more secluded window tables, is both a date spot and a place for Belltown revelry pre-funk. But a lot of the food is just too funky for this price point.

Modern
Upmarket restaurant

Belltown
2400 1st Ave.
(206) 443-3301

Hours
Tue–Sat
5:00pm–10:30pm
Sun
5:00pm–10:00pm

Bar
Beer, wine, liquor

Credit cards
Visa, MC, AmEx

Reservations
Not accepted

Features
Date-friendly

7.0	7.5
Food	Feel

$40	6.0
Price	Wine

Bizzarro Italian Café

There's some pretty good creative Italian hiding amid all the zaniness

www.bizzarroitaliancafe.com

Italian
Casual restaurant

Wallingford
1307 N. 46th St.
(206) 632-7277

Hours
Daily
5:00pm–10:00pm

Bar
Beer, wine

Credit cards
Visa, MC

Reservations
Not accepted

Features
Veg-friendly

Bizzarro's interior is studiously wacky. It looks like a flea market threw up—there's a tandem bike and a traffic signal, among many other things, hanging from the ceiling; all manner of knick-knacks, trinkets, statuettes, and scribbled notes cover every other square inch of the place. It helps that the friendly staff clearly digs the strangeness of it all.

But the surprises don't stop at the ceiling. Bizzarro makes some good Italian food. This is a locavore joint, with most ingredients sourced from within a 300-mile radius, so everything is very fresh and showcases the best of Washington State. The wine list boasts decent prices, and is reasonably well chosen, but ultimately too short and narrow. Still, there's a nice focus on Old World bottles and lesser known producers.

There are some classic preparations here, like clams in a spicy tomato sauce and spinach ravioli—this place definitely caters to the comfort-food eater. But there are more creative dishes, too, like capellini in a modified pesto made with arugula, pistachios, garlic, and parmesan; or gnocchi stuffed with tongue, cheeks, or other often-wasted parts of animals. Most dishes are hits, with one in five being a miss that just doesn't come together.

Black Bottle

Seattle's original gastropub has kept its
strange menu and approachable wine list

www.blackbottleseattle.com

6.5	8.5
Food	Feel

$35	7.0
Price	Wine

Modern
Bar

Belltown
2600 1st Ave.
(206) 441-1500

Hours
Daily
4:00pm–midnight

Bar
Beer, wine, liquor

Credit cards
Visa, MC, AmEx

Reservations
Accepted

Features
Date-friendly
Outdoor dining
Veg-friendly

We don't know how the Black Bottle's managed to stay somewhat classy. It's deep in the belly of the Belltown beast, yet most of the time it feels like a break from the 1st Avenue mayhem. Oh, it's still a meat market—how can it not be when it's lit to make everyone look beautiful?—but the high ceilings, white walls and bare bulbs give it the air of an art gallery and the guy next to you might be wearing architectural eyewear instead of a popped collar.

Black Bottle was Seattle's first official gastropub. Even in the more forgiving days of 2005, patrons weren't keen on the incredibly unfocused menu: a Thai standard like larb gai next to Northwest classics like locally made sausages, or simple steamed clams next to South Asian lamb and curried vegetables. The prices are a bit all over the place, too: $5 for fried chicken, $9 for a flatbread. Vegetable dishes (there are plenty) are the most consistently good. The "Broccoli Blasted"—charred florets brushed with olive oil and generously salted—is a favorite, but a word of advice: don't try to eat a whole plate at once; it's as gross as eating a whole chocolate cake by yourself.

Although it's clearly wine-centric, the Black Bottle has an odd list that seems targeted to people who don't really know wine but want to feel like they do. That said, there are some very affordable boutique selections, too. And the bar's almost equally known for its sangría, margaritas, and mojitos.

5.0 Food
6.0 Feel

$20
Price

Blue C Sushi

Uneven conveyor-belt sushi with J-Pop
sensibilities and American palates in mind

www.bluecsushi.com

Japanese
Counter service

Fremont
3411 Fremont Ave. N.
(206) 633-3411

Downtown
1510 7th Ave.
(206) 467-4022

University District
4601 26th Ave. NE
(206) 525-4601

Hours
Mon–Thu
11:30am–9:00pm
Fri
11:30am–10:00pm
Sat
noon–10:00pm
Sun
noon–9:00pm
Hours vary by location

Bar
Beer, wine, liquor

Credit cards
Visa, MC, AmEx

Reservations
Not accepted

Features
Kid-friendly

Blue C is a tough one. On one hand, grabbing a
"Seattle Roll" (like bagel and lox, only
disgusting) from a conveyor belt is an offense in
a town where there are sushi bars serving
spectacular uni and even cod semen. On the
other hand, cute, cheap, and innocuously weird
has its place.

Blue C's mod restaurants are certainly
adorable. Color-coded plates of simple rolls,
nigiri, and hot items like chicken katsu and
"Tokyo sweets" (mostly puff pastries), chug by
while silly videos showcase all manner of
Japanese obsessives, from LARPers to rockabilly
boys.

The clearly labeled and cautiously seasoned
dishes will delight sushi beginners. But the
biggest problem is that freshness varies:
although several of our panel members have
dined at the Fremont and Downtown locations
frequently without incident, there have been
enough outside reports of grossness to urge
some caution. You could stick to the veggie rolls
and hot dishes and have a reasonably satisfying
lunch. Or just trust your instincts and your
nose—the staff at most branches are friendly
and accommodating. Maybe this is why Blue C's
popularity so far outstrips its quality.

Blueacre Seafood

A worthy, focused maritime successor to
Steelhead Diner

7.5	7.0
Food	Feel

$50	8.0
Price	Wine

www.blueacreseafood.com

Blueacre is the newest space from the owners of
Steelhead Diner, and it shares some of the same
quirks, like an annoyingly cutesy menu (with
sections divided into themes like the "craggy
moor" and "belly full o' steam") and the
perpetuation of bad trends (making wagyu beef
into a burger—a waste of expensive meat—and
smothering it in Tillamook cheese).

Beyond a few boring meats, Blueacre's menu
is utterly focused on seafood. At the raw bar are
Hood Canal and Puget Sound all-stars,
Kumamotos, and Wellfleets from Cape Cod.
Mains range from Rainier-beer-battered fish and
chips to several selections of (refreshingly) whole
fishes (usually American varieties like Idaho trout
and catfish, and highly recommended).

Blueacre's menu descriptions are much more
playful than the preparations, which rely (not in
a bad way) on garlic and lemon, brown butter,
or the dreaded soy glaze. When you do get a bit
of hazelnut romesco or a Peruvian-inspired aji
amarillo, it perks up the dish without
overwhelming it. The wide-ranging wine list is
especially conducive to having a nip at lunch,
with a nice selection of by-the-glass pours.

The space is attractive: the blue accents in a
mounted marlin or a blown-up photo of a
butterfly play pleasantly off of the shiny
sharkskin blue booths. At any rate, it's a nice,
open space, bright and cheerful while looking
reasonably grown-up.

Seafood
Upmarket restaurant

Belltown
1700 7th Ave.
(206) 659-0737

Hours
Daily
11:00am–10:00pm

Bar
Beer, wine, liquor

Credit cards
Visa, MC, AmEx

Reservations
Accepted

Features
Date-friendly

8.5	9.0
Food	Feel

$50	9.0
Price	Wine

Boat Street Café

Unpretentious, possibly romantic, and on the best-of-the-Northwest list

www.boatstreetcafe.com

French
Upmarket restaurant

Queen Anne
3131 Western Ave.
(206) 632-4602

Hours
Sun–Mon
10:30am–2:30pm
Tue–Sat
10:30am–2:30pm
5:00pm–10:00pm

Bar
Beer, wine

Credit cards
Visa, MC

Reservations
Not accepted

Features
Brunch
Date-friendly
Good cocktails
Outdoor dining

Some of our panelists are more enamored with Boat Street than others, but all can muster a hearty huzzah for its good, simple French-inflected fare. The simpler the dish, the better: duck breast on greens or roasted chicken with chicory polenta, dishes that might fall flat in lesser hands, are light but satisfying when in this kitchen's watch.

More ambitious mains are sometimes less impressive, but appetizers and desserts get consistent praise. And Boat Street has one unusual and delightful gimmick: the chef is a pickling fiend. Order anything that includes pickled vegetables and fruits (from onions to fennel to figs and raisins), and prepare for a magical journey to the land of supertang.

The white-on-white dining room goes for "whimsical Northwest" rather than *Fraaanch*, with upside-down paper umbrellas and Christmas-light-entwined tree branches hanging from the ceiling. Despite being at the end of Western Avenue in a weird building, this is one of the most romantic restaurants in town. It's a great first-date pick, cozy and intimate but not stuffy or too chi-chi.

And there's plenty of premium booze to help keep the conversation going. Although there's room for improvement on the Champagne side of things, Boat Street's bar really knows how to make a Kir Royale. And there's a long list of well-priced wines ranging from the Loire Valley to Provence and the Rhône.

Boiling Point

"So hot. So bubbly. So stinky. So wanty."

7.5 Food

7.0 Feel

$25 Price

Chinese
Casual restaurant

Bellevue
1075 Bellevue Way NE
(425) 455-8375

Hours
Daily
11:00am–11:00pm

Credit cards
Visa, MC

Reservations
Not accepted

Features
Kid-friendly

Before you start penning irate letters, we should make it clear that the above quote is from Boiling Point's own menu. This twee mantra describes the "Stinky Tofu Hot Pot"—a mélange of meatball, pork blood, pork intestine, and quail egg along with the stinky (fermented) tofu. Though this isn't the best thing on the menu—they get the acrid, eye-watering smell of the tofu right, but the flavor's not as strong as we like it—it represents the outer limits of Boiling Point's menu, and why it has an almost exclusively Chinese clientele.

The menu is pretty much just hot pots and cold drinks (including bubble teas). Everyone's eating the same thing; it's just the contents of the hot pot that differ—curry fish balls, kimchi, lamb beef. More heat is available at the little spice bar if five stars isn't enough (and it might not be).

It's a sight to see, all the steaming hot pots coming from the kitchen to the tables—and it's especially fun on a cold day. Boiling Point may not be compelling enough to warrant a long trip, but it's a great lunch stop in Bellevue. Note that it's really small, and gets packed at dinner, so don't arrive with a large group.

BOKA Kitchen + Bar

Hotel 1000's übertrendy lounge and bar isn't bad—especially at happy hour

www.bokaseattle.com

Modern
Upmarket restaurant

Downtown
1010 1st Ave.
(206) 357-9000

Hours
Mon–Fri
6:30am–midnight
Sat–Sun
8:00am–midnight

Bar
Beer, wine, liquor

Credit cards
Visa, MC, AmEx

Reservations
Accepted

Features
Date-friendly
Good cocktails

If discovering that the name is an acronym for Bold, Original Kitchen Artistry makes you want to throw a pomegranate-infused Molotov cocktail through a giant plate-glass window, BOKA's probably not for you. Service can be snooty at times; the interior is the kind of sexy that probably carries a corporate trademark; and the menu lacks focus.

But if you're tired of the "rustic chic" being peddled so hard all over town, and don't want to go into the heart of darkness (i.e. Belltown), then BOKA's a passable place to spend some money, feel fancy, and have a few interesting cocktails (lemongrass dry soda, yellow bell pepper, and Aviation gin? Nice.).

Happy hour is the best time to visit, bringing with it $3 and $6 small plates, $9 burgers, and discounted cocktails, and taking away a good bit of BOKA's sticker shock.

The kitchen is competent. Small plates are all over the place (house-made pretzels, ahi tartare with salsa verde, quail egg, parmesan crackers), while some gourmet flourishes scale the heights of laziness or pretentiousness (waygu beef hot dogs, fries with truffle oil), but mains are simpler and more focused: simply cooked quality cuts of local meat and fish with light sauces and sides. Still, it's far from enough to justify the prices and pretense here.

Boom Noodle

A trendy spot for noodle soups and Asian snacks and...did we mention trendy?

7.0 Food
7.0 Feel

$35 Price

www.boomnoodle.com

Boom Noodle, with its attempt to bring sexy back to the noodle bowl, appears at first glance to be Asian food for Caucasians—the type of Caucasians that are impressed by backlit Stoli bottles at the bar. But Chef Jonathan Hunt is far more sincere than his hip spot with its fancy cocktails would suggest. Although he has little formal training in Asian cuisines, he's traveled extensively in Japan researching classic recipes to riff on, and he has great intuition.

Not everything here works—some simple pleasures like pork gyoza and calamari are disappointing—but the kitchen has a way with salmon, and the simple noodle soups, along with some fun fusion snacks like edamame purée with sweet potato crisps and white prawns wrapped in crunchy phyllo, are consistently good. And the location in the University District has weekend breakfast service.

Boom does the lounge vibe well—it's modern but not overly trendy—but it always feels a bit strange to have lunch here. Even with the garage-style windows rolled up on sunny days, the place still has that late-night aura, and it just feels kind of wrong to dine here in daylight.

Japanese
Upmarket restaurant

Capitol Hill
1121 E. Pike St.
(206) 701-9130

University District
2675 NE Village Lane
(206) 525-2675

Bellevue
504 Bellevue Way NE
(425) 453-6094

Hours
Mon–Wed
11:30am–10:00pm
Thu
11:30am–11:00pm
Fri
11:30am–midnight
Sat
noon–midnight
Sun
noon–10:00pm
Hours vary by location

Bar
Beer, wine, liquor

Credit cards
Visa, MC, AmEx

Reservations
Not accepted

Features
Good cocktails
Wi-Fi

7.5	8.5
Food	Feel

$40	8.0
Price	Wine

Brad's Swingside Café

A Fremont institution known for its laid-back quirkitude and simple Northern Italian

Italian
Upmarket restaurant

Fremont
4212 Fremont Ave. N.
(206) 633-4057

Hours
Tue–Sat
5:30pm–10:00pm

Bar
Beer, wine

Credit cards
Visa, MC

Reservations
Not accepted

Features
Outdoor dining
Veg-friendly

Out of all the Italian places in Seattle trying to create authentic hominess, Brad's gets closest to the mark—it's a shack (excuse us, cottage), with creaky floors and screen doors. Dining here feels like being a kid playing "restaurant" in your friend's garage. There's even baseball memorabilia on the walls.

No, you don't understand: it *really* feels like dining with your family—one panelist saw the chef burn the Bolognese and throw it out, all the while cursing and talking about it loud enough for the entire dining room to hear.

Even the most grown-up parts of the menu have a hominess to them: hearty dishes like wild boar and venison pasta in a light tomato cream sauce, or seasonal seafood farfalle with baby fennel root and wild mushrooms, are much like haute versions of meals once shrouded in the innocuous comfort of childhood: they're rich and tasty, if short of spectacular.

Although the wine list is extensive on paper, you never know what they'll actually have in stock. Generally speaking, you'll find good, rustic Northern Italian wines without any bells or whistles. But that too is fitting—if anything were too polished here, it would feel out of place.

Branzino

Creative Italian in a space with just the right amount of Belltown glitz

8.0	7.5
Food	Feel

$50	7.5
Price	Wine

www.branzinoseattle.com

Branzino had barely collected its first round of fawning reviews when original chef Ashley Merriman answered the siren's call of *Top Chef*. That was a bummer, but her replacement, Quinton Stewart, who worked at Tilth and also under Merriman, has plenty of experience following the tenets of local, seasonal cooking. The quality has remained consistent and high.

The name isn't a misnomer: seafood is Branzino's strong suit, with the namesake fish sharing the menu with local catches like halibut. Homemade pastas are also strong, and the best of them often showcase seasonal treats like wild mushrooms. The wine list is concise and careful, with bottles that will match well with this food.

Branzino is like an amuse-bouche for Belltown. The space is hip, but not chilly, oddly themed, or too '80s or '90s. The high-backed wooden booths are attractive, if not terribly comfortable, and offer a bit of privacy in a small space that often gets packed and loud. On weekends, there's eye candy galore, but during the week, this is a cozy local spot where everyone knows each other. Or at least that's how it feels.

Italian
Upmarket restaurant

Belltown
2429 2nd Ave.
(206) 728-5181

Hours
Mon
5:00pm–10:00pm
Tue–Thu
5:00pm–11:00pm
Fri–Sat
5:00pm–midnight
Sun
4:00pm–10:00pm

Bar
Beer, wine, liquor

Credit cards
Visa, MC, AmEx

Reservations
Accepted

5.0
Food

8.0
Feel

$25
Price

Brickyard BBQ

If this place were only a bar, we'd be just fine with that

www.brickyardbarbq.com

Southern
Casual restaurant

West Seattle
2308 California Ave. SW
(206) 933-3109

Hours
Daily
11:00am–2:00am

Bar
Beer, wine, liquor

Credit cards
Visa, MC, AmEx

Reservations
Not accepted

Features
Outdoor dining
Wi-Fi

Brickyard is maddeningly inconsistent. The pulled-pork sandwich is quite good, holding onto a hint of smoke and doused with a light, tangy sauce, but the beef brisket is sometimes so dry that, when cut into, it flakes apart like salmon. Brickyard's version of "spicy" would be safe to feed to an infant.

Although mac and cheese and cornbread are decent, some of the other sides are laughable: baked beans swimming in a ketchupy sauce, or a "salad" of peas, cubed cheddar, and raw red onion swimming in mayonnaise. (While the latter may be traceable to some down-home tradition or other, part of being a good chef is knowing which traditions are worth inflicting on gullible urbanites.)

Brickyard is a pretty decent watering hole, though. There's a good beer selection—the prerequisite domestics plus lots of microbrews—and a large selection of hard liquor, from Basil Hayden to Wild Turkey. The inside is cramped, but the outdoor seating area is a fun place to catch a few rays of sun. And the staff is friendly enough to make us wish we could give the place higher food marks.

Brouwer's Café

The best beer list in the city, and Belgian bar food to match it

6.5 Food
8.0 Feel

$40 Price

www.brouwerscafe.blogspot.com

Belgian
Casual restaurant

Fremont
400 N. 35th St.
(206) 267-2437

Hours
Mon–Thu
11:00am–10:00pm
Fri–Sat
11:00am–11:00pm
Sun
11:00am–10:00pm

Bar
Beer, wine, liquor

Credit cards
Visa, MC, AmEx

Reservations
Not accepted

Features
Good beers
Outdoor dining

There isn't a bar in Seattle that can top Brouwer's for beer. The bottled beer list is longer than a Northern European winter, and the on-tap list is longer than many restaurants' wine lists. Belgium and the Pacific Northwest are the most thoroughly represented, and we love how thoughtful the Northwest selection is—half a dozen Hair of the Dogs and not a Red Hook in sight. And as if all that weren't enough to wet your whistle, there's a damned fine list of single-malt whiskies.

The menu is a quick survey of some of the world's best drinking food: pommes frites from Belgium (chipotle sauce is the best choice), a good croque monsieur from France, sausages in the German and Polish traditions, and a lamb burger with a mélange of incongruous toppings (a shout-out to overambitious 1990s "PacNW" cuisine, perhaps). There are lighter plates, too, like some tasty salads, but here's where we remind you of the higher alcohol content of Belgian beer—for Pete's sake, lay a better foundation than seasonal vegetarian risotto.

Brouwer's is appropriately dark and foreboding inside, but it's just a little too mod to capture the "mead-swilling pleasure palace" vibe we hoped for. Be forewarned: it's a low-key spot for lunch and not too obnoxious at happy hour, but after 8pm it turns into a frat party.

7.5 Food | 8.0 Feel

$30 Price | 7.5 Wine

Buddha Ruksa

Lychee-martini-style Thai-American, plus the occasional authentic surprise

www.buddharuksa.com

Thai
Casual restaurant

West Seattle
3520 SW Genesee St.
(206) 937-7676

Hours
Tue–Fri
11:00am–10:00pm
Sat–Sun
4:00pm–10:00pm

Bar
Beer, wine, liquor

Credit cards
Visa, MC

Reservations
Accepted

Features
Date-friendly

In the arena of dressed-up Thai in an ornate setting, Buddha Ruksa still has to answer to May Thai in Wallingford—in fact, if the two weren't so far from each other, Buddha Ruksa might not seem like such a big deal.

But everything that lands in West Seattle feels like a revelation, so let's count Buddha Ruksa's strengths. First, plates are beautifully presented. Second, the menu is more adventurous than most Thai-American; for example, in season, they might try skin-on trout. The "Sample Platter" panders to Western palates with cream-cheese-stuffed crab wontons and such, but it's all surprisingly tasty, perhaps even worth blowing out a stent or two.

Buddha Ruksa also makes possibly the best pad see ew in town, with superfluously wide noodles; a rich, syrupy soy sauce; and lightly steamed, vividly green broccoli. This is the kind of inauthentic Thai-American slop of which we heartily approve. Still, many dishes are slightly out of balance, particularly curries, which are often too sweet.

Buddha Ruksa has a very good wine list (with a heavy—and appropriate—nod to Rieslings), along with the usual gimmicky Thai-themed cocktails, and a loungey vibe matches its ample drink menu. If anything, the place is almost too dark and too woody inside, with intricate carving everywhere—it feels a bit like dining in the inside of a humidor.

Not that there's anything wrong with dining inside a humidor.

Café Besalu

Neck-and-neck with Bakery Nouveau for best croissants in the city

Café Besalu shares many characteristics with the city's most-fawned-over French bakery, Bakery Nouveau: you won't find many croissants this French without a passport. The place has long lines on weekends and during breakfast rushes. The space is sweet—and mid-morning on calmer weekdays a pleasant place to read the paper—but it's not terribly interesting. Not that "interesting" is necessarily what you need on a lazy morning.

Yet Café Besalu is also unique in certain ways. It's less of a production than Bakery Nouveau; despite its accolades and loyal patrons, there's a "who, us?" feeling to the place that's very (Old) Ballard.

The pain au chocolat is amazing—snagging one that has just come out of the oven is worth planning your day around. Also of note are pear or apple pastries (when they have them), brioche, and almond delicacies. The coffee's fine, but really it serves merely to make sure you don't end up with a throat full of croissant splinters.

Breads
Sweets
Coffee
Café

Ballard
5909 24th Ave. NW
(206) 789-1463

Hours
Wed–Sun
7:00am–3:00pm

Bar
None

Credit cards
Visa, MC

Features
Kid-friendly
Outdoor dining

7.5 Food | 8.0 Feel

$40 Price

Café Campagne

A cute but celebrated brunch spot that knows its way around a croque monsieur

www.campagnerestaurant.com

French
Casual restaurant

Downtown
1600 Post Alley
(206) 728-2233

Hours
Mon–Thu
11:00am–4:00pm
5:00pm–10:00pm

Fri
11:00am–4:00pm
5:30pm–11:00pm

Sat
8:00am–4:00pm
5:30pm–11:00pm

Sun
8:00am–4:00pm
5:30pm–10:00pm

Bar
Beer, wine, liquor

Credit cards
Visa, MC, AmEx

Reservations
Accepted

Features
Brunch

Café Campagne knocks it out of the park each weekend with oeufs en meurette: poached eggs on slices of brioche toast, blanketed with red wine and foie gras butter sauce, and accompanied by fries for good measure. At lunch, this kitchen does the standards really well: croque monsieur and madame, bacon and onion tarts, salade Niçoise. At dinner…well, you might as well go down the street to Le Pichet.

The space is cute, a reasonable impersonation of a French café, if one that panders a lot to the American expectations. (Think vintage French posters of the type that plaster the rooms of coeds who are too artsy and sophisticated to collect Absolut ads.)

Despite being so close to Pike Place Market, Café Campagne isn't terribly touristy. Midweek, it's infected with some of the market mania, but because the place is slightly tucked away, and just brusque and French enough to intimidate the cruise-ship crowd, it attracts the kind of tourists who are, at least, far more interesting to observe than the business lunchers that make up the rest of the crowd—aging European and Russian divas carrying giant metallic purses, for example. At least Seattle's not provincial.

Café Flora

Vegetarian that's low on gimmicks, high on
flavor, with a flowing courtyard too

7.0	8.0
Food	Feel

$40	5.0
Price	Wine

www.cafeflora.com

Café Flora is warm and approachable, and when
not full of young families, it's even romantic.
The interior courtyard, with its fountain and
foliage, has the most personality of the various
spaces here, and is the best bet for date night.

Brunch is fantastic. Try the egg scrambles,
cheese grits, "Hoppin' John fritters" (made with
black-eyed peas), or biscuits and mushroom
gravy. Be forewarned, however, that during this
busy time, it often feels like dining in the midst
of a giant play date.

At dinner, Portobello mushrooms are, for
better or for worse, a go-to ingredient; one of
the best dishes turns them into the fungal
equivalent of beef Wellington. Café Flora stuffs
ravioli, quesadillas, and crêpes with roasted
seasonal vegetables, and sculpts veggies and
beans into pâtés, crumbles, and risotto cakes.
Seasonal specialties usually shine, especially in
autumn, when the kitchen has hearty things like
pumpkin and foraged chanterelles to work with.
Pizzas round out the menu, making it a kind of
meat-free free-for-all, but then again, when
you're accommodating so many different tastes
(veggie, vegan, gluten-free, skeptical omnivore),
that's understandable.

Café Flora recently jazzed up its cocktail menu
with fun specialty ingredients like Bison Grass
vodka, elderflower liqueurs, and house-made
ginger beer. This is good news, as the wine list
is terrible.

Vegefusion
Upmarket restaurant

Madison Park
2901 E. Madison St.
(206) 325-9100

Hours
Mon–Fri
9:00am–10:00pm
Sat
9:00am–2:00pm
5:00pm–10:00pm
Sun
9:00am–2:00pm
5:00pm–9:00pm

Bar
Beer, wine, liquor

Credit cards
Visa, MC, AmEx

Reservations
Not accepted

Features
Brunch
Date-friendly
Good cocktails
Kid-friendly
Veg-friendly

Café Juanita

Some of the best Italian-inspired, locally-sourced cooking, in a genteel house

www.cafejuanita.com

Italian
Upmarket restaurant

Eastside
9702 NE 120th Pl.
(425) 823-1505

Hours
Tue–Sat
5:00pm–10:00pm
Sun
5:00pm–9:00pm

Bar
Beer, wine, liquor

Credit cards
Visa, MC, AmEx

Reservations
Essential

Features
Date-friendly
Veg-friendly

If you're going to haul your cookies to the Eastside for one meal, you should come here. The menu is a mix of the pride of the Northwest (Oregon lamb, Washington-raised rabbit, and mussels from British Columbia) and Italy (lardo, Umbrian lentils, Barbera risotto). This might all come together like so: local squab with miner's lettuce, veal sweetbreads, and Moscato foie gras pan sauce. Pastas are homemade, as are gelati in unusual flavors like fennel seed and honeycomb.

At the risk of sounding like we're writing a personal ad, the kitchen also has a way with organ meats, tails, and trotters. And Café Juanita has one of the region's most extensive wine lists: great Italian wines and the best of the Northwest big hitters are represented, with tons of gems at every price point.

The converted house doesn't look very promising from the outside, and the dining room, although appropriately elegant, is not transportive in any particular way. But with soft music accompanying the gentle chatter of delighted guests of all ages; gracious, professional service; and sink-in-and-stay-awhile gray leather bench seating, Café Juanita creates just the refined, ethereal vibe you expect when you're spending so much money.

Café Ori

Greasy, finger-lickin' Hong Kong comfort food in a place that feels full-on Chinese

7.5 Food

4.0 Feel

$15 Price

www.cafeori.com

Café Ori serves some of the best quick-and-cheap Hong Kong-style Chinese food on the Eastside. The menu is so extensive that you could use it as a lesson plan if you're trying to learn Cantonese. Though not necessarily side-trip-worthy, Café Ori is a favorite among Eastsiders for lunch and takeout.

The portions are huge, and the food is cheap and savory. Hainanese chicken rice, the beef brisket curry, and the Taiwanese pork chop rice are standouts. Bubble teas are very popular, too. Lots of Chinese folks eat here, which isn't surprising considering how many Chinese people live in Bellevue, but it's still a pretty good sign.

The "café" in the name is a bit misleading—it's a typical characterless eatery in a strip mall. But it's less dingy than some of the I.D. joints, and service is fast and friendly.

Chinese
Casual restaurant

Bellevue
14339 NE 20th St.
(425) 747-8822

Hours
Daily
11:00am–10:00pm

Bar
BYO

Credit cards
None

Reservations
Accepted

Features
Kid-friendly

8.5	9.0
Food	Feel

$40	8.0
Price	Wine

Café Presse

Le Pichet's little sister mixes a modern
aesthetic with French comfort food

www.cafepresseseattle.com

French
Casual restaurant

Capitol Hill
1117 12th Ave.
(206) 709-7674

Hours
Daily
7:00am–2:00am

Bar
Beer, wine, liquor, BYO

Credit cards
Visa, MC

Reservations
Accepted

Features
Date-friendly
Outdoor dining
Veg-friendly
Wi-Fi

Café Presse is the hippest recreation of a French
bar in town. Delicate baby-blue wallpaper
provides the backdrop for the fully stocked bar,
which has a marble top and black pipe barriers
separating it from the dining area. A skylight
illuminates wood beams lining a 30-foot ceiling,
exposed duct work, and chartreuse-yellow
tables. Soccer matches on the bar's TV, along
with a magazine rack carrying everything from
the *London Financial Times* to *Juxtapoz*,
compete for the short attention spans of the
trendy crowd, much of which is probably too
busy discussing Egon Schiele to notice such
things.

The café does very basic French food very
well. Steak frites is a favorite: a hanger steak
with a nice char and a medium-rare interior
comes with greasy, crispy, utterly masterful fries.
The chicken liver terrine is so rich and slick that
you'll wish the baguette were 12 feet long.
Expertly roasted chicken is served two ways:
fresh out of the oven (expect an hour's wait) or
cold with mayonnaise (the way to go). The
French-focused wine list hovers on the smaller
side of mid-sized, but it goes very well with the
food, and there are plenty of by-the-glass
options.

Café Presse is notably better than Le Pichet
(the owners' other French café) in one aspect: it
isn't as much of a pain in the ass. Most menu
items are available all day, unlike at Le Pichet,
with its wafer-thin windows of opportunity in
which to order certain things.

Caffé Vita

A hip coffee joint that's likely coming soon
to a menu near you

www.caffevita.com

Known as "the coffee mafia" for its practice of
strong-arming its way onto restaurant menus in
town—not to mention unsubstantiated rumors
of shady business practices—Caffé Vita might
lead you to expect coffee as bad-ass as its
reputation. The coffee is certainly not terrible—
fine restaurants all over town serve this stuff,
and we've all stopped in their five locations for
an espresso on occasion—but it's not the best in
town either.

Hipsters are a funny lot, and you'll find the
moodiest of them here at Caffé Vita
moonlighting as baristas. If you don't mind a bit
of attitude with your morning latte art, then by
all means, the quiet upstairs loft in the Capitol
Hill location is a perfectly pleasant place to pass
the hours.

With many robust, smooth, farm-direct and
fair trade blends, Caffé Vita is also ideal for the
coffee drinker with a conscience. If observing
beautiful Cap Hill denizens sporting carefully-
mussed bedhead is more your speed, you can't
find a better spot than the sidewalk tables here
on a sunny day. If it's pure coffee bliss you're
after, you might be a touch disappointed.

A warning, or perhaps a perk: unisex
bathrooms.

Coffee
Café

Capitol Hill
1005 E. Pike St.
(206) 709-4440

Pioneer Square
125 Prefontaine Pl. S.
(206) 652-8331

Queen Anne
813 5th Ave. N.
(206) 285-9662

Fremont
4301 Fremont Ave. N.
(206) 632-3535

Hours
Mon–Fri
6:00am–11:00pm
Sat–Sun
7:00am–11:00pm
Hours vary by location

Bar
None

Credit cards
Visa, MC, AmEx

Features
Outdoor dining
Wi-Fi

<table>
<tr><td>**8.5**
Food</td><td>**8.0**
Feel</td></tr>
<tr><td>**$60**
Price</td><td>**7.5**
Wine</td></tr>
</table>

Campagne

Simple white-tablecloth elegance, great views, and good globetrotting French

www.campagnerestaurant.com

French
Upmarket restaurant

Downtown
86 Pine St.
(206) 728–2800

Hours
Tue–Sun
5:00pm–10:00pm

Bar
Beer, wine, liquor

Credit cards
Visa, MC, AmEx

Reservations
Accepted

Features
Date-friendly
Outdoor dining

Gastronomically and economically, Seattle's casual French cafés are more satisfying than the few pricey special-occasion spots in this genre. In fact, overall, we prefer sister space Café Campagne to this, its fancier older sibling.

But Campagne really dials in the effortless sophistication that we could use more of in this town, and it's nice to travel back in time to when creating an upmarket feel didn't require much more than a few white tablecloths and professional (i.e. not overly chatty) service. Campagne's small bar and café tables draped in starched white are attractive enough, but the main focus of the room is the view. At night, city lights reflect in the water of Puget Sound.

French classics are consistently strong here, especially if they involve steak: a petite rib eye with marrow bones, frites, and red wine jus, for example, is right on the money (and we mean money—it's priced in the stratosphere). The more experimental inclusions of Pacific Northwest ingredients or global influences are more hit-or-miss, but the hits—oysters and duck confit in harissa, for example—are of the kind that indelibly imprint themselves on your brain and palate.

The quality of Campagne's wine list has varied greatly over the past few years, but at press time, it seemed to be back on an upward swing.

Canlis

After more than 50 years, still *the* special-occasion spot in Seattle

www.canlis.com

9.0	8.0
Food	Feel

$110	9.5
Price	Wine

Modern
Upmarket restaurant

Queen Anne
2576 Aurora Ave. N.
(206) 283–3313

Hours
Mon–Fri
5:30pm–9:30pm
Sat
5:00pm–10:00pm

Bar
Beer, wine, liquor

Credit cards
Visa, MC, AmEx

Reservations
Essential

Features
Date-friendly
Good cocktails

Canlis is the restaurant where you: (a) propose, (b) make partner, or (c) try to instill the idea of prosperity on your progeny before they head off to pursue a liberal-arts education. It has the best service in Seattle. There's no fleece in sight (men must wear sports jackets, a practice that's almost extinct in America, even in New York's most expensive restaurants. (This is the 21st century.) Nonetheless, the atmosphere is utterly unique. The place practically floats on Lake Union. Prices are sky-high.

Canlis was known and valued for years for being old-school—caviar, shrimp cocktail, surf and turf. There have been some improvements to the menu, like a new version of the "Peter Canlis Prawns," the restaurant's signature appetizer. The new one is more delicate, cooked in butter, and tossed in a garlicky, red chili-flecked sauce. But for the most part, Canlis keeps doing what it has always done well: beef tenderloin (Waygu, these days), pricey lobster, and Seattle's best duck preps. In the past, the kitchen has too often played it safe, but this is starting to change. The wine list is extensive, spanning the spectrum from 30-year-old Bordeaux to new artisanal Washington releases.

You can bypass the wallet-busting dining room and have drinks and nibbles in the lounge, which is the best spot in the house to hear surprisingly good Radiohead piano covers.

8.5	8.0
Food	Feel

$50	7.5
Price	Wine

Cantinetta

Tuscan-influenced cooking that's nearly worth the two-hour waits

www.cantinettaseattle.com

Italian
Upmarket restaurant

Wallingford
3650 Wallingford Ave.
(206) 632-1000

Bellevue
10038 Main St.
(425) 233-6040

Hours
Tue–Thu
5:00pm–10:00pm
Fri–Sun
5:00pm–11:00pm
Hours vary by location

Bar
Beer, wine, liquor

Credit cards
Visa, MC, AmEx

Reservations
Not accepted

Features
Veg-friendly

Cantinetta is part of Seattle's recent no-reservations trend. Waits can be over two hours, an experience that can be pretty unpleasant, as the restaurant is in the middle of residential Wallingford (not even a 7-Eleven within walking distance), and the bar area is too tiny to comfortably accommodate weekend crowds.

But Cantinetta is deserving of this loyalty. Organic local ingredients and Tuscan influences yield such excellent dishes as pappardelle lamb ragù with oxtail gnocchini. The kitchen creates interesting combinations (think avocado, grapefruit, and cured olives), and the house-made pasta can be revelatory, especially in bowls of broth.

Appetizers are some of the strongest dishes here, whether they're light salads featuring fennel and beets or flavor nuggets like pancetta-wrapped dates with balsamic reduction. The wine list focuses on Washington State and Italy. It's not particularly extensive, but it is carefully chosen.

As for the space, somewhere in Cantinetta's back room is a dog-eared copy of *Rustic Chic for Dummies*: rough-hewn wooden tables, ogre-bludgeoning wood-and-wrought-iron chandeliers, wine bottles as decoration, curvy gilt mirrors, and black-and-white photographs of Roman alleyways. It's all a little obvious, but also pretty and intimate nonetheless. And besides, the food's so good that we'd show up even if it looked like the Olive Garden.

Canton Noodle House

Simple, cheap Hong Kong comfort food
that will cure whatever ails you

7.0 Food

3.0 Feel

$10 Price

The black bars over the front window are not
the most welcoming sign, and inside, Canton
Noodle is your typical bare-bones Asian
restaurant. But we could watch the owner fill
and hand-pleat wontons on the table in the
back pretty much all afternoon.

This place does make a decent bowl of Hong
Kong-style wonton noodle soup; the broth,
noodles, and wontons are all comparable to the
ingredients used at our other go-to spots in the
I.D. The best choices, though, are the sui kau
(dumplings with pork and wood ear
mushrooms) and beef brisket noodle soup. The
cold sliced beef shank is a favorite, too, often
better than the standard wonton noodle soup.
Comfort foods like congee and deep-fried
doughnuts round out the small menu.

Though there's not much to it, Canton
Noodle is one of the more pleasant super-cheap
I.D. eateries. The proprietors are very nice, and
this overlooked spot is not as chaotic as some
closer to the train station and Uwajimaya.

Chinese
Casual restaurant

**International
District**
506 12th Ave. S.
(206) 329-5650

Hours
Mon–Thu
10:00am–7:00pm
Fri–Sat
10:00am–8:00pm
Sun
10:00am–7:00pm

Bar
None

Credit cards
None

Reservations
Accepted

7.0 Food | 7.5 Feel

Captain Black's

If you want inexpensive Southern pub grub, board this ship

$25
Price

www.captainblacksseattle.com

Southern
Casual restaurant

Capitol Hill
129 Belmont Ave.
(206) 327-9549

Hours
Daily
4:00pm–2:00am

Bar
Beer, wine, liquor

Credit cards
Visa, MC, AmEx

Reservations
Not accepted

Features
Good beers
Good cocktails
Outdoor dining
Wi-Fi

Captain Black's is a strange duck. Its motto is "Eat, Drink, Pillage," but except for a few ship's-wheel chandeliers, the pirate theme is pretty poorly executed. In fact, the small space merely has that low-key DIY vibe you'd expect on the Hill, with a few wooden booths and tables and some bar seating. It's bookended by two great decks, however, which get packed when weather allows.

The menu bears no relation to the pirate theme, either—where's the rum and rat's meat?—and it's short on real Cajun cred, but it offers some Southern comforts like decent fried fish po'boys or chicken and waffles. The latter is the best dish on this menu: it's done with a plump, juicy chicken breast with the wing attached; the batter has a crunch that registers on the Richter scale, while its accompanying waffle is jazzed up with sweet, orangey butter and a ramekin of real maple syrup. Together they're wonderful—the citrusy sweetness of the waffle puts out the heat of the chicken. Otherwise, stick to the list of excellent snacks: fried cheese curds (using Beecher's cheese), hush puppies, fries with spicy aïoli.

Captain Black's other signature is the Captain's Tea (sweet tea-infused vodka, lemon, and soda water). This potent concoction is dangerously easy to drink. There's also a good selection of whiskies, and a few curiosities like Peroni on tap.

Carmelita

Reliable white-tablecloth vegetarian that's been aging gracefully

www.carmelita.net

For a long time after it opened in 1996, Carmelita was not only one of the few fancy vegetarian restaurants in town, but also one of the few special-occasion spots north of the canal. Although it is no longer doing the most cutting-edge vegetarian cuisine in Seattle, it's still a very reliable choice for sophisticated farm-to-table food.

The main dining room, with its textured ceilings, still has a bit of that '90s pomegranate glow, though the space is not as egregiously dated as some eateries from the same era. A newly added patio is wonderfully secluded, while a recently added bar area has perked up the interior quite a bit—and there's also a reinvigorated happy hour, when sunchoke chips, spaghetti squash bonbons, and fried Marcona almonds pair with all manner of fancy cocktails featuring ingredients like muddled rhubarb and habanero syrup. The wine list is short, succinct, and eminently affordable.

Unusually for a vegefusion place, Carmelita's menu is coherent. The wow factor, however, varies. There's inventiveness (using pickled fruits to dress up a salad, for instance, or making a passable crêpe out of fava beans), but also challenging veggie takes on traditional dishes (a saffron paella with Calasparra rice, red spring onion, sun-dried tomatoes, aged Manchego, and romesco sauce). And then there are just the local, seasonal vegetable dishes that Seattle is so good at.

Vegefusion
Upmarket restaurant

Phinney Ridge
7314 Greenwood Ave. N.
(206) 706-7703

Hours
Tue–Sat
5:00pm–10:00pm
Sun
5:00pm–9:00pm

Bar
Beer, wine, liquor

Credit cards
Visa, MC

Reservations
Accepted

Features
Date-friendly
Good cocktails
Outdoor dining
Veg-friendly

7.0 Food | 6.0 Feel

$30 Price | 5.0 Wine

Cedars

One of the best of the U-District ethnic lunch options

www.cedarsseattle.com

**Indian
Middle Eastern**
Casual restaurant

University District
4759 Brooklyn Ave. NE
(206) 527-4000

Hours
Mon–Sat
11:00am–10:00pm
Sun
noon–9:30pm

Bar
Beer, wine, BYO

Credit cards
Visa, MC, AmEx

Reservations
Accepted

Features
Kid-friendly
Outdoor dining
Veg-friendly

Although it's not a great deal compared to the all-you-can-eat lunch buffets in the area, this converted house on the north end of the U-District is always packed with UW students. A short menu of Middle Eastern standards such as falafel, gyros, and kebabs complements a much longer menu of Indian staples: vindaloo, butter chicken, tandoori meats. The Indian food is better, and it's what makes the place so popular.

There's nothing really novel here, just well-done versions of the well-known dishes. And if you like your food spicy, Cedars will deliver. We're impressed by the beer selection, but puzzled by the lengthy but almost adorably clueless wine list. But no biggie—when our mouths are on fire, we want a can of crappy beer, not a bottle of crappy wine. And crappy it is here—Cedar's list is pretty anemic. All the wines are big obvious super-power wineries that everyone knows. They carry every big name brand, homogenized wines crafted for maximum approachability. They're chosen lazily, but priced well—$5 makes a lot of people happy to drink.

Aside from its nice deck, Cedars is fairly forgettable décor-wise, but it has a good vibe, happy patrons, and a friendly waitstaff.

Chez Shea

A fine, if somewhat mercurial, old-school "fine" French experience

7.5	8.5
Food	Feel

$65	8.0
Price	Wine

www.chezshea.com

Chez Shea has a wonderful location above Pike Place Market, with peek-a-boo views of the Sound. It also has some pretty good French food.

Much of Chez Shea's appeal is in the way the mood is set. This is one of the most romantic restaurants in Seattle, especially at sunset. At the same time, the bar is a classy, peaceful place to have a cocktail and unwind after a tedious workday. If you prefer to unwind with wine, the list here is a well-rounded one, but the prices are on the higher end of affordable.

Chez Shea keeps the spell intact with French classics that bear only the most subtle of twists: pan-roasted Muscovy duck, seared squab breast with spring onion pistou, or beef tenderloin with marrow butter and red wine jus will satisfy, but they're not dashing enough to interrupt conversations or inspire what-am-I-doing-with-my-life reveries. That's fine: there's a time when all we need is simply elegant food for a simply elegant evening. Or just a nice drink, a beautiful view, and nice company.

French
Upmarket restaurant

Downtown
94 Pike St.
(206) 467-9990

Hours
Tue–Sun
5:00pm–10:00pm

Bar
Beer, wine, liquor

Credit cards
Visa, MC, AmEx

Reservations
Essential

Features
Date-friendly

7.0 6.0
Food Feel

$30
Price

Chiang's Gourmet

There are some traditional gems among the Americanized junk

www.chiangsgourmet.com

Chinese
Casual restaurant

Ravenna
7845 Lake City Way NE
(206) 527-8888

Hours
Mon–Thu
11:30am–9:30pm
Fri
11:30am–10:30pm
Sat
10:30am–10:30pm
Sun
10:30am–9:30pm

Bar
Beer, wine, BYO

Credit cards
Visa, MC

Reservations
Accepted

Features
Brunch
Kid-friendly

Your experience of Chiang's depends on which menu you order from: the American one or the *real* menu, which has dishes like "Fried Pig's Intastine" [sic]. If you settle for the weak American menu, you'll get dishes that are either overly sweet, too greasy, or too salty—and, worse still, you'll miss out on Chinese classics like "Bean Curd Sheets Roll" and "Fried Tofu of Strong Odor" (stinky tofu, which is not bad, though not as good as at Henry's Taiwan). The "Shepherd's Purse Bun," in spite of the singular usage and obscenely low prices, comes with two delightful puffy steamed buns filled with finely diced greens. Hot pots are also a good choice. Skip dim sum, though, which is mediocre compared to what you'd find in the I.D.

Despite some cool framed woodcuts—one of which features a red-robed, bearded man-beast described as "Chinese Santa Claus with a sword"—there's that typical banquet-hall feel of a restaurant that bustles when busy and feels stale when quiet. Luckily, the former is more common; the flip side is that there's nearly always a wait for a table, in part because this is the best option on the northside (that is, north below Richmond).

Chiso

Well-rounded Japanese, equally good at ippin, omakase, and sake

8.5	7.0
Food	Feel

$45	6.0
Price	Wine

www.chisoseattle.com

At Chiso, you don't have to choose your sushi persona—you can be either a glib roll-eater or (better) an unyielding traditionalist and feel satisfied with either experience. Perhaps more than any other Japanese restaurant in the city, Chiso offers consistent quality across all pages of its menu, which makes it a great place to bring a group of people with varying expectations.

Omakase sushi is offered at lunch and dinner, and will please purists with relentlessly fresh catches of the day; the chef's selection is on another plane from the basic lunch combo, as it should be, although the latter is no slouch either. But Chiso also makes excellent rolls—including some of the best veggie maki in the city—and great ippin ryori (a Japanese term translated literally to "one-dish food") like nicely sauced tuna poke, toothsome tempuras, very lightly seared duck breast, and fried shrimp heads. Drinks begin, and should end, with an equally good selection of both chest-hair-growing sake and delicate, if sweet, mixed drinks featuring lychee, basil, and seasonal fruits. (There's a lot of room for improvement on the regular wine list, however; the flavors from the kitchen are abused by the big, oaky New World reds on the list.)

The décor follows suit: it's a bit sparse, neither too homey nor too trendy, with olive green walls, paper lanterns, comfy banquette seating, and an attractive and dimly lit (at night) sushi bar. All of this makes Chiso mutable for friends, families, or couples.

Japanese
Upmarket restaurant

Fremont
3520 Fremont Ave. N.
(206) 632-3430

Hours
Mon–Thu
11:30am–2:00pm
4:00pm–9:30pm
Fri
11:30am–2:00pm
4:00pm–10:30pm
Sat
4:00pm–10:30pm
Sun
4:00pm–9:00pm

Bar
Beer, wine, liquor

Credit cards
Visa, MC, AmEx

Reservations
Accepted

<table>
<tr><td>**6.5**
Food</td><td>**7.0**
Feel</td></tr>
<tr><td>**$40**
Price</td><td>**7.5**
Wine</td></tr>
</table>

Cicchetti

Better for drinks with a view on the city
than meals with a view on pan-Med fusion

www.serafinaseattle.com/cicchetti

**Italian
Middle Eastern**
Upmarket restaurant

Eastlake
121 E. Boston St.
(206) 859-4155

Hours
Tue–Thu
5:00pm–midnight
Fri–Sun
5:00pm–1:00am

Bar
Beer, wine, liquor

Credit cards
Visa, MC, AmEx

Reservations
Accepted

Features
Good cocktails
Outdoor dining

At least Cicchetti puts it right out there—the name basically translates to "small plates." Constructing a full or coherent meal can be even more difficult here than it often is at other small-plates eateries. Influences from around the Mediterranean—perhaps too far around—show up in dishes from octopus with salsa verde and chickpeas to Moroccan-spiced shredded lamb with harissa-spiked yogurt (the former is recommended, the latter is not). The more ordinary dishes tend to be more consistent, with salt cod fritters and simple pizzas making for a pretty satisfying meal. The one must, at press time, was a vaguely Sicilian dish on the dessert menu: ricotta fritters with huckleberry sauce.

Cicchetti clearly harbors a desire to be taken extremely seriously as a restaurant, but the city already seems to have decided otherwise. The place is popular, but most people drop in just to drink. And for good reason: the bar's contribution is exceptional, with strong specialty cocktails that are inventive (the Visigoth has wolfberry whiskey, dry sherry, Italian vermouth, lemon, and bitters), but well balanced, and not too pricey. As for wine, there's a medium-sized list with an obvious focus on Italy and the food: most pairings work quite nicely.

The multi-floor mother-in-law-style building is modern and hip, with city views, but its Eastlake location keeps it from being too full of scenesters. Cicchetti is owned by the same folks who run Serafina, but the two restaurants have very different foci and feels.

Citizen Coffee

The DIY space is great, the food could use some polish

6.0	8.0
Food	Feel

$20	6.0
Price	Wine

www.citizencoffee.com

Maybe it's just the row of salvaged theater seats, but Citizen feels like a cool black-box theater—a performance space cobbled together on a shoestring budget and built in the middle of someone's loft apartment. The top floor of the bi-level space has most of the seating, including a few couches and the theater seats, which are not the best crêpe-eating perches.

Unfortunately, as with so many community theaters, the space is more intriguing than the works presented. The crêpes are okay, but they're often packed with far too many ingredients. The buckwheat "Citizen Crêpe," for example, has grilled asparagus, spinach, bacon, and gruyère and the whole thing is topped with a squiggle of a crème-fraîche-based concoction. Somehow, it still manages to be bland. On the other end of the spectrum, a caramelized apple crêpe with sautéed apples and melted brie and walnuts comes to the table drenched in honey and winds up cloyingly sweet. Banh-mi-style sandwiches are good, especially salty roasted pork shoulder—but by good, we mean good for a coffeeshop.

And that's really what Citizen is: a good coffeeshop. We have no complaints with the beans, and the fact that there's also a very affordable wine list (it's not a program with much depth, but they have sangría and $5 glass pours and all bottles are under $20) makes it easy to end the day here by transitioning from laptop hermit to social butterfly.

French
Sandwiches
Sweets
Café

Queen Anne
706 Taylor Ave. N.
(206) 284-1015

Hours
Mon–Thu
6:00am–9:00pm
Fri
6:00am–10:00pm
Sun
7:00am–9:00pm
Sat
7:00am–10:00pm

Bar
Beer, wine

Credit cards
Visa, MC, AmEx

Reservations
Not accepted

Features
Outdoor dining
Veg-friendly
Wi-Fi

www.thecollinspub.com

7.5	8.0
Food	Feel

$40
Price

Collins Pub

A bright, caring spot in the dire Pioneer Square scene—with great beer, too

American
Casual restaurant

Pioneer Square
526 2nd Ave.
(206) 623-1016

Hours
Daily
11:00am–2:00am

Bar
Beer, wine, liquor

Credit cards
Visa, MC, AmEx

Reservations
Accepted

Features
Good beers
Outdoor dining

Could it be? A pub in Pioneer Square that doesn't cater to the lowest common denominator? (Drunks puking in the square on Saturday night, you know who you are.)

Why, yes! Although Collins sees its share of post-game revelry, the kitchen takes itself very seriously, and the fresh, constantly evolving menu makes for some of the best pub grub in town.

Steaks and burgers are highlights, but Collins Pub also does a good job with fish, unusual within its genre. Most of it is sourced from Pike Place Market. Sides, which can be as straightforward as mashed potatoes and braised greens or as Northwest-y as foraged mushrooms, local mixed greens, and leek cream, deserve a special note—they balance out the main dish well both in flavor and portion size.

The beer list focuses on Northwest and Belgian brews, with many high-end internationals. There aren't many places in town where the staff can walk you through the brewing differences between various German wheat beers, or talk about the Trappist monks' beermaking process.

Although it has a bit of a canned, contemporary sheen—a lot of dark woods and glowing amber lights—Collins is ultimately a friendly neighborhood pub where patrons might hunker down in a booth to play board games if they're not at the bar cheering on the Mariners or the Seahawks.

Copper Gate

Honoring Scandinavian heritage with all the
essentials: lingonberries, aquavit, and T&A

7.5 | **8.0**
Food | Feel

$30
Price

www.thecoppergate.com

The centerpiece of Copper Gate's bar is a replica
of a Viking ship hull—this actually *is* the bar,
which is not only undeniably cool, but also a lot
more tasteful than it sounds on paper. There's a
lot of vintage ephemera scattered around the
place (much of it handed down from the
previous owner), including dozens of black-and-
white photos of women, possibly Scandinavian
and mostly naked. There's a lesson about
Scandinavian culture here somewhere—a nod,
perhaps, to Sweden's progressive sex-ed
program?—but a living museum for the kiddies
it's not.

Tradition reigns in other ways: the place is
dark and a tad cold. Service can charitably be
described as stoic. And you'll be eating small
plates of classic dishes like pickled herring with
beets and pumpernickel, gravlax, Swedish
meatballs with ligonberry preserve, and a
delicious red-beet salad. A few dishes color
outside the lines—aquavit-coffee-braised short
ribs, for example. But Scandinavian cuisine is
fundamentally about restraint, and that's the
deal here, too.

The drink list is fun and different. Along with
the many cocktails made from aquavit and other
Scandinavian liquors like Gamel Dansk, there's a
solid craft beer list here, too.

Scandinavian
Casual restaurant

Ballard
6301 24th Ave. NW
(206) 706-3292

Hours
Daily
5:00pm–11:00pm

Bar
Beer, wine, liquor

Credit cards
Visa, MC, AmEx

Reservations
Not accepted

Features
Good beers
Good cocktails
Outdoor dining

8.5 9.0
Food Feel

$80 8.5
Price Wine

Corson Building

A special place for the communal dining
experience, if a pricey one too

www.thecorsonbuilding.com

Modern
Upmarket restaurant

Georgetown
5609 Corson Ave. S.
(206) 762-3330

Hours
Thu–Fri
6:00pm–10:30pm
Sat
6:30pm–9:30pm
Sun
9:30am–2:00pm
6:00pm–9:30pm

Bar
Beer, wine, liquor

Credit cards
Visa, MC, AmEx

Reservations
Essential

Features
Brunch
Good cocktails

A garden getaway in hipper-than-thou industrial
Georgetown, the Corson Building is an oasis
between railroad tracks and an interstate ramp.
It's quirky, decrepit, and elegantly DIY.
Thursdays and Fridays feature à la carte menus,
while Saturday is a fixed price dinner; there are
also two prix-fixe Sunday suppers a month.

Dinner here is a multi-course, set-menu lesson
in why locavores get away with being so
insufferably smug. Corson is as self-sustaining as
possible: there are herb and vegetable gardens,
chicken and pigeon coops. The ritual includes a
half-hour before dinner to wander around the
compound, drink in hand.

The Corson Building mostly lives up to its
hype. The chef knows how to cook using
simple, quality ingredients: dishes like (backyard)
chicken braised with apricots and anise hyssop,
or confit of duck leg with shinseiki pear, whole
turnips, and walnuts, are expertly prepared.
Although the more risk-taking dishes are
generally successful and exciting, occasionally it
all feels a little too cool and trendy. When they
bring out the reindeer aspic, you might wonder
if you're at dinner or a photo shoot. Wine
pairings are carefully chosen and it's rare to get
a dud.

Communal family-style dining is less
attractive, of course, when you have to drop a
car payment on dinner. But look past the prices,
and you've got one of the city's most engaging
dining experiences.

Crow

A mix of night-out and neighborhood
haunt with a careful, crowd-pleasing menu

7.0	8.0
Food	Feel

$45	7.0
Price	Wine

www.eatatcrow.com

It's hard to define The Crow Restaurant & Bar's
current place in the dining scene. It still
continues to draw big, boisterous crowds—but
sometimes, if only by accident, we tend to talk
about it in the past tense. Perhaps it's because
the place inspires nostalgia for the heady days
of the early 'aughts, when serving heavy, mildly
rustic comfort food in a converted industrial
space was innovative rather than commonplace.

But Crow still knows how to please its
neighborhood regulars. It's a pretty place, with
machine-polished steel plates, saturated colors
(namely bold red curtains), a large bar, and
high-backed booths. Service can be unbelievably
slow at times, but at least you won't feel
rushed. The crowd is…well, it's Queen Anne.
Expect some youngsters who have finally
graduated from Peso's, some real oldsters, and
quite a few Just for Men Touch of Gray models
having a discreet glass of wine.

Unlike many restaurants honoring local
ingredients with constantly shuffling menus,
Crow has held on to a few rather plebian
customer favorites: lasagne with house-made
noodles (occasionally great, occasionally bland),
a pan-roasted quarter-chicken wrapped in crispy
prosciutto (a dish that's nonetheless
praiseworthy). It is these preps and the
desserts—simple with a twist like pineapple-
ginger upside-down cake or warm chocolate
tart with spicy peanut brittle—that might let
Crow perch there indefinitely.

Modern
Upmarket restaurant

Queen Anne
823 5th Ave. N.
(206) 283-8800

Hours
Sun–Thu
5:00pm–10:00pm
Fri–Sat
5:00pm–11:00pm

Bar
Beer, wine, liquor

Credit cards
Visa, MC, AmEx

Reservations
Accepted

Crush

This supremely artistic sensory experience
makes our cold hearts flutter

www.chefjasonwilson.com

Modern
Upmarket restaurant

Madison Park
2319 E. Madison St.
(206) 302-7874

Hours
Tue–Sun
5:00pm–10:00pm

Bar
Beer, wine, liquor

Credit cards
Visa, MC, AmEx

Reservations
Essential

Features
Date-friendly

You can't have a crush for five years—either it develops into a relationship or it ends in tears and recrimination. At first, some of us feared we were headed toward the latter scenario with celeb chef Jason Wilson's Madison Park showpiece. Awash in extreme "creativity," the place seemed to have the temperament of those notoriously hard-to-date artists—there's a fine line between creative genius and delusional mania.

After Crush's bumpy first year (or two), some of us had to take a little break. But things change, people mature, and we're glad Wilson's still with us. Every time we dine here, we learn something new about the use of an ingredient or a flavor combination—and a long-term relationship is all about the learning. In this case, it's also about the following: sublime raw hamachi sprinkled with sea salt and floating in a creamy celeriac sauce; a brick of foie gras chased with sweet quince cubes and toasted cinnamon brioche slices; or bacon purée added to a mix that already includes lacquered pork belly—talk about hot bacon-on-bacon action.

Speaking of bad food-writing jokes, the interior has inspired more Jetsons references than should ever appear in print, so we won't rag too hard on the white fiberglass chairs that clash so noticeably with an otherwise sedate dining room.

Cupcake Royale

One of the better cupcake trendsters in town

www.cupcakeroyale.com

Cupcake Royale is by far Seattle's most successful cupcake shop—it's a chain, and the sheer turnover in one shop is impressive. The cupcakes sure are pretty, with signature swirls of gooey butter cream atop cakes that fan out into egregiously wide hats. They're pretty good, too. Cupcake Royale sources local and organic ingredients, and recent efforts to make the cakes "moist-ier" have worked: they make the best cakes out of all the cupcake shops and the quality of these never varies from day to day or branch to branch. These creations are the closest thing to the best of the mom-made birthday treats so many remember fondly.

What these cupcakes lack, however, is depth. The frosting is overpoweringly sweet, and with the exception of the interesting seasonal concoctions (e.g., spicy Mexican-chocolate frosting for cinco de mayo) all of the frostings tend to taste the same whether they're pastel purple or orange or pink. Of the regularly featured cupcakes we like the salted caramel (a lot of salt to balance out a lot of sugar) and the carrot cake (cream cheese frosting) varieties the best.

Cupcake Royale does have cute shops, though, particularly the Capitol Hill branch, which looks like it was jointly designed by a princess-obsessed six-year-old and a concrete-obsessed hipster. These are actually full coffeeshops, complete with good beans and laptop junkies.

Sweets
Coffee
Counter service

Capitol Hill
111 E. Pike St.
(206) 328-6544

Ballard
2052 NW Market St.
(206) 782-9557

Madrona
1101 34th Ave.
(206) 709-4497

West Seattle
4556 California Ave. SW
(206) 932-2971

Hours
Daily
7:00am–11:00pm
Hours vary by location

Bar
None

Credit cards
Visa, MC, AmEx

Features
Kid-friendly
Wi-Fi

7.0	7.5
Food	Feel

$70	7.5
Price	Wine

Dahlia Lounge

The Hollywood date-night spot, but don't expect fireworks in the food

www.tomdouglas.com

Modern
Upmarket restaurant

Belltown
2001 4th Ave.
(206) 682-4142

Hours
Mon–Thu
11:30am–2:30pm
5:00pm–10:00pm
Fri
11:30am–2:30pm
5:00pm–11:00pm
Sat
9:00am–2:00pm
5:00pm–11:00pm
Sun
9:30am–2:00pm
5:00pm–9:00pm

Bar
Beer, wine, liquor

Credit cards
Visa, MC, AmEx

Reservations
Accepted

Features
Brunch
Date-friendly

Dahlia hasn't changed much since Tom Hanks wooed his annoying girlfriend here in *Sleepless in Seattle,* which is odd, because the restaurant has moved locations since then. Dahlia will be forever tethered to "that movie," which is fitting because our feelings for it flip-flop as mercilessly as Meg Ryan's feelings for her sneezing, wheat-averse fiancé.

On one hand, Dahlia was chosen as a filming location because it was able to make Seattle seem chic and romantic. And it still delivers on that fantasy for many people. Dahlia screams Valentine's Day dinner, especially with its red, red walls. The lights are so romantically dim that you can barely see your food, and there's plenty of cozy booth seating.

On the other hand, this kitchen feels stuck: salmon in a tangy vinegar soy sauce? Even the interior, as romantic as it is at night, in the light of day feels like some 45-year-old single gal revamped her apartment with a "pomegranate" color theme.

But wait, the fire hasn't completely gone out. Steak, fish, and duck are always competently cooked. We can still expect some surprises—the brunch congee with prawns and Chinese doughnuts, for example, is a return to form. And then there are the 1,200-calorie comforts: coconut cream pie and homemade donuts with fancy jams and marscapone. Maybe we can stick it out for a few more years…

Daniel's Broiler

Old-school surf and turf that won't make a
fool of you

www.schwartzbros.com

7.0	6.5
Food	Feel

$95	9.5
Price	Wine

On paper, Daniel's Broiler doesn't seem that
promising. It's part of a local chain of high-end
steak and seafood restaurants strategically
placed in lovely locations for maximum price-
gouging—there are branches on both Lakes
Union and Washington. And you and the other
tourists and/or cigar-smoking locals will drop
more than a few bucks here: steaks and chops
in the $40 to $60 range, $50+ for an Australian
rock lobster tail, and the standard steakhouse
insult of sky-high prices for creamed spinach.

But Daniel's is still a better deal than many
pricey steakhouses (we're looking at you, John
Howie), and they know how to serve up a great
medium-rare steak. The views over either
sparkling lake (the Bellevue location is in a
shopping complex, so we don't recommend
choosing that one unless it's a matter of
convenience) are wonderful—you might see Mt.
Rainier from the Leschi marina.

And if you're seeking neutral ground for a
potentially awkward or tense intergenerational
gathering, this is a solid pick. Service is
outstanding—refined without being snotty (you
can declare your pitiful wine budget to the
sommelier without shame)—and the high
quality of the food will make this a splurge that
everyone can enjoy.

Steakhouse
Upmarket restaurant

Madrona
200 Lake Washington
Blvd.
(206) 329-4191

South Lake Union
809 Fairview Pl. N.
(206) 621-8262

Bellevue
10500 NE 8th St., 21st
Fl.
(425) 462-4662

Hours
Sun–Thu
5:00pm–9:00pm
Fri–Sat
5:00pm–10:00pm
Hours vary by location

Bar
Beer, wine, liquor

Credit cards
Visa, MC, AmEx

Reservations
Accepted

Features
Date-friendly
Live music
Outdoor dining

Dante's Inferno Dogs

As long as these brats exist, heaven can wait. So can our diets...

www.dantesinfernodogs.com

American
Food cart

Ballard
Ballard Sunday Market,
5330 Ballard Ave.
(206) 283-3647

University District
2623 Northeast
University Village
(206) 523-0622

Hours
Sun
10:00am–3:00pm

Credit cards
None

Features
Kid-friendly
Outdoor dining

Like Satan, Dante's is always lurking at the periphery, chipping away at our negligible will power. There's the cart on a hot day, luring you away from sensible sustenance, like water. Or outside the gym. Or across the street from the bar where you already exceeded your weekly calorie intake in beer.

For more than nine years, Dante Rivera has made the best bratwurst on wheels, and he now has seven carts in his fleet. A variety of toppings is available; the bratwurst is best served with grilled onions and Seattle's default condiment, cream cheese (great on brats, unforgivable on regular hot dogs). The veggie and chicken varieties of sausage are surprisingly good.

Regular weekly stops for the carts include University Village shopping center (on Friday, Saturday, Sunday), and the Ballard Sunday Market. Check out the Dante's Twitter feed (@danteinfernodog) to find out where else the carts pop up.

Delancey

Unworthy of two-hour waits, but good
pizza for Seattle

7.5	6.5
Food	Feel

$40	7.5
Price	Wine

www.delanceyseattle.com

First, the face-palm aspect of Delancey: at this
writing, weekend waits for tables were
exceeding two hours. Two-hour waits. For pizza.
That thing you can get in less than two minutes
in New York, the city with the street this
restaurant was named after.

Okay, moving on. Delancey makes a pretty
good fancy wood-fired pie. Although the dough
could use more salt and more fermentation
flavor, it's chewy and airy. (Char is variable, but
most pies come out with a fair bit of it.) A
flavorful and bright tomato sauce pulls
everything together. Toppings, although a bit
sparsely spread, are fresh and occasionally
inventive (clams with crème fraîche, for
example).

Starters are hit or miss; salads are often
underseasoned. Skipping the apps, however,
will leave room for mildly precious but uniformly
excellent desserts like a bittersweet chocolate
chip cookie with gray sea salt. The wine list isn't
extensive, but it's solid—and interesting, with
bottles like an Oregon Grüner Veltliner.

The interior is simple and sweet: with its
blackboard with nightly specials, cool vintage
light fixtures, and mix-matched chairs, Delancey
is a perfect fit for Ballard. That said, with a
noisy, hungry crowd eyeing your table, Delancey
isn't yet the relaxing neighborhood spot it
aspires to be.

Pizza
Casual restaurant

Ballard
1415 NW 70th St.
(206) 838-1960

Hours
Wed–Sat
5:00pm–10:00pm
Sun
5:00pm–9:00pm

Bar
Beer, wine

Credit cards
Visa, MC

Reservations
Not accepted

Features
Veg-friendly

5.0 Food / 6.5 Feel

$15 Price

Delicatus

We want to love this downtown sandwich shop, but it doesn't live up to the hype

www.delicatusseattle.com

Sandwiches
Casual restaurant

Pioneer Square
103 1st Ave. S.
(206) 623-3780

Hours
Mon–Thu
11:30am–8:00pm
Fri–Sat
11:30am–10:00pm

Bar
Beer, wine, liquor, BYO

Credit cards
Visa, MC

Reservations
Accepted

The potential bursts out of Delicatus like a wad of pastrami in an unworthy rye. The space, in one of Pioneer Square's old buildings, has the high-ceilinged, exposed-brick-and-beams mystique that helps so many Capitol Hill joints toe the line between café and nighttime hangout (Delicatus does have a small bar). The ingredients are sourced from some great local purveyors—Zoë's meats, as well as baked goods from Essential Baking Company and Brenner Brothers. Alas, sandwiches are merely ordinary.

Delicatus has many fans among downtown office workers, and it doesn't make a bad sandwich. But with such good ingredients, we expect a little more flavor. Even the more complex creations seem a little one-note (that note often being salt). The "Duwamish," for example, Delicatus' version of the Cuban sandwich, often has too much bread and salty pork and ham and not enough Swiss or mayo; the tangy cucumber/cabbage relish doesn't blend as effortlessly as do the pickles in the original version. Even the classic pastrami on rye needs more, or a more dynamic, Russian dressing.

The menu is divided into two categories, "The Traditionalists" (classic combinations like the BLT) and "The Progressives" (more convoluted combinations like the "Duwamish"). Delicatus seems to have more success with the traditional side of the menu: the fresh-cooked meats that feature in the Progressives, like lamb shank and pulled pork, tend to be lackluster.

Dick's Drive-In

A heart attack on a bun, but a staple for those with Seasonal Affective Disorder

6.5	7.5
Food	Feel

$5
Price

www.ddir.com

No matter how long the lines at Cantinetta and Delancey get, the lines will always be longer at Dick's, the most iconic of several local hamburger chains. It's a far step up from McDonald's in that the ingredients are less mysterious—they slice up real potatoes for the fries, the beef isn't terrible, and the milkshakes are hand-dipped. However, the result looks about the same, and you can expect the standard salt-and-fat-fueled heart palpitations.

Don't bother with deluxe or special; just go with cheeseburgers (you'll need at least two). The fries occasionally rock; usually, they're a bit soggy and oversalted. Milkshakes are good, but we can't imagine what sort of cast-iron stomach can handle both a milkshake and a pile of burgers.

Waiting in line is half the fun, at least at the Capitol Hill and Wallingford locations, which have the most personality, especially shortly after last call. At any hour of the day, the Capitol Hill branch is a crash course in all the beauty and drawbacks of the neighborhood's much-touted "eclecticism."

The Wallingford location is often just as amusing, though its proximity to UW makes it a different animal. Things we've learned from Dick's: freaks and drug-addled kids can form an orderly queue; nasally girls in "dress sweats" and the men who don't love them can't.

American
Counter service

Capitol Hill
115 Broadway Ave. E.
(206) 323-1300

North Seattle
12325 30th Ave. NE
(206) 363-7777

Wallingford
111 NE 45th St.
(206) 632-5125

Queen Anne
500 Queen Anne Ave. N.
(206) 285-5155

Hours
Daily
10:30am–2:00am

Bar
None

Credit cards
None

Features
Kid-friendly

8.5	9.0
Food	Feel

$45	8.0
Price	Wine

Dinette

This ambient Euro-influenced space isn't just cute—it's getting better with age

www.dinetteseattle.com

Modern
Upmarket restaurant

Capitol Hill
1514 E. Olive Way
(206) 328-2282

Hours
Tue–Sat
4:00pm–11:00pm

Bar
Beer, wine, liquor

Credit cards
Visa, MC

Reservations
Accepted

Features
Date-friendly
Good cocktails
Veg-friendly

Dinette entered the Capitol Hill dining scene on the strength of its gimmicks. It was one of the first restaurants to offer a "supper club" (it still does family-style Sunday dinners bimonthly). And it offered a signature starter: fancy toast topped tapas-style with rich concoctions like salami, fontina, and tapenade, or creamy gorgonzola, walnuts, and balsamic syrup.

The mood is just right: convivial but with enough soft lighting and ineffable ambience for a date night. The dining room has a low-key, modern-rustic feel—one panelist felt like he had wandered into Anthropologie's home décor section. The tiny adjacent bar, with its peek-a-boo view of the kitchen, is the embodiment of cozy on a drizzly night.

House-made pasta like tender gnocchi stuffed with ricotta and seasonal vegetables, pan-roasted pork chops with French lentils, crispy duck confit—the kitchen draws from myriad European influences with the same satisfying, well-executed results.

While the wine list doesn't have a lot of depth, it's a good mix of Old and New World, with most bottles being very affordable. Dinette is more exciting in the drinks department, with house-infused liquors, homemade liqueurs (including an excellent limoncello and, on occasion, a nocino), and an interesting selection of apéritifs and digestifs.

Dish

It's just breakfast, but at one of the city's best diners

7.0	6.5
Food	Feel

$15
Price

The Dish serves an old-fashioned American breakfast. It's perfect on a weekend morning, whether you're up early or you've slept in and want to soak up the booze in your blood stream with some biscuits and gravy. Unfortunately, everyone knows this, so you will wait and wait on weekends.

But how long do you really want to stand around, looking at a particularly depressing stretch of Leary Way, just to get an omelette or corned beef hash? The food is pretty good and filling, but if Seattle had a large supply of diners, no one would put up with the line and harried, borderline-rude service here. In fact, public opinion of The Dish has seemed to slip dramatically in the past five years as more places around town have started offering brunch.

But we don't have many diners, and this is as good a place as any to get a scramble. The space is small, loud, busy, and aromatic. The hot sauce collection is neat, and not just for show—definitely ask for a few bottles to sample. It kind of reminds us of a Northwest version of the cafe in *Back to the Future* where Marty McFly first runs into Young Biff. Or maybe the stuck-in-time feeling comes from the cash register—checks accepted but no credit cards.

American
Casual restaurant

Fremont
4358 Leary Way NW
(206) 782-9985

Hours
Tue–Sat
7:00am–1:45pm
Sun
8:00am–1:45pm

Bar
None

Credit cards
None

Reservations
Not accepted

Features
Kid-friendly
Outdoor dining
Veg-friendly

D'Ambrosio Gelato

Delicious gelato that gets it all right, with some lovely touches from the Old World

www.dambrosiogelato.com

Sweets
Counter service

Ballard
5339 Ballard Ave. NW
(206) 327-9175

Hours
Mon–Thu
noon–10:00pm
Fri–Sat
noon–midnight
Sun
10:00am–10:00pm

Bar
None

Credit cards
Visa, MC

Features
Kid-friendly

D'Ambrosio Gelato is about as far away from the gluttonous experience that is Cold Stone Creamery as you can get. No one is going to break out into an off-key song and dance if you plunk a dollar into the tip jar. Portions are small and civilized. Ask the owner to throw Oreos and Reese's Pieces mix-ins into his Sicilian pistachio gelato, and he'd probably clutch his heart, curse your forebears, and keel over from the sacrilege.

Locals line up for this stuff even on rainy days—chances are if you see a queue of hungry patrons snaking out of a tiny jewel box of a Ballard gelateria, you're here. Sidle up to one of the blonde wood counters, and indulge in at least two scoops.

As far as we're concerned, D'Ambrosio serves the dreamiest frozen treats in town. Small batch, Italian ice-cream made with organic dairy and fruit—and mineral spring water used in its sorbetto—makes this sweet a scoop above the rest. This gelato is light and milky-clean, and the sorbets are not overly rich so that the flavors—intriguing ones, like panna cotta, caramel and figs, hazelnut, banana, and chestnut—truly shine. This stuff is sexier than Sophia Loren on your tongue, and probably nearly as messy.

Earth & Ocean

Possibly the best hotel restaurant within the city limits

www.earthocean.net

The W is the velvet-rope discotheque of hotel chains, with a reputation predicated mostly on the canned-chic connotations of the brand. But the Seattle hotel has always stood out for having a real restaurant—one that represents the Pacific Northwest well, while still delivering on the typical W experience.

The space is '90s modern, with plush red chairs pulled up to dark wood tables, clashing artfully with a striped carpet of primary colors. Oversized paintings hang on the wall, and in one corner gold velveteen booths have a view of an impressive wine collection. In other words, this place looks ridiculous in daylight. Although, like all hotel restaurants this place is open all day, ordering something as pedestrian as an American breakfast is a mistake. If there's any magic happening, it's at dinner.

The menu is divided into surf and turf, excuse us, Earth and Ocean. The former includes starters like lamb burgers, and a very good charcuterie plate (they make their own), and mains like reasonably priced smoked duck and grilled lamb sirloin and a stupidly overpriced burger. The latter includes bites like salmon tartare and mac and cheese with blue prawns and mains like Pacific sockeye in a spicy broth. The three-course tasting menu, which includes a wine pairing, is a great deal. The vodka and Red Bull, though, you'll have to buy à la carte.

7.5	8.0
Food	Feel

$60	7.5
Price	Wine

Modern
Upmarket restaurant

Downtown
1112 4th Ave.
(206) 264-6060

Hours
Mon
6:30am–10:30am
Tue–Fri
6:30am–10:30am
11:30am–2:00pm
5:00pm–10:00pm
Sat
7:00am–1:30pm
5:00pm–10:00pm
Sun
7:00am–1:30pm

Bar
Beer, wine, liquor

Credit cards
Visa, MC, AmEx

Reservations
Accepted

Features
Brunch
Date-friendly

6.5 | 8.0
Food | Feel

$110 | 9.0
Price | Wine

El Gaucho

"El Gouge-o"

www.elgaucho.com

Steakhouse
Upmarket restaurant

Belltown
2505 1st Ave.
(206) 728-1337

Bellevue
450 108th Ave. NE
(425) 455-2715

Hours
Mon–Thu
5:00pm–11:00pm
Fri–Sat
5:00pm–1:00am
Sun
5:00pm–11:00pm

Bar
Beer, wine, liquor

Credit cards
Visa, MC, AmEx

Reservations
Essential

Features
Date-friendly
Live music

A lot about El Gaucho sounds promising, at first; this local chain aims for something between Morton's and an Argentine steakhouse, grilling dry-aged beef over coals. But the steaks are inconsistent—the char on some cuts is wonderfully crisp, but a totally flavorless six-ounce filet is not at all worthwhile—and prices are sky-high. The wine list is more interesting than the ones at most national-chain steakhouses, but it is also amazingly overpriced, with some bottles over three times retail.

El Gaucho used to be a bigger part of Seattle's dining scene; for a brief period it was synonymous with a swanky night out, with dancing in the Pampas Room and a stay at the affiliated boutique hotel upstairs creating a sophisticated escape on a very sketchy corner of Belltown. But even then, the food and execution couldn't fully justify the prices.

The décor is as expected—rich, dark, and sleek. Live jazz fills in the silences between tinkling glasses and silverware as tuxedo-clad waiters scurry by with carts for tableside Caesar salads, the darkness punctuated by an occasional burst of flame from a bananas Foster in the making. El Gaucho is more like dinner theater, where the food is not the point. There, too, you pay way too much for the antics and scenery.

El Mestizo

Kind of a newcomer, kind of off the beaten path, and thoroughly great

8.5	9.0
Food	Feel

$30
Price

www.elmestizorestaurant.com

Mexican
Casual restaurant

Central District
526 Broadway
(206) 324-2445

Hours
Mon–Thu
11:00am–10:00pm
Fri
11:00am–11:00pm
Sat
9:00am–11:00pm
Sun
9:00am–8:00pm

Bar
Beer, wine, liquor

Credit cards
Visa, MC, AmEx

Reservations
Accepted

Features
Brunch

Though it's in the type of high-ceilinged narrow space that typifies so many upmarket Seattle restaurants, El Mestizo has an even better vibe than most. It's a touch modern, with its chocolate-and-butter color scheme and shiny stainless-steel open kitchen, and a touch traditional, with Diego Rivera's calla lilies and a few crafts hanging on the walls. El Mestizo isn't the only place in town doing region-hopping traditional favorites in a date-friendly atmosphere, but nowhere else do all the pieces of that particular puzzle fit so well together.

At lunch, El Mestizo sticks to tacos, burritos, and a few soups (including a good sopa Azteca). The burritos may be a better value, but we prefer the tacos: they're cheap, and the savory fillings like the cochinita pibil (probably the best version of this we've had in a sit-down restaurant) don't get buried under rice and sour cream. The dinner menu is a well-edited list of iconic dishes like chile en nogada. We recommend the alambres, a deceptively simple preparation of sliced beef and peppers topped with cheese that picks up a nice bit of a salt and smoke from bacon. The mole poblano is also noteworthy: El Mestizo's mole is thicker and sweeter, which may not be to everyone's liking, but it is more complex than its competitors' versions.

7.5 6.0
Food Feel

$10
Price

El Puerco Llorón

Low-key, craving-inducing, pretty authentic
Mexican at the market

www.elpuercolloron.com

Mexican
Counter service

Downtown
1501 Western Ave.
(206) 624-0541

Hours
Sun–Thu
11:00am–7:00pm
Fri–Sat
11:00am–8:00pm

Bar
Beer

Credit cards
Visa, MC

Reservations
Not accepted

This little eatery on the Pike Place hillclimb feels
like something you'd find in Mexico, though in a
city that sees its share of tourists—down a side
street in Cabo, maybe. Though it's usually just
used as a quick lunch break for downtown
office workers, it's not a bad place to linger on a
late afternoon in summer.

It's pretty campy, with banners, posters, and
flags covering the hand-painted turquoise walls.
The mismatched tables are perched under all
sorts of hanging ephemera like a set of tiny
chairs with woven-straw seats. You order at the
counter, and service is nonexistent (many people
complain that it's actually a bit on the surly
side).

Taquitos (filled with chicken, carnitas, carne
asada) and the carne asada platter are the
standouts here. And all the other accoutrements
of authenticity are in evidence, too: tiny, hand-
formed tortillas; aguas frescas like horchata;
shelves lined with Jarritos and a good selction of
Mexican beers; a good salsa bar.

We've had enough good meals to feel
comfortable recommending it, but be
forewarned that word of mouth is all over the
place and it seems to have more "off days" in
the past three years than it ever has before.

Elliott's Oyster House

A cheesy old-school Seattle institution, but one that serves decent food

www.elliottsoysterhouse.com

7.5	8.0
Food	Feel

$60	6.5
Price	Wine

The oysters here are ridiculously good, and Elliott's devotes its happy hour to them. If you miss happy hour (be forewarned that the place gets tourist-trap expensive after 6 pm), try the oyster stew, which is rich, redolent of shallots and smoky bacon, and has two plump, tender Willapa Bay oysters submerged in its creamy depths.

As for the other dishes…well, the kitchen is fairly creative for a corporate-feeling place, but really the oysters are the reason to come here. And the bar is well-equipped to wash down all those bivalves: bartenders are knowledgeable, there's a good selection of draft beer, and the wine cellar, though not deep, carries many selections that pair well with the different types of oysters.

This place is both old-school and touristy—they do shellfish towers, for Pete's sake, and provide lobster bibs—but it's a fun place to dine and the service is wonderful. The waterfront location is great, too, though the views won't mean much when your back is to them while you're sitting at the oyster bar.

Seafood
Casual restaurant

Downtown
1201 Alaskan Way, Pier 56
(206) 623-4340

Hours
Sun–Thu
11:00am–10:00pm
Fri–Sat
11:00am–11:00pm

Bar
Beer, wine, liquor

Credit cards
Visa, MC, AmEx

Reservations
Accepted

emmer&rye

Precise small plates with very modern
pedigree in a quirky Victorian house

www.emmerandrye.com

Modern
Casual restaurant

Queen Anne
1825 Queen Anne Ave.
N.
(206) 282-0680

Hours
Mon–Thu
11:00am–10:00pm
Fri
11:00am–11:00pm
Sat
9:00am–11:00pm
Sun
9:00am–10:00pm

Bar
Beer, wine, liquor

Credit cards
Visa, MC

Reservations
Accepted

Features
Brunch
Good cocktails
Outdoor dining

Emmer is also known as farro, and emmer&rye's
signature starter is a plate of fried farro with a
savory peanut-yogurt sauce. The menu rarely
falters from there, with local, seasonal
ingredients thoughtfully put to use in dishes like
rabbit loin with porcini and pea shoots and goat
crépinette with black trumpet mushrooms and
butternut squash gratin.

Attention to detail here is usually impeccable:
the sausage is house-made, and the cocktail list
is remixed monthly to accommodate both the
seasons (cherry harvest) and the trends (bacon
vodka). The kitchen is not always in top form,
and there are some questionable recipes from
time to time, but most of the mistakes—or,
more correctly, missed opportunities (say, not
adding a citrusy or acid note to balance out a
salty dish)—are easy to forgive. The wine list is
small but interesting (and organized largely by
varietal, not region— a pet peeve of ours). Stick
with cocktails.

emmer&rye has a charming set-up in a
converted Victorian house with some jarring
interior details—tacky blown-up and framed
posters of emmer fields, for one. Service, while
reasonably competent, is nothing extraordinary.
A few more adjustments, and a meal here could
be really special.

Espresso Vivace

Spectacular espresso and some frou-frou-coffee-drink guilty pleasures

www.espressovivace.com

Vivace roasts some of the best coffee in the city, and the brew is for serious coffeeheads. The coffee is full-bodied, with a rich oiliness. And although pretentious coffee drinkers like us might sneer at add-ins as a general rule, we confess a particular fondness for the lightly sweetened Café Nico—a shot of espresso with a tiny bit of milk, orange zest, and nutmeg.

Despite the "seriousness" of this coffeehouse, Vivace holds wide appeal: a popular drink is the "White Velvet," a creamy, foamy, sweetened confection that's like the more sophisticated sister to the in-your-face coffee-flavored milkshakes of Starbucks. (For the hardcore coffee geeks, you'll be pleased to know that Vivace only serves ristretto shots.)

With two brick-and-mortar locations plus a walk-up café, Vivace still retains that small-quantity quality, even in a big-coffee city. The new Capitol Hill location is an expansive, 2000-foot space with a curved stand-up Italian bar and under-counter murals. The downtown location is similarly large, with glassed-in meeting areas that can be reserved at no charge. Delicious carby offerings rotate seasonally, but we've indulged in both "Top Pot" and "Mighty-O" (vegan) donuts here, as well as locally made cupcakes, cookies, chocolate biscotti, and Whoopie Pies.

Coffee Sweets
Café

Capitol Hill
532 Broadway Ave. E.
(206) 860-2722

South Lake Union
227 Yale Ave. N.
(206) 388-5164

Eastlake
321 Broadway Ave. E.
Espresso cart. No phone.

Hours
Daily
6:00am–11:00pm

Bar
None

Credit cards
Visa, MC, AmEx

Features
Outdoor dining
Wi-Fi

Etta's

Extra, extra, read all about it: Tom's tourist trap squeaks by with average seafood

www.tomdouglas.com

Seafood
Upmarket restaurant

Downtown
2020 Western Ave.
(206) 443-6000

Hours
Mon–Thu
11:30am–9:30pm
Fri
11:30am–10:00pm
Sat
9:00am–3:00pm
4:00pm–10:00pm
Sun
9:00am–3:00pm
4:00pm–9:00pm

Bar
Beer, wine, liquor

Credit cards
Visa, MC, AmEx

Reservations
Accepted

Features
Brunch
Date-friendly

Once one of the more beloved restaurants of Tom Douglas's empire, Etta's is now solely the domain of tourists and Seattleites who want to treat out-of-towners to seafood but don't want to put too much effort into doing so.

Douglas does know seafood, although oysters are hit-or-miss; we've had good fried versions, and some bad experiences, too. Most of the standard "Seattle" dishes—salmon, fish and chips, black cod, Dungeness crab cakes…zzzz…sorry, we must have drifted off—are at least competent. Venture beyond the familiar, though, and you'll get inexpertly cooked fish and strangely dated riffs on Asian-fusion dishes, although some, like tuna tartare, are still right on the money. This is true even at brunch (the best meal for the money), where the corned beef hash and the Dungeness eggs Benedict are much better than a much-heralded but wildly disappointing and overcooked wild salmon with cornbread pudding and shiitake relish, or overpriced crab cakes, another house favorite, which are doughy and uninspired.

Speaking of Asian fusion, the mid-1990s are well represented in Etta's dining room, with copper railings and weird orange, yellow, and pale green glass pendant lamps. The place definitely needs renovations, although most visitors won't notice since the large windows nicely frame the spillover "bustle" of Pike Place Market.

Eva Restaurant

A magnificent, semi-hidden gem in Green Lake

8.5	9.0
Food	Feel

$45	8.5
Price	Wine

www.evarestaurant.com

Eva isn't really all that hidden—well, it is in residential Green Lake, a neighborhood with a mostly undistinguished scene—but it's one of those places that so quietly does its own thing that we tend to stop hearing its whispers among the clatter of small plates and vintage martini shakers.

Fairy lights and white tablecloths are all Eva offers in décor, but we wouldn't want more: the place is classy without losing the simple neighborhood bistro vibe. The menu follows suit; it offers class before flash, with starters like Cabrales flan with pear relish, and mains like goat cheese, arugula, and hazelnut ravioli with a morel mushroom cream sauce. Eva is particularly good with birds, and this is the place to order quail.

From May through October, weekend suppers are three-course set-menus featuring ingredients from the big farmers' market in the U District. These dinners are very affordable and strike a perfect balance between "aw, shucks" simple (babyback pork ribs with collard greens and strawberry-rhubarb crumble) and the best kind of farmer's-market ingenuity (sugar snap pea soup with goat cheese gnocchi and chive blossoms).

Eva has one of the best wine lists in the city, with some of the world's best producers, from Burgundy to Rioja to Tuscany to Nahe, and the waitstaff does an excellent job of suggesting pairings.

Modern
Upmarket restaurant

Green Lake
2227 N. 56th St.
(206) 633-3538

Hours
Daily
5:00pm–10:00pm

Bar
Beer, wine, liquor

Credit cards
Visa, MC, AmEx

Reservations
Accepted

Features
Date-friendly

Ezell's Famous Chicken

A fast-food institution, Oprah approved,
where you get your chicken to go

www.ezellschicken.com

Southern
Counter service

South Seattle
11805 Renton Ave. S.
(206) 772-1925

Central District
501 23rd Ave.
(206) 324-4141

North Seattle
7531 196th SW
(425) 673-4193

Hours
Mon–Thu
10:00am–10:00pm
Fri–Sat
10:00am–11:00pm
Sun
11:00am–10:00pm
Hours vary by location

Bar
None

Credit cards
Visa, MC

Surprising non-greasy fried chicken with awesomely crispy skin concealing moist hunks of meat. That's it, that's what Ezell's does. Is it the only place in town to sate the craving for a fried drumstick? Not anymore. But Ezell's is an institution: not a school day goes by when a line of Garfield High students doesn't form at lunch time. Not a drizzly evening goes by without some Seattleite driving four neighborhoods from home to pick up a 24-piece. And Oprah was here.

Chicken comes light or dark, regular or spicy. Spicy is more of a short burst of cayenne and paprika than a full-mouth inferno, so be sure to grab some containers of Ezell's excellent hot sauce. As for sides, forgo the mashed potatoes and gravy and stick to the rolls and cole slaw. The latter is a nice complement to the salty chicken, and the former are spectacular. For anyone who finds wings and thighs too pedestrian, Ezell's offers fried gizzards and/or livers by the pound—dipped in hot sauce, they're almost better than the rest of the chicken, and a lot cheaper, too.

This is definitely a spot for take-out. There's no place to comfortably enjoy your chicken unless you want to sit on the curb by the bus stop—most people eat in their cars.

Facing East

Taiwanese, Momofuku-ed, from the pork-heavy fare to the classy digs

8.0 Food

5.5 Feel

$25 Price

Seattle has played out all iterations of modern Vietnamese and modern Japanese, so eventually someone had to try modern Taiwanese, and the young, hip, well-to-do Chinese of the Eastside are the perfect audience for a menu that ranges from crispy fried chicken to century egg over cold tofu to more fusiony dishes like sweet dumplings made with sweet-potato flour. There are quite a few good dishes here, our favorites being lamb with water spinach, pork "burgers" (in steamed buns), and fried pork chop on rice. (Soups are watery and a little bland, though you might get a reasonable bowl of beef noodle.)

Although some dishes come to the table in the expected pile of vegetables and meat atop a pool of oily broth, Facing East does like to play with presentation a bit: the pork "burgers" here actually resemble burgers, the pork spilling out of open-face steamed buns. Shaved ice desserts come out, somewhat annoyingly, on a flat plate as a pile of chunky detritus that resembles a high school science fair volcano.

The space is definitely more upscale than a typical fast-food Chinese joint—the tea service, for example, is lovely, with mod clear plastic cups and teapot—but it's still in a strip mall, and horribly crowded, so it's not a particularly pleasant place to dine.

Chinese
Casual restaurant

Bellevue
1075 Bellevue Way NE, B2
(425) 688-2986

Hours
Tue–Thu
11:30am–3:00pm
5:00pm–9:00pm
Fri–Sat
11:30am–3:00pm
5:00pm–10:00pm
Sun
11:30am–3:00pm
5:00pm–9:00pm

Bar
None

Credit cards
Visa, MC

Reservations
Not accepted

Features
Kid-friendly

FareStart

Decent eats for a great cause—you'll leave fat, happy, and feeling good about yourself

www.farestart.org

American
Casual restaurant

Downtown
700 Virginia St.
(206) 267-7601

Hours
Mon–Wed
11:00am–2:00pm
Thu
11:00am–2:00pm
6:00pm–8:00pm
Fri
11:00am–2:00pm

Bar
Beer, wine

Credit cards
Visa, MC, AmEx

Reservations
Accepted

FareStart isn't perfect, but it's virtuous: the restaurant is a school that teaches culinary skills to the homeless. Weekday lunches are handled by regular staff and students; weekly dinners are handled by guest chefs (with students assisting) who donate both their time and the ingredients for the menus they've created.

The quality of the food can vary from overcooked to careful, delicious to underseasoned, but in general, by the time students are cooking for the masses, they know their basics, and the dishes are pretty well executed and very well presented. The lunch menu changes every few months but always includes salads, sandwiches, burgers, and several vegetarian options.

Rest assured that FareStart is not preparing its students for a life at McDonald's. When we say sandwiches, we mean apple-braised pork shoulder on potato bread or pan-seared ahi with pickled cucumber and chipotle-honey aïoli. The wait staff is a mix of students and volunteers, so service is generally earnest and reliable, but not polished. The Thursday guest-chef dinner is a great way to sample this chef's food at a more reasonable price than at his own restaurant.

The attractive bi-level loft space defies you to remember that this restaurant is a little different than most—the exposed duct work and concrete are the extra-credit lesson in how to create the quintessential Seattle restaurant.

Flying Fish

Moderately trendy and majorly reliable for
Washington State bounty

7.5	6.0
Food	Feel

$60
Price

www.flyingfishrestaurant.com

The Flying Fish is just fine. We've had whole fish
that was slightly overcooked and dishes that
favored style over substance—there are better
ways to wrangle the Washington coast's
excellent razor clams than on an open-faced
sandwich—but overall, Flying Fish delivers a
consistently satisfying seafood bonanza. It
provides a taste of the freshest catches, a few
reasonably well-executed Thai flourishes (the
chef spent some time studying Thai cuisine), and
an atmosphere that's casual and fun but still
feels like it's trying to dress up a bit.

Although normally we'd embrace a move out
of the tourist trap of the Pike Place Market area,
Flying Fish's new digs aren't necessarily an
improvement. The new space is more modern,
perhaps, but it has much less personality.
Granted, it's hard to make large generic
commercial spaces—in this case the bottom
floor of one of the city's new biotech
buildings—look as lived-in as an older building
in a historic part of town, but it's always a little
depressing when a restaurant can't get beyond
that cafeteria/fancy diner feel. And we have no
words for whatever happened at the bar: red
globular lanterns hang over chartreuse bar
stools that are inverted cones. Oh well, at least
"packed and cheerful" is a good distraction for
these kinds of design missteps.

Seafood
Upmarket restaurant

South Lake Union
300 Westlake Ave. N.
(206) 728-8595

Hours
Mon–Fri
11:30am–11:00pm
Sat–Sun
5:00pm–11:00pm

Bar
Beer, wine, liquor

Credit cards
None

Reservations
Accepted

Features
Date-friendly
Outdoor dining

Flying Squirrel

If this place weren't such a trek, it would outbuzz Delancey in the Seattle pizza wars

www.flyingsquirrelpizza.com

Pizza
Casual restaurant

Columbia City
4920 S. Genesee St.
(206) 721-7620

Hours
Daily
5:00pm–10:00pm

Bar
Beer, wine

Credit cards
Visa, MC, AmEx

Reservations
Not accepted

Features
Kid-friendly
Outdoor dining
Veg-friendly

Flying Squirrel combines the obsession with fancy toppings with the quest to create a classic New York pie, and the results shame the overpriced Neapolitan pizzas.

The standard tomato and mozzarella pie has an excellent ratio of sauce, cheese, char, oil, and bubbles in the dough. Flying Squirrel sources from local legends (cured meats from Salumi and Zoë's) and local purveyors (free-range eggs and organic greens), and the toppings really do stand out.

Combinations may look overly ambitious in print, but they make perfect sense on the pie— nothing's done simply for novelty's sake. The #8—free-range egg, organic arugula, fresh mozzarella, parmesan, and red onion—is one of our favorites, as is the #5, a wonderfully salty and citrusy combination of garlic-roasted pulled pork, cilantro, red onion, cotija cheese, and fresh lime. Flying Squirrel's owner loves cassette mix-tapes, and music influences some of the pizza specials (like the ever-popular "Herb Alpert," with red sauce, mozzarella, Salumi's oregano salami, roasted garlic, and fresh basil).

The restaurant is nicer than a typical pizzeria—there's some funky artwork on the walls and candles flicker at night—but less interesting than some of the gourmet pizza spots within city limits. Early diners will share the space with lots of young families, but everyone seems to coexist peacefully.

Fonté Café & Wine Bar

8.0	8.5
Food	Feel

$25	8.0
Price	Wine

Classy coffee shop that's the best thing about the new Four Seasons hotel

www.fontecoffee.com/cafe_winebar.html

Fonté is an excellent local micro-roaster; it's been around for a while, but until it opened this flagship shop, its coffee wasn't always easy to find. So it's nice to have a dedicated retail shop.

Beige, beige, beige: from the leather couches and chairs to light-colored wood tables, it's the pallor of choice for Fonté, interrupted only by a few curvy brown leather swivel chairs and a barista station that is so white and sterile it looks like a parody of how coffee will be served in the future. The upscale space is very attractive, and the polished contemporary feel makes more sense than some shaggy neighborhood aesthetic because Fonté doubles as a wine bar. The list here is lovely, extensive, deep, and deep, and you should play around with it: there are a few flights, and a selection of smaller pours.

The menu was developed by Jason Wilson of Crush, so the food is far from an afterthought; it's by far the best and most sophisticated fare you could get at a place that focuses so intensely on coffee. Eggs are organic and fresh from his family's farm. Hearty sandwiches like gruyère, bacon, and caramelized onion and the all-day breakfast menu seem custom-built for freelancers keeping weird hours. Happy-hour patrons get the usual (i.e. lamb sliders) along with interesting soups (spiced chickpea and ginger) and a nice selection of Salumi cured meats to accompany wine choices. The wine and beer lists are color-coded to aid pairings.

Modern Coffee
Café

Downtown
1321 1st Ave.
(206) 777-6193

Hours
Sun–Mon
7:00am–9:00pm
Tue–Sat
7:00am–10:00pm

Bar
Beer, wine, liquor

Credit cards
Visa, MC, AmEx

Reservations
Accepted

Features
Veg-friendly
Wi-Fi

Fresh Bistro

"Fresh" in this case means fussy, green-walled farm-to-table, not "really cool"

www.herbanfeast.com/freshbistro

Modern
Upmarket restaurant

West Seattle
4725 42nd Ave. SW
(206) 935-3733

Hours
Mon–Thu
11:00am–10:00pm
Fri
11:00am–11:00pm
Sat
9:00am–3:00pm
5:00pm–11:00pm
Sun
9:00am–3:00pm

Bar
Beer, wine, liquor

Credit cards
Visa, MC, AmEx

Reservations
Accepted

Features
Brunch
Date-friendly
Outdoor dining
Veg-friendly

Everything here is indeed very fresh, but it's all a little fussy and a little salady. Maybe the paper menu just needs a good edit, but every dish seems to have at least a half-dozen featured ingredients. The pork belly sandwiches, which, in the ultimate hedging of bets, are called "pork belly banh mi sliders" are super, but even they are a bit overdressed with foie gras mayo and a larger-than-needed pile of pickled carrots, daikon, cilantro, jalapeño, cucumbers, and Romaine.

But vegetables are treated well here, and in its salads and sides, Fresh tries to incorporate the parts of the plant that usually get tossed in the compost heap (like beet greens, for example). That's some sustainability street cred.

The space is pleasant enough, but with a few obvious "fresh" visual cues: the walls are painted green, the sculptures are biomorphic, and ceramic mugs of grass sprouts decorate the tables instead of flowers. We respect what Fresh is trying to do, but in the parlance of our time, they need to slow their roll a bit—there are enough people doing the local and seasonal thing that there's no need to create a farm-to-table theme park.

Fu Man Dumpling House

7.5 Food

4.0 Feel

$15 Price

A different style of dumpling in a familiar style of hole in the wall

Eating at Fu Man is half spectator sport: a large part of its appeal is standing in front of the window watching the dumplings being made. (There's certainly nothing else to look at in this nondescript restaurant in a nondescript neighborhood). The dumplings are Shandong-style, which means they have a thicker, chewier skin, and this alone draws dumpling aficionados. We prefer the pan-fried dumplings, though the boiled version is also perfectly serviceable thanks to a pungent and addictive garlicky dipping sauce.

We wouldn't recommend straying too far past the dumplings, although the green onion pancake is a fine appetizer. The other dish of note is the "Chinese burger"—a ridiculous name for a seasoned pork patty inside pan-fried dough and served with the requisite garlic sauce. How does that differ from the regular dumplings? Well, there's a hockey puck's worth of meat in the dough instead of a dollop.

Chinese
Casual restaurant

North Seattle
14314 Greenwood Ave. N.
(206) 364-0681

Hours
Tue–Sun
11:00am–3:00pm
4:30pm–9:00pm

Credit cards
Visa, MC, AmEx

Full Tilt Ice Cream

The rambunctious teen to Molly Moon's soccer mom

www.fulltilticecream.com

Sweets
Ice Cream
Counter service

South Seattle
9629 16th Ave. SW
(206) 767-4811

Columbia City
5041 Rainier Ave. S.
(206) 226-2740

University District
4759 Brooklyn Ave. NE
no phone

Hours
Tue–Sat
noon–10:00pm
Sun
noon–9:00pm
Hours vary by location

Bar
Beer

Credit cards
Visa, MC

Features
Kid-friendly
Live music

This cheeky ice cream parlor first made headlines for opening its flagship shop in White Center, a suburb ignored by even the most adventurous community-minded hipsters. But it beckoned all with pinball machines and all-ages indie-rock concerts, and soon everyone was talking about the inventive ice cream flavors, too.

Full Tilt likes to push the envelope with unfamiliar ingredients like ube (a purple yam from the Philippines that gives ice cream a delightful Willy Wonka-esque hue) and (unfamiliar, at least, to American palates, but delicious nonetheless) salted licorice. But the most adored flavors are usually a bit simpler like green tea, cookies and cream, or the Memphis King (an Elvis-worthy orgy of banana, peanut butter, and chocolate). While Full Tilt does its part to source responsibly, the place has a slightly different definition of "local" ingredients, often looking to the diverse communities south of the city for inspiration: horchata and Thai iced tea are two standout flavors, and Full Tilt even makes paletas.

The shops have a naturally DIY feel—these are definitely not boutiques—and although they appeal to a wide range of Seattleites, they seems most suited to the kind of kids who sign up for rock n' roll fantasy camps. But what would you expect from an ice cream parlor that serves beer?

Genki Sushi

Revolving fish in a flying-fish city

6.0 Food

5.5 Feel

$15 Price

www.genkisushiusa.com

Japanese
Casual restaurant

Queen Anne
500 Mercer St.
(206) 453-3881

Capitol Hill
1620 Broadway
(206) 708-7554

Hours
Sun–Thu
11:00am–10:00pm
Fri–Sat
11:00am–11:00pm

Bar
Beer, wine, liquor

Credit cards
Visa, MC, AmEx

Reservations
Not accepted

Features
Date-friendly
Veg-friendly

Genki Sushi arrived in Seattle just above the QFC grocery store in lower Queen Anne and started serving sushi that's, well, a bit better than the sushi you can get in that QFC. Most would say that Blue C offers higher quality, but for a 10 and a five, you probably get an extra plate or two here.

Grab what you like as it rolls by on the conveyor belt. A favorite is the saba-no bo-sushi, which is mackerel rolled with rice to make a sushi stick. There are non-fish offerings, too. A little bowl of tonkotsu ramen is good for those unwilling to make a commitment to a bigger bowl elsewhere.

The best part of Genki, as with all conveyor-belt sushi joints, is watching what goes round and round—and seeing how others react to the offerings. Bizarre-looking pork belly? Check. Tunafish salad roll? Check. Unidentifiable dessert? Check. But at these low prices, it's fun to give anything and everything a try.

7.5 Food | 6.0 Feel

Georgetown Liquor Co.

Maybe the healthiest bar food in town

$25 Price

www.georgetownliquorcompany.com

Vegefusion
Bar

Georgetown
5501B Airport Way S.
(206) 763-6764

Hours
Mon–Thu
11:00am–10:00pm
Fri
11:00am–11:00pm
Sat
10:00am–11:00am
Sun
10:00am–10:00pm

Bar
Beer, wine, liquor

Credit cards
Visa, MC

Reservations
Not accepted

Features
Brunch
Veg-friendly

Are you a vegetarian or vegan, but also a bad-ass? Do you like black walls, Battlestar Galactica, and Field Roast? Then come on down to Georgetown Liquor Company, a hipster-anointed hard-drinking den where the microbrews are on tap and the ham is surrounded by quotation marks. Um, but don't come if you're a youngster—this place *is* a bar and no one under 21 is allowed in.

Georgetown Liquor is very Georgetown. It looks like 10 drunk geeks pooled all of their dorm-room junk, threw in some booths and a bar, and turned out the lights. There's a sandwich called "The Frac" and an appetizer called "Obi-Won-Ton." (No funny names for the salads, though. Is salad not inherently funny?) There are also arcade games and old Ataris.

But seriously, folks, the food's good. Although split pea and "vegan ham" soup is nothing special (are you surprised?), the soup of the day is often something simple but well executed, like carrot ginger. Sandwiches are excellent: the above-ridiculed "Frac" is certainly a winner, delightfully combining apricot chutney, lentil-sage Field Roast (an imitation meat), brie, arugula, and roma tomatoes on ciabatta.

Glo's

Not worth a wait in the rain, but maybe for classic American breakfast on sunny days

6.5	3.0
Food	Feel

$15
Price

This tiny run-down diner with late '80s décor isn't a pretty sight; the lines running out the door on weekends seem laughable when the Hill has so many restaurants offering brunch in a better setting. But breakfast at Glo's is good and simple—the fanciest thing on the menu is a stack of pancakes with seasonal fruit.

Glo's is all about poached eggs, bacon, and hash—the signature and best dish is the eggs Benedict. There are a few items for vegetarians, like the biscuits and gravy made with mushroom gravy, and a vegan special that's not on the menu: a mound of hash browns, purple cabbage, tomatoes, avocado and onions (ask for it with the veggie chili).

We can't overemphasize how annoying the wait for a table can be. You'll probably spend more than twice the amount of time waiting, and waiting for your food, than it takes to eat your scramble or short stack. And some of the waitstaff are among the visibly hung-over and short-tempered. At least the coffee is good—from Bainbridge Island roaster Pegasus—and available while you wait.

American
Casual restaurant

Capitol Hill
1621 E. Olive Way
(206) 324-2577

Hours
Mon–Fri
7:00am–3:00pm
Sat–Sun
7:00am–4:00pm

Bar
None

Credit cards
Visa, MC

Reservations
Not accepted

Features
Kid-friendly
Veg-friendly

Green Leaf

Probably the best midrange Vietnamese in
the I.D. *and* the place isn't a dump

www.greenleaftaste.com

Vietnamese
Casual restaurant

**International
District**
418 8th Ave. S.
(206) 340-1388

Hours
Daily
11:00am–10:00pm

Bar
Beer, wine

Credit cards
Visa, MC

Reservations
Not accepted

Features
Veg-friendly

Green Leaf is an I.D. favorite. When it opened, it
filled a void between pricey Tamarind Tree and
the hole-in-the-wall pho and banh mi joints. It's
hard to find an unkind word about the place
because almost nothing on the menu
disappoints.

The pho is really good, with ideally cooked
vermicelli noodles and great toppings. They
don't skimp on the fresh herbs and greens in
anything—bowls of pho and spring rolls both
have so much foliage that they look like
terrariums. However, you can get decent pho all
over town, so most of us stop at Green Leaf
when we want quality mains like lemongrass
chicken, which has a wonderfully strong, bright
taste; or bun (vermicelli with choice of meat and
a fried egg roll). Banh xeo (savory rice-flour
pancakes) and the lotus root salads, particularly
the version with papaya and mango, are not to
be missed.

The downstairs is cramped but cute, looking
slightly more stylish than the average I.D. eatery,
with soft lighting at dinner bouncing off light
green walls to give the place a nice glow.
There's more space upstairs, but it's more
kitschy, with tables carved to look like the back
of traditional wagons (the arm rests are the
crests of big wooden wheels). Need we say
more?

Guanaco's Tacos Pupusería

8.0 **6.5**
Food Feel

A jovial staff doles out roll-out-the-door
Salvadoran snacks for super cheap

$10
Price

www.guanacostacos.webs.com

Guanaco's Tacos Pupusería has become a fast
favorite for several reasons: it's incredibly fun to
say (for gringos anyway), it serves one of the
most underrepresented cuisines in the city, and
it's one of the best deals in town.

For only a few bucks, you can get a sampler
with at least one pupusa, another item like a
taco or enchilada, and two slabs of fried yuca.
The name doesn't lie: the pupusas are definitely
the thing to order here. Inside a crisp layer of
hand-patted masa from corn or rice flour (a
hard-to-find pupusa version) is a juicy pile of
meat (chicken and/or chicharrón, pork skin),
melted cheese, loroco (an aromatic Central
American herb), spinach, zucchini, and
jalapeños. (You can build your own pupusa,
making a simpler or vegetarian version.) We also
recommend the pastelito, a savory and salty
empanada stuffed with beef and onions. The
sampler is a lot of food; a pupusa on its own
would be a hearty snack, and an economical
one.

Both locations are friendly and cheerful, but
we're partial to the Capitol Hill branch. Tucked
away from the Broadway hubbub next to a
Korean joint and a smoke shop, it's a great
place to catch up with a group of friends over a
San Lucas beer. The guys running the show here
are also really good at explaining each item and
making recommendations.

Salvadoran
Casual restaurant

Capitol Hill
219 Broadway E., #314
(206) 328-6288

University District
4106 Brooklyn Ave. NE
(206) 547-2369

Hours
Sun–Thu
11:30am–9:00pm
Fri–Sat
11:30am–10:00pm

Bar
Beer, BYO

Credit cards
Visa, MC

Reservations
Not accepted

Features
Kid-friendly

7.0 5.5
Food Feel

$15
Price

Harbor City

This newer dim sum spot is a better value than the old standbys

Chinese
Casual restaurant

International District
707 S. King St.
(206) 621-2228

Hours
Daily
8:30am–11:00pm

Bar
Beer, wine

Credit cards
Visa, MC, AmEx

Reservations
Accepted

Features
Brunch

Why stand in a long line at Jade Garden when you can stand in a shorter line here? There's little to differentiate Harbor City from the other dim sum joints in town, and it won't settle the never-ending and frankly futile "best dim sum" debate, but it does turn out some fresh and flavorful—and cheap—dumplings along with a few decent dinner options.

The many versions of pork dumplings are a strong suit here—with siu mai being the favorite—but there are plenty of interesting nibbles from tendon to tripe to chicken's feet. Avoid har gow, which is like, well, a wet noodle; we've had better luck with other varieties of shrimp dumplings, which have ingredients like chives or bean curd adding some stronger flavors. At dinner, the simple barbecued items like ribs or roast duck are best and also a very good value.

This is more dim sum parlor than dim sum palace, which means less sensory overload than Jade Garden but fewer tables (don't sleep in too late on Sundays). Service is surprisingly friendly, and magnanimously accommodating of newcomers—for a dim sum restaurant, anyway.

Harvest Vine

From heavenly to horrible—sit at the bar
and hope for the best

www.harvestvine.com

8.5	7.0
Food	Feel

$65	8.0
Price	Wine

At this writing, a review of Harvest Vine comes
with several caveats. The place is in a state of
transition and the panel's recent visits ranged
from "best meal of the year" to "ruined my
whole week." But as of late, the restaurant
seems to be righting itself again.

Most of the time Harvest Vine creates
delectable Basque tapas with inventive yet
focused flavors. You'll get the best selection if
you sit at the bar and make nice with the
chefs—off-menu sampling is often revelatory—
but usually anything involving duck or venison is
excellent. Morcilla is a must, crumbling under
the fork, and usually accompanied by a crispy,
salty counterpoint like pork belly. But the
kitchen has managed on several occasions to
wring the salty goodness out of salt cod (pretty
much an act of treachery), but dishes like pulpo
de feira (boiled octopus) and seared scallops
with duck confit and lentils are outstanding. The
all-Spanish wine list is a treat, with many bottles
that are well within the affordable range. A few
Basque selections keep things extra-interesting.

Some of the Jekyll-and-Hyde feeling has to do
with where you're seated. The charming and
lively main room has the bar and open kitchen;
the downstairs has two rooms, the larger of
which feels like the banquet room at a HoJo
where the baseball team goes to eat spaghetti
after the big game. And no matter where you
sit, the service has been spotty. But while
Harvest Vine has had its moments of being off,
when it's on, there are few finer dining
experiences in the Seattle area.

Spanish
Upmarket restaurant

Madison Park
2701 E. Madison St.
(206) 320-9771

Hours
Mon–Fri
5:00pm–10:00pm
Sat–Sun
10:00am–2:00pm
5:00pm–10:00pm

Bar
Beer, wine

Credit cards
Visa, MC, AmEx

Reservations
Accepted

Features
Brunch
Date-friendly

Henry's Taiwan

(Mostly) traditional Taiwanese cuisine
served up by a really nice guy

Chinese
Casual restaurant

International District
504 S. King St.
(206) 624-2611

Bellevue
549 156th Ave. SE
(425) 213-5392

Hours
Daily
11:00am–9:00pm
Hours vary by location

Bar
None

Credit cards
Visa, MC

Reservations
Accepted

Henry's Taiwan is on one of those blocks in the I.D. that's just enervating. It's next to a bar that is a virtual members-only club for the chronically alcoholic hobo philosopher. This is noteworthy because having one of those "why do I bother to come down here" moments right before you walk in the door helps you properly appreciate the restaurant's laid-back charm. A former hole-in-the-wall, Henry's is not much more than a few booths and some cheery yellow walls, but it's a very pleasant place for a quick meal.

There is a Henry, and he's a charismatic fellow who likes to chat with his customers. If you're new to this cuisine, this is helpful, as he'll gladly explain the composition of a soup or what exactly makes delicious stinky tofu smell like a root canal.

This is a real bang-for-your-buck restaurant, with most items staying in the single-digit range. Soups are delicate, with bonito broth and other touches taking away from sheer authenticity, but adding Henry's hallmark twist on Taiwanese. And, the stinky tofu is the best in town, and is especially good in the ma la pietan version, which includes a century egg.

Herbfarm

It certainly is memorable—that much can't be disputed.

8.0	8.5
Food	Feel
$250	9.0
Price	Wine

www.theherbfarm.com

Dining at Herbfarm requires serious commitments: dinner lasts approximately four hours, includes nine courses, and costs a pretty penny. The space is cozy, with a sort of grandmother's-cottage kind of feel: think overstuffed, vintage chairs in zany, mismatched patterns. Communal dining tables are covered with dark green and gold tablecloths.

There is a farm here; herbs grown on-site contribute to each meal. Menus change weekly and have very cohesive themes, some of which can be literal (like "A Banquet of Basil" in which many of the dishes feature the titular herb), but most of which are nice snapshots of the seasons ("A Menu for an Autumn Sketchbook" may be a delightful blur of squash, squab, currants, and spiced apple). Wine pairings are excellent, plucked from Herbfarm's larger-than-life list. Winos can dive in and play around a bit, making their own selections from the list.

Dinner starts with a walk in the garden, and after you're seated, there is an (awkwardly formal) explanation of the dishes, with words from the chef, the sommelier, the resident field mice...Herbfarm kind of overdoes everything, and the delicate tableware and autumnal sketching can start to feel like a bit much. Or actually, much. Not just a bit. But it's truly an unique experience.

Or is it? Several chefs have cribbed the Herbfarm's moves to great effect: Art of the Table does a short pre-meal run-down, and the Corson Building offers garden meandering and communal dining. And both are a lot cheaper.

Modern
Upmarket restaurant

Eastside
14590 NE 145th St.
(425) 485-5300

Hours
Thu–Sat
7:00pm–9:00pm
One seating per night
Sun
4:30pm–9:00pm
One seating per night

Bar
Beer, wine

Credit cards
Visa, MC, AmEx

Reservations
Essential

Features
Date-friendly

Hing Loon

An I.D. institution that still delivers and draws big crowds

Chinese
Casual restaurant

International District
628 S. Weller St.
(206) 682-2828

Hours
Sun–Thu
10:00am–1:00am
Fri–Sat
10:00am–2:00am

Bar
Beer, wine

Credit cards
Visa, MC, AmEx

Reservations
Accepted

Features
Kid-friendly

We can't help be a little suspicious of Hing Loon: it's long been the automatic recommendation for Chinese food in the I.D., and this place thus attracts a lot of tourists (with Seattleites eating the most cautious items on what is a rather diverse menu).

The greasy Cantonese food here is passable. "Country Style Pan Cake" is a supple doughy flatbread, crispy outside but chewy inside, studded with diced scallion and dried shrimp. "Handmade Noodle Noodle" features slippery round rice noodles with sautéed onion, chicken, shrimp, and slivers of char siu (pork belly), all doused in soy sauce and topped with lacy ribbons of scrambled egg. Beef with ginger and scallions has enough ginger to give the tender chunks of beef that seductive gingery slow burn. Offal aficionados will like dishes like "Lo Mein with Assorted Beef Organs," with juicy tripe and melt-in-the-mouth tendon. Hing Loon even makes its own red pepper paste, which is sweet and smoky, with a late-hitting heat. (You can pick up a bottle of it on the way out.)

This is a classic Chinatown eatery, meaning it's a fluorescently lit eyesore. Laminated tables, generic chairs, stereotypically Chinese artwork, and white-and-gray speckled linoleum floors—you get the idea. However, the décor does require careful study: the walls are papered with additional items not on the printed menu.

Hiroki

A Japanese bakery that makes expats think of home while updating classic recipes

www.hiroki.us

If you like green-tea desserts, this is only bakery to visit. Hiroki Inoue's signature green tea tiramisù is the definitive word on matcha-infused sweets.

As that creation shows, Hiroki blends Japanese and European influences. A soufflé cheesecake with a chiffon bottom and apricot glaze, for example, eschews the rich, creamy quality of a New York-style cheesecake, and is instead light and fluffy and not too sweet—a quality that resonates with Hiroki's Japanese customers. There are plenty of éclairs, biscotti, tarts, and New York-style cheesecakes in the pastry case, too. (The sweetness in all of these is generally more subtle than at, say, an Italian or a French bakery.) Beyond green tea, other Japanese ingredients (like kobacha, a type of squash) make their way into cakes and muffins.

The bakery is comfortable enough for a sit-down, but not really compelling enough for a long stay, especially on weekends around brunchtime, when the lines are long.

Sweets
Counter service

Green Lake
2224 N. 56th St.
(206) 547-4128

Hours
Wed–Fri
noon–9:00pm
Sat–Sun
9:00am–9:00pm

Bar
None

Credit cards
Visa, MC

<table>
<tr><td>**7.0**
Food</td><td>**5.5**
Feel</td></tr>
</table>

Homegrown

$15
Price

Simple sustainability with minimal bells and whistles...oh, and with steak

www.eathomegrown.com

Sandwiches
Counter service

Fremont
3416 Fremont Ave. N.
(206) 453-5232

Capitol Hill
1531 Melrose Ave.
(206) 682-0935

Hours
Mon–Thu
8:00am–4:00pm
Fri–Sun
8:00am–3:00pm
Hours vary by location

Bar
Beer

Credit cards
Visa, MC

Features
Outdoor dining

Homegrown's menu is a nicely curated list of classics—turkey-bacon-avocado, catfish po'boy, Reuben—served with house-made kettle chips. A few seasonal choices round out the sandwich menu—grilled cheese gets some interesting twists during melon season—and there are also salads and a few daily soups. Some people complain that this kitchen complicates things too much, but compared with some of the culinary hijinks out there, hazelnut romesco on a crab cake sandwich seems pretty run-of-the-mill. Sandwiches are well made, well balanced, and, with the exception of the "Bluffernutter" (house-made marshmallow fluff, peanut butter, and bacon), free of idiotic Gen-X nostalgia. The only truly lame sandwich is the regular vegetarian option: sprouts, hummus, and avocado on toasted bread.

The Capitol Hill branch gets more attention for being part of the recently opened Melrose Market, which is in a renovated building and includes a butcher, cheese shop, florist, and the awesome Sitka & Spruce. However, the seating at this tiny outpost sucks. There are a few outdoor tables—cute, but awfully close to dumpsters—and a few high butcher's blocks that are way too close together (and to the line).

The Fremont space is more of a real café: the perfect cross between nondescript Seattle Euro-bistro and nondescript Seattle coffeehouse.

Honoré Artisan Bakery

Best macaroons in the city, sold in a setting that's cute without being precious

Perhaps knowing it will never rival Café Besalu or Bakery Nouveau for croissants, Honoré has staked its claim on another French treat, the macaroon. The raspberry macaroon is the closest replica to what you'd get at Ladurée in Paris in terms of texture, balance, and intensity of fiavor.

There's a wonderful variety of macaroons; flavors range from simple chocolate to salted caramel, lavender, or pistachio. Honoré also makes a very good quiche (we love the ultra-browned crust), and the croissants aren't half-bad either—they're buttery, if not as delicate as the ones at Café Besalu.

The small space has a few counter seats for sipping cappuccinos. It also frequently has lines out the door. Honoré attracts a lot of moms with little kids in tow, and we can see why: it's less chaotic than Besalu, but still a feast for the eyes, with all of those multi-colored macaroons lined up in the pastry case like delicious little yo-yos.

Sweets
Coffee
Counter service

Ballard
1413 NW 70th St.
(206) 706-4035

Hours
Wed–Fri
7:00am–4:00pm
Sat–Sun
8:00am–4:00pm

Bar
None

Credit cards
Visa, MC

Features
Kid-friendly

Hosoonyi

The best spot for soondubu, as long as you can find it—and find your server

Korean
Casual restaurant

Edmonds
23830 Hwy. 99
(425) 775-8196

Hours
Daily
10:30am–10:00pm

Bar
Beer, wine

Credit cards
Visa, MC

Reservations
Not accepted

Features
Kid-friendly

This Korean restaurant is worth the hassles—be sure to look up the directions before you go, because it's hard to find the *exact* strip mall that it's in—for its best-loved dish, soondubu (spicy tofu stew). This is simply the best version of the dish in the metro area. Hosoonyi makes quite a few varieties; along with the silky tofu you can add beef, seafood, pork, or vegetables like kimchi and mushrooms. You also get an egg to crack over the bubbling cauldron of stew.

If you don't order the soondubu—and really, why go, if you don't?—the seafood pancake is very good and the banchan that come with any meal are plentiful and terrific. Barbecue doesn't stand out here: the marinade they use for the meats is sweeter than we prefer, and they also grill the meat just until done—no yummy char. The Korean beer list is pretty long—four or five of the major brewers—and complements the spicy soups well.

With Korean pop music videos playing loudly and gratingly, it's not exactly elegant, but it does feels like a real part of a Korean community, with many expats dining here. Service is generally friendly, but sometimes very slow—you might have to flag down another server.

How to Cook a Wolf

Ethan Stowell's homage to rustic cooking does almost everything right

www.ethanstowellrestaurants.com/howtocookawolf

How to Expand your Empire, by Ethan Stowell

1. Decide you want to open another Italian-inspired restaurant that features luscious pastas and ahi and/or hamachi crudo.
2. Differentiate this from your other ventures by co-opting the weird title of a book by a food writer, and develop a loose theme around the simplicity of simple meals with fresh ingredients celebrated by said writer.
3. Create a modern, attractive, upscale-yet-casual space that only very loosely relates to this rusticity theme. Settle on a sleek urban cabin/basketball court look.
4. Work your usual magic in the kitchen. Bestow on the ungrateful foodies of this town plates of melt-in-your-mouth ahi/hamachi crudo with a hint of spicy chili and avocado, bucatini in tomato sauce with oregano and guanciale, and quail with corona beans and spinach.
5. Add in the usual flourishes: smaller, shareable plates; good service; and a solid wine list and a staff capable of making recommendations from it.
6. Count your money.

Italian
Upmarket restaurant

Queen Anne
2208 Queen Anne Ave. N.
(206) 838-8090

Hours
Sun–Thu
5:00pm–11:00pm
Fri–Sat
5:00pm–midnight

Bar
Beer, wine, liquor

Credit cards
Visa, MC, AmEx

Reservations
Not accepted

Features
Date-friendly

<table>
<tr><td>**7.2**
Food</td><td>**5.5**
Feel</td></tr>
</table>

$15
Price

I Love New York

Start spreading the gehakte leber, East-Coast style

www.ilovenewyorkdeli.net

Sandwiches
Counter service

University District
5200 Roosevelt Way NE
(206) 523-0606

Downtown
Economy Building, 93
Pike St., #4
(206) 381-3354

Hours
Mon–Sat
6:00am–8:00pm
Hours vary by location

Bar
None

Credit cards
Visa, MC, AmEx

Features
Kid-friendly

One growing category of Seattle restaurants is the "East Coast deli," typically some sort of New Yawk theme park that serves sandwiches that are basically a wall of pastrami or Boar's Head meats. I Love New York certainly does lay it on thick—it's a veritable anthropology lesson on the types of foods your average big-city Jew takes for granted. There's lox, pastrami, and whitefish salad. There are smears of chicken liver added to already formidable sandwiches: the "Hester," our favorite, has turkey and pastrami and chopped chicken liver on house-made Zissel rye. Kosher franks are imported from New York, as are the meats, lox, pickles, mustard, and cheesecakes.

Some cranky ex-New Yorkers can't really understand what the fuss is about: the whitefish salad isn't all that, it's not entirely clear why you can't make cheesecake here in Seattle. But I Love New York makes very good sandwiches, and does so in an area of downtown where it's difficult to get a decent lunch. The breakfast sandwiches (available until 11 am) are great: what does an egg and cheese on a roll need? Why, pastrami, of course. And we will admit that it's nice to be able to pick up rugelach, matzoh meal, and an overstuffed sandwich in one outing.

Beyond that, what can we say? It's just a freakin' deli. And to be honest, some of the transplants on our panel actually don't love New York that much.

I Love Sushi

Good happy hour sushi and anytime udon
and snacks

www.ilovesushi.com

6.0 Food

8.0 Feel

$60 Price

Japanese
Casual restaurant

Bellevue
11818 NE 8th St.
(425) 454-5706

Eastlake
1001 Fairview Ave. N.
(206) 625-9604

Hours
Mon–Thu
11:30am–2:00pm
4:00pm–10:00pm
Fri
11:30am–2:00pm
4:00pm–10:30pm
Sat
noon–2:30pm
5:00pm–10:30pm
Sun
noon–9:30pm

Bar
Beer, wine, liquor

Credit cards
Visa, MC, AmEx

Reservations
Accepted

Features
Outdoor dining

We're not sure what it says about Seattle that this is the first Fearless Critic book with two restaurants in a single city beginning with the words "I Love." It would be easier to recommend I Love Sushi for its sushi if it weren't so pricey, but everything from the bento to the rolls is pushing ultralounge prices. Anytime outside of happy hour, those seeking sashimi and nigiri or only very simple rolls will find better value elsewhere, or at least better fish for the money.

But happy hour is a steal, with a good portion of sashimi and rolls available. I Love Sushi also does a pretty good job with fancier rolls, which are not that much more expensive than at any other restaurant. There are the usual overstuffed tempura creatures and dragon rolls plus a few more fusiony ones employing tropical fruits. Udon and cooked appetizers like calamari are consistently decent and more reasonably priced.

I Love Sushi has a neat, albeit inconvenient, location on Lake Union. Although we prefer to eat our sushi in a more temperature-controlled environment than a deck on a warm summer day, the glimpses of the lake and the yachts moored right outside the restaurant pair just fine with draft beers.

In the Bowl

A vegetarian "noodle bistro" that doesn't skimp on the spice

www.inthebowlbistro.com

Vegefusion
Casual restaurant

Capitol Hill
1554 E. Olive Way
(206) 568-2343

Hours
Daily
noon–9:30pm

Bar
None

Credit cards
Visa, MC

Reservations
Not accepted

Features
Veg-friendly

Vegetarian and pan-Asian aren't exactly the most promising combination of words, but In the Bowl has a loyal Capitol Hill following because this kitchen knows how to bring the heat. Seriously, they're really not holding back on the spice, so unless that appeals to you, order a star below what you normally would.

The menu is mostly Thai, with some Japanese noodle dishes plus stir-fries and fried-rice dishes that could be attributed to a number of Asian countries. Though you can order "beef," "chicken," or "prawns," each is merely a slightly different version of tofu or other type of soy protein. If you're not partial to the fake meats, which vary in quality here, just stick with the tofu, which comes sans quotation marks. Anyway, the plain tofu and vegetables allow the sauces and broths of the best dishes—pineapple curry, yellow curry noodle soup, and Tokyo noodles—to take center stage.

The predominantly yellow-and-orange interior, like the menu, is a hodgepodge of styles and cultures: Pacific Northwest Modern light fixtures, Buddhist temple bells, and the requisite padded black banquet chairs you find in every Asian eatery. Hilariously enough, the best part of the restaurant is the bathroom: it's quite the little sanctuary.

Inay's

The best down-home Filipino cooking in the metro area, in a down-home Filipino setting

8.0 Food

4.5 Feel

$15 Price

Inay's is an odd mix of the typical turo-turo cafeteria set-up—steam trays and stainless steel countertops and all—and grandma's house.

The food is authentic Filipino. Pata (pork) is fried just right, crunchy on the outside and tender on the inside. The pinakbet (shrimp paste and mixed green beans, bitter melon, and pork) is also excellent. And there's dinuguan, the famous pig-blood stew, which strikes an ideal balance of sweet, salt, and dull spice. The hot lunch special has a good food-to-rice ratio.

In contrast to other area Filipino restaurants, Inay's does not engulf its food in salt, and considering how salty Filipino food can get, this is a major plus. And for the salt that remains, order a San Miguel, the national beer of the Philippines, another rarity in these parts.

Filipino
Counter service

Beacon Hill
2503 Beacon Ave. S.
(206) 325-5692

Hours
Daily
9:00am–9:00pm

Bar
Beer

Credit cards
Visa, MC

Reservations
Accepted

Features
Kid-friendly

Jade Garden

Sometimes-passable Chinese at always-welcome late hours

Chinese
Casual restaurant

International District
424 7th Ave. S.
(206) 622-8181

Hours
Daily
9:00am–2:30am

Bar
Beer, wine

Credit cards
Visa, MC

Reservations
Accepted

Features
Brunch
Kid-friendly

Here's what Jade Garden is: it's a typical Chinese restaurant with the usual cheesy red and black color scheme and paper lanterns and laughing Buddhas everywhere. It's a dim sum palace with 45-minute waits for weekend brunch. It's a place into which you stagger at 1:30 am when you need some greasy Chinese food to avert a Hindenburg-sized hangover.

Here's what it isn't: a hidden gem. A place that will teach you anything new about Chinese food. There are some stand-outs: tender pea vines in a very garlicky sauce, the "dry style" chow fun, and the "Special Beef," a huge plate of really tender strips of beef, fried in a crunchy batter and doused in a sticky tangy sauce (kind of like a General Tso's beef). There are amazing deals: the "House Special Chow Mein" is such an expansive pile of thin wheat noodles topped with slices of beef, shrimp, pork, and sautéed onions that when you have to pick out the rubbery slices of squid you're glad to get rid of some ballast.

The quality of the service varies, though we've had good experiences. If you manage to get the had-to-wait-for-brunch scowl off your face you might get some good recommendations from the staff.

JaK's Grill

A homegrown place that serves good steaks with a side of no nonsense

www.jaksgrill.com

8.5	8.0
Food	Feel
$75	**7.5**
Price	Wine

Seattle has a handful of top-end steakhouses, but JaK's wins the prize for being the least stuffy and least pricey of the bunch, while still turning out excellent food. What's more, JaK's is local to Seattle, not a huge chain, and as a result, it might be the only serious steakhouse to which you'll feel comfortable showing up in jeans and a T-shirt (though you can also get spruced up in a suit, if you prefer). Still, even with a laid-back attitude, JaK's offers the excellent service and professional, old-world vibe you'd expect at a jeweled-cuff-links-and-Cuban-cigar steakhouse.

The beef is dry-aged on premises. (It's corn-fed beef, but it's good stuff, not feedlot beef.) And for the highest-quality beef cuts and other mains, the prices are fair, especially since salad and sides are included—no ridiculous à-la-carte prices. Portions are large and can often be shared.

JaK's has a good wine program, with many well-known Washington State options, some big juicy reds to accompany the steaks, and other more delicate selections to round out the list. There's not a lot of diversity on the list outside of the U.S., and the selection occupies a pretty young window, but it's well-rounded. This is one of the best options in town for steak.

Steakhouse
Upmarket restaurant

West Seattle
4548 California Ave. SW
(206) 937-7809

University District
3701 NE 45th St.
(206) 985-8545

Hours
Mon
5:00pm–9:00pm
Tue–Thu
11:00am–2:00pm
5:00pm–10:00pm
Fri
11:00am–2:00pm
4:30pm–11:00pm
Sat
4:00pm–11:00pm
Sun
4:00pm–9:00pm
Hours vary by location

Bar
Beer, wine, liquor

Credit cards
Visa, MC, AmEx

Reservations
Not accepted

Features
Date-friendly

7.5 | 7.5
Food | Feel

$110 | 8.0
Price | Wine

John Howie Steak

Celebrating disposable income, one steak at a time

www.johnhowiesteak.com

Steakhouse
Upmarket restaurant

Bellevue
11111 NE 8th St., Suite 125
(425) 440-0880

Hours
Mon–Thu
11:00am–2:30pm
5:00pm–10:00pm
Fri
11:00am–2:30pm
5:00pm–11:00pm
Sat
5:00pm–11:00pm
Sun
5:00pm–9:00pm

Bar
Beer, wine, liquor

Credit cards
Visa, MC, AmEx

Reservations
Accepted

Features
Date-friendly

What would a traditional steakhouse look like stripped of its manly pretenses? Perhaps a place where if you tire of your comfy booth, you can rest your martini on a baby grand piano turned into a table by a piece of protective glass.

This preciousness is clearly aimed at the lovely ladies who stumble in for a shrimp Cobb salad after a hard tour of label-hunting at The Shops at The Bravern (the restaurant is inside the most expensive mall on the Eastside). Their presence, plus personal wine lockers for regulars, mean there are quite a few Microsoft bachelors trolling happy hour. Speaking of wine, the list here is long and lovely, with plenty of steakhouse heavy hitters.

The kitchen is competent, and the steaks, most of which are grilled over mesquite, are suitably picturesque, nicely charred on the outside with at least two or three different shades of pink inside. They know their way around Wagyu, which may appear as tartare, or in an infantilized slider form. Modern American cooking sets John Howie apart from the most traditional steakhouses, but the menu is too schizophrenic, embracing both the *old* old school (bananas Foster) and fleeting new trends (sliders, over-the-top starters like tempura-fried Kurobuta bacon with maple-sambal-ponzu sauce).

Joule

Finally, fusion that's not the slightest bit gimmicky

9.5 Food

9.0 Feel

$50 Price

www.joulerestaurant.com

Joule represents the best kind of fusion cooking. It cleverly combines French and Korean staples and techniques, and chefs Rachel Yang and Seif Chirchi know when to let one cuisine hold court (shrimp and edamame dumplings or simple, nostril-searing kimchi); when to let an unexpected ingredient create a subtle crossover (spicy beef soup with daikon, leeks and crème fraiche, or duck breast with daikon soubise); and when to let things get weird (the incredible mochi with oxtail and soy-cured egg yolk). Out of the current crop of "inventive" chefs, this husband-and-wife team is perhaps the most consistent and inspiring.

If you sit at the counter that encircles the partially open kitchen, you can see some of this chemistry in action—Yang and Chirchi actually do most of the cooking. Otherwise, the small space is simple but graceful—canary yellow and brown walls and candles flickering on dark wood. The tables are close together so Joule is alternately romantic and casual/loud as it fills up and thins out.

It's worth following Joule's Facebook or Twitter (@joulerestaurant) feeds for news of special events like Sunday night globetrotting barbecue menus.

Modern
Upmarket restaurant

Wallingford
1913 N. 45th St.
(206) 632-1913

Hours
Tue–Thu
5:00pm–10:00pm
Fri–Sat
5:00pm–11:00pm
Sun
5:00pm–10:00pm

Bar
Beer, wine

Credit cards
Visa, MC, AmEx

Reservations
Accepted

Features
Date-friendly

7.0 Food | 7.5 Feel

$25 Price

Julia's Indonesian Kitchen

Indonesian curries and fried chicken for the adults, the kids, and the ravenous

Indonesian
Casual restaurant

Ravenna
910 NE 65th St.
(206) 522-5528

Hours
Tue–Sun
11:30am–9:30pm

Bar
Beer, wine, BYO

Credit cards
Visa, MC, AmEx

Reservations
Accepted

Features
Kid-friendly
Veg-friendly

www.juliasindokitchen.com

Julia's is one of the best purveyors of a cuisine that's hard to find within the city limits. The menu includes many traditional Indonesian favorites like Javanese fried chicken (marinated in a bevy of spices), fried whole fish with balado (a chile sauce), and rendang (slow-cooked beef in a dynamic red curry). The fried chicken, though, is hands down the best dish here, and it comes with little bits of the marinade dipped in flour and fried for extra flavor.

Nasi rames, a tray of a curries with a vegetable and tofu salad and corn fritters around a cone of steamed rice, is popular with UW students looking for not only a taste of home but for a cheap and filling lunch.

The converted bungalow is very cute and funky—red and lime green accent walls and batik prints for tablecloths and curtains—and looks more like a neighborhood coffeehouse than a restaurant.

June

Neighborhood flavors with a bit of downtown flair—and nose-to-tail fare

www.juneseattle.com

8.0	7.5
Food	Feel

$50
Price

June had some big shoes to fill when it occupied the former space of Cremant, and judging by how little the space has changed—the concrete walls, banquette seating that looks like you're settling down on a slab of sheet metal, and the gray color scheme are still there—June just kind of settled right in, no shoehorn required. It's a little spare, but there are a few ennui-lifting spring-green accents, and the restaurant is nicely elegant.

Although the menu may seem like the usual rustic/seasonal/French hodge-podge, this kitchen is doing things a wee bit differently. It's on the cutting edge of nose-to-tail food fad-dom with its most talked-about dish: lamb's neck over egg noodles. And while "rustic" in many restaurants amounts to "extra-chewy bread," June leaves the vertebrae in the lamb's neck and the ribs in the roasted rabbit (which, incidentally, comes with a side of the bunny's liver).

Not everything on the dinner menu is inspired. Pan-roasted chicken with fiddlehead ferns? Snooze. The brunch menu, on the other hand, is fit for Louis XIV: think lamb stew with a fried egg, duck hash, house-made chocolate doughnuts with pecan-caramel sauce.

Vegetarians take note: although mains are meat-heavy (you might have to make do with farro or gnocchi), June has you covered with great veg-friendly apps, like lightly-charred grilled yams, asparagus-nettle vichyssoise, and chilled corn soup with strawberry relish.

French
Upmarket restaurant

Madrona
1423 34th Ave.
(206) 323-4000

Hours
Mon–Thu
5:00pm–10:00pm
Fri
5:00pm–11:00pm
Sat
10:00am–2:00pm
5:00pm–11:00pm
Sun
10:00am–2:00pm
5:00pm–10:00pm

Bar
Beer, wine, liquor

Credit cards
Visa, MC, AmEx

Reservations
Accepted

Features
Brunch
Date-friendly
Kid-friendly

7.5 | 5.5
Food | Feel

$25
Price

Ka Won Korean BBQ

Tabletop grilling and banchan in a place whose décor keeps the focus on the food

Korean
Casual restaurant

North Seattle
15004 Hwy. 99
(425) 787-6484

Hours
Mon–Sat
11:00am–11:00pm
Sun
11:00am–9:00pm

Bar
Beer, wine, liquor

Credit cards
Visa, MC

Reservations
Accepted

Features
Kid-friendly

One of our favorite Northside Korean restaurants, Ka Won is no secret: it's always bustling with regulars cooking pork belly, kalbi, and other marinated meats on tabletop BBQ grills; or, perhaps, tossing seemingly endless supplies of meats and seafood into bubbling pots of spicy broth.

In the mix are always a few folks dutifully chowing their way through the prix-fixe dinner, which is huge, with bulgogi, fish, soup, salads, and, of course, banchan. The banchan, which is a highlight at most of the Northside restaurants, are legendary here: you get about ten starters here ranging from kimchi to anchovies.

Like almost all Asian restaurants outside the city limits, Ka Won is in a strip mall; the interior is a bit worn, but it's tidy, and it seems that at some point, some effort went in to painting the walls butter yellow and installing a few chandeliers instead of fluorescents. But the most dynamic element of the room is the series of silver vents hovering to catch the smoke rising from the grills. Delicious.

Kau Kau BBQ

Not the best Chinese barbecue in town, but it's cheap, filling, and hits the spot

6.5	6.0
Food	Feel

$10
Price

www.kaukaubbq.com

One of those I.D. joints that's been holding on for about 30 years, Kau Kau has a loyal following—even if it's a following that will readily admit that it's not the best Chinese barbecue in town. But people don't go to Kau Kau to split hairs about imaginary "best of" designations; they go for the ridiculously cheap lunch specials (soup, pork barbecue, pork fried rice, some vegetables, and an additional item like an egg roll), dishes that we are sad to report bring down Kau Kau's overall food rating quite a bit, or for a big-ass plate of pork to soak up after-work boozing. Long hours, great prices, decent barbecue: that's our Kau Kau.

As at most places, you can't really go wrong with the barbecued pork or duck, though Kau Kau's menu is much more lengthy than at other ducks-hanging-in-the-window places. Chow mein, hot pot, and prawns prepared a half-dozen ways—nothing really stands out too much; the chow foon dishes might be the most comfort food-y of the lot. Don't come expecting fireworks, and it's not hard to go home happy.

Chinese
Casual restaurant

International District
656 S. King St.
(206) 682-4006

Hours
Daily
10:00am–10:00pm

Bar
Beer, wine

Credit cards
Visa, MC, AmEx

Reservations
Not accepted

7.0 6.0

Food | Feel

$25
Price

Kimchi Bistro

A good Korean food fix that doesn't require a road trip

Korean
Casual restaurant

Capitol Hill
219 Broadway E.
(206) 323-4472

Hours
Daily
11:00am–10:00pm

Bar
Beer, wine

Credit cards
Visa, MC

Reservations
Not accepted

Features
Veg-friendly

Not all good Korean food requires a drive to the suburbs. Kimchi can't compete with some of our North Seattle favorites, but it's no consolation prize, either. It may not have the tabletop grills or the outstanding and endless banchan, but it does a good job with the standards many Korean-restaurantgoers crave most: soft, spicy tofu soup, for instance, or bi bim bap hot pot (which is loaded with rice, kimchi, egg, vegetables, and meat or tofu). Other standards, like kalbi beef and bulgolgi, are also consistently good. The kimchi has a nice kick to it, and in general, dishes are sufficiently hot and spicy.

Kimchi does have one thing in common with the North Seattle standbys: a strange location. It's tucked into one of Broadway's depressing mini-malls next to a cigar shop—if you didn't know to look for the place, you'd never find it. But inside its tiny confines, Kimchi is warm and pleasant, thanks in large part to surprisingly genial service.

Kingfish Café

This Southern belle needs to be revived—
the food is not on the same level as the fun

6.0	7.5
Food	Feel

$45
Price

www.thekingfishcafe.com

There's much to like about Kingfish, which serves Southern staples like fried chicken, fried green tomatoes, and collard greens in an upscale country diner setting. But in the many years it's been with us, the place has started to feel a little less soulful. Maybe it's the crowd skewing older. Maybe it's the obvious presence of tourists in the dining room. Maybe it's the kitschy names of the dishes ("Miss Choo Choo's Company's Commin' Ribeye Steak"). Whatever it is, the Southern-as-spectacle vibe is starting to dominate more, which is too bad, because the place was built on sincerity: the owners drew upon a lot of family recipes, and enlarged family portraits still decorate the dining room.

The fried chicken is decent, but after a mini-obsession with the dish put it on many of Seattle's menus, other restaurants in town have eclipsed Kingfish's version. The shrimp and chicken gumbo is still a contender, however, and the famous red velvet cake is often transcendent. Maybe the chefs could put these plates together in their sleep, but sometimes that quality can translate to a bit less excitement on the plate, even for tried-and-true recipes.

Kingfish is a fun and friendly place. But it's a little too expensive, and the waits are a little too long to be justified by cuisine that no longer dazzles.

Southern
Casual restaurant

Capitol Hill
602 19th Ave. E.
(206) 320-8757

Hours
Mon–Thu
11:30am–2:00pm
5:30pm–9:30pm
Fri
11:30am–2:00pm
5:30pm–10:30pm
Sat
10:00am–2:00pm
5:30pm–10:30pm
Sun
10:00am–2:00pm
5:30pm–9:30pm

Bar
Beer, wine, liquor, BYO

Credit cards
Visa, MC

Reservations
Not accepted

Features
Brunch
Date-friendly

King's Barbeque House

Not the best Chinese BBQ meats, but simple, filling, and cheap

Chinese
Counter service

International District
303 12th Ave. S.
(206) 720-4715

Hours
Daily
10:00am–6:30pm

Bar
None

Credit cards
None

King's does reasonably good Cantonese barbecue. You either order by the pound or order one of the lunch specials, which is basically meat with white rice and maybe some sauce ladled over the top. King's is known for its roast duck and roast pork, but of the two, the roast pork seems to be more consistent; roast duck is sometimes very good, but at other times, it's too dry. BBQ chicken doesn't have quite the word of mouth as the duck or pork, but it's pretty enjoyable. There's also the standard full menu of staples, including decent wok-sautéed Chinese greens.

King's can't rival Ton Kiang (a few blocks north), but it's one of the most reliable barbecue joints in the I.D., and we should note that all of the leftovers hold up pretty well in the fridge.

The set-up is totally no-frills, even for the I.D. There's no seating, just a walk-up counter. "Decoration" consists of meat hanging in the windows and a nice man with a sharp cleaver and a butcher block.

Kisaku

This slightly under-the-radar sushi restaurant rivals Shiro's for best in the city

9.0 Food

7.0 Feel

$45 Price

www.kisaku.com

Omakase here is incredible: among the many must-orders are hotate konbu jime (sweet scallop with kelp marination and a surprising umami kick on the back end that negates the need for soy sauce) and amaebi (be sure to eat the fried head afterward). Those treats, and other rarities like shirako (sperm sacs from cod), which are more about texture than flavor, break up the nigiri parade nicely. Be sure to request the hotate konbu jime early, as it can take up to an hour to prepare.

As with any good sushi restaurant, you must sit at the counter for the best experience. But if you want to order off the menu, hot dishes like a soft shell crab tempura or spicy deep-fried oysters won't disappoint. Kisaku's rolls are very subdued compared to most sushi restaurants, with deep-fried eggplant and red pepper being the craziest one to regularly appear on the menu.

Kisaku is a very pleasant place to have a leisurely meal—although, again, you'll be better off at the counter, which is more attractive than the rest of the room (which suffers in character a bit from having an odd layout). Besides, which would you rather face: the affable sushi chefs standing over jewel-colored fish or unsmiling Green Lake families?

Japanese
Casual restaurant

Green Lake
2101 N. 55th St.
(206) 545-9050

Hours
Mon, Wed–Thu
11:30am–2:00pm
5:30pm–10:00pm
Fri–Sat
11:30am–2:00pm
5:30pm–10:30pm
Sun
5:00pm–10:00pm

Bar
Beer, wine

Credit cards
Visa, MC, AmEx

Reservations
Accepted

6.5 | 9.0
Food | Feel

$30
Price

Knee High Stocking Co.

A good take on the speakeasy vibe, but still behind Tavern Law in cocktail supremacy

www.kneehighstocking.com

American
Bar

Capitol Hill
1356 E. Olive Way
(206) 979-7049

Hours
Mon–Thu
6:00pm–1:00am
Fri–Sat
6:00pm–2:00am
Sun
6:00pm–1:00am

Bar
Beer, wine, liquor

Credit cards
Visa, MC

Reservations
Accepted

Features
Good cocktails

Where's the moonshine, the bathtub gin, the watered-down Canadian whisky, the methanol?

This bar, which follows squarely in the New York-inspired speakeasy theme tradition, nonetheless gets some mileage out of some archaic cocktails that you might not have tried before, like a gin drink called "The Stork," created by a Prohibition-era club of the same name; or an 1890s "after-dinner mint" with crème de menthe. In a more modern vein, there is a "seasonal" menu that makes good and sparing use of ingredients like ginger beer and yellow chartreuse.

The brief food menu isn't as special, but it includes some decent nibbles like a hot dog topped with relish and pickled peppers or a neat twist on the traditional Caesar salad, with asparagus instead of lettuce. The cheese plate is great and has interesting seasonal accompaniments like pear butter.

As is the norm for this genre, you have to ring a doorbell on an unmarked door to be admitted, but as at most speakeasy-wannabe joints, the artifice breaks down as soon as the doorman starts checking IDs. How clandestine is a place if you can send a text message to make reservations?

Although the debauchery might be limited to absinthe and a creepy mural of (sigh) a man making out with an infant, Knee High does a serviceable job of feeling dark and secretive— you do feel as if you've been hand-selected to drink here.

Kushibar

Food on a stick is their shtick

7.0 | **8.0**
Food | Feel

$35
Price

www.kushibar.com

Kushibar opened to much fanfare, especially amongst the Japanese community. Finally, a place doing proteins on sticks: yakitori (grilled chicken) and kushiyaki (non-poultry items).

But take a look inside, and you'll see that it's the pretty typical Belltown crowd: white people eating white-meat sticks. No chicken tail, no chicken intestines. We've often found it hard to get some of the menu's most interesting conceits, like ox tongue. But if you persevere, you might get hatsu (heart) and kawa (chicken skin), which are certainly more challenging than the plain old sasami (white meat).

There are plenty of non-stick dishes, too, including a lot of the usual izakaya fare that makes for a fine excuse to drink sake, shochu, and soju. All of this happens in a really nice venue, including a unique outdoorish space along the sidewalk. It's hard to blame a place for its clientele, but when a restaurant's potential is as great as this one's, it's also hard not to lament the fact that Kushibar seems to be more about Belltown boys putting down some beers than about getting the serious Japanese food of which this kitchen is capable out to the community.

Japanese
Casual restaurant

Belltown
2319 2nd Ave.
(206) 448-2488

Hours
Mon–Fri
11:30am–1:00am
Sat–Sun
4:00pm–1:00am

Bar
Beer, wine, liquor, BYO

Credit cards
Visa, MC, AmEx

Reservations
Accepted

Features
Date-friendly
Outdoor dining

La Carta de Oaxaca

Holy mole! Authentic Mexican flavors, tapas style

www.lacartadeoaxaca.com

Mexican
Casual restaurant

Ballard
5431 Ballard Ave. NW
(206) 782-8722

Hours
Mon
5:00pm–11:00pm
Tue–Thu
11:30am–3:00pm
5:00pm–11:00pm
Fri–Sat
11:30am–3:00pm
5:00pm–midnight

Bar
Beer, wine, liquor, BYO

Credit cards
Visa, MC, AmEx

Reservations
Not accepted

There is a distinct lack of hominess here: a mix of too-tightly-packed blonde-wood tables under backlit photos of native oaxaqueños, which are so well composed and framed that you might imagine a *Dwell* magazine editor having designed the place. The lights are really bright, the acoustics are bad—the place gets unbearably noisy—and there's something cold about the open kitchen where the silent staff pats out hand-formed tortillas.

But there's no rule that says good Mexican restaurants have to be holes in the wall, and all the tradition that's needed here is in the small menu of small plates. Although some of the recipes come from other regions of Mexico, most of them are based on Oaxacan traditions. Mole negro, served over chicken or pork, is popular, but it's not even the kitchen's best work. Those honors go to the tacos al pastor, lamb birria (stewed lamb tacos), albóndigas (meatballs) in a spicy vegetable soup, and caldo de pescado, a spicy fish soup that comes with unedited chunks of fish (skin, bones, and all).

Paying for chips and guac may seem like an annoying pomposity, but the expenditure is worthwhile to sample the salsa bar.

La Isla

A bit for pricey for plantains, but with
portions this big, we don't care

8.0	7.5
Food	Feel

$35
Price

www.laislaseattle.com

La Isla might be the only place in Seattle making
truly authentic Puerto Rican food. All the hits
are here, from plátanos to carne frita, albeit at
slightly inflated prices (it is on the trendy end of
Ballard, after all).

Plátanos, sweet plátanos. The appetizer plate
of a few smashed green plantains and a few
sliced ripe ones is worth it even if your main
comes with a side of them—it's the one thing
that you'll most definitely need after wrangling
with a huge portion of fried bacalao (cod),
pastelón, or ropa vieja (a Cuban dish, actually,
and in slider form to remind you that you're still
in Seattle).

The space is…bizarre. Tables are awkwardly
grouped, and the long bar looks like something
you'd find in a dance club in Tacoma or
Olympia—except for the fine rums replacing
neon-colored shots. But with light Caribbean
kitsch—Spanish-language street signs, a few
Puerto Rican flags—and friendly service, La Isla
is festive without being goofy. And we just have
to love a place that writes "Holy Shit!" on its
own menu to call attention to one of the
owners' favorite dishes (the deep-fried catfish
strips).

Puerto Rican
Casual restaurant

Ballard
2320 NW Market St.
(206) 789-0516

Hours
Daily
11:30am–11:00pm

Bar
Beer, wine, liquor

Credit cards
Visa, MC, AmEx

Reservations
Not accepted

Features
Outdoor dining

La Medusa

A bright spot in the growing Columbia City dining scene

www.lamedusarestaurant.com

Italian
Casual restaurant

Columbia City
4857 Rainier Ave. S.
(206) 723-2192

Hours
Tue
5:00pm–9:00pm
Wed
5:00pm–10:00pm
Thu
5:00pm–9:00pm
Fri–Sat
5:00pm–10:00pm

Bar
Beer, wine, liquor

Credit cards
Visa, MC

Reservations
Accepted

Features
Date-friendly
Kid-friendly
Veg-friendly

Well worth the light-rail trip to Columbia City, La Medusa offers the usual locally sourced seasonal fare with an inspired Sicilian spin. (Like Café Juanita, this is a restaurant that sources everything locally, except when they're importing ingredients from Italy.)

Cod fritters are salty, creamy nuggets encased in a shaggy yet perfectly crisp batter, fried just so, and nestled in a ramekin atop a puddle of garlicky and fresh-tasting marinara. The acciuga pizza, with caciocavallo cheese and white anchovies, also comes with a couple of eggs, sunny side up and blinking at you coquettishly. "Grandma's Greens" are topped with raisins, olives and pine nuts; this might be the most delicious way to eat kale that doesn't involve the use of vast amounts of bacon. A tender, beefy grilled sirloin comes in a demi-glace with roasted potatoes, parsnips, carrots, and sunchoke, the earthy tang of which lends a novel layer of flavor to the usual root vegetable menagerie.

The wine list is an homage to every great wine-producing area of Italy and has many affordable bottles, including the very quaffable house red.

This is a casual, café-tables-and-chalkboard-menus kind of place, which makes the prices seem a bit high. But we guess that La Medusa hits its inclusivity quota in other ways. The crowd often skews older, but the staff is extremely accommodating of kids.

La Rustica

Linguine-and-tiramisù Italian, off the beaten path

www.larusticarestaurant.com

6.5	8.0
Food	Feel

$55
Price

Italian
Upmarket restaurant

West Seattle
4100 Beach Dr. SW
(206) 932-3020

Hours
Tue–Thu
5:00pm–10:00pm
Fri–Sat
5:00pm–10:30pm
Sun
5:00pm–9:30pm

Bar
Beer, wine, liquor

Credit cards
Visa, MC, AmEx

Reservations
Not accepted

Features
Date-friendly
Outdoor dining
Veg-friendly

A great counterpoint to the spate of (sometimes overly) creative Italian restaurants downtown, La Rustica is solidly neighborhood Italian-American. It's intimate—or cramped, depending on how much you value elbow room and privacy—and suitably romantic.

La Rustica's location, in a residential area beyond Alki Point, is also a nice change of pace from the converted-warehouse scene. Outdoor seating is across the street from a little beach, and with its vine-clad trellises and wrought-iron mesh tables, the space has that traditional gazebo feel that's championed these days mostly by suburban restaurants. The interior, too, seems to fly in the face of urban trends, riding the line between quaint and tacky, but this lack of pomposity is perhaps why many are so fond of the restaurant.

The big menu is Italian-American in a broad sense. Bivalves, poultry, and steaks tend to get a bit lost under rich stone-ground mustards, cream sauces, and gorgonzola. Conversely, the kitchen seems to get things just right in soups and broths—the light cioppino allo zafferano is excellent. There are enough mussels and scallops on the menu to bolster the dining-by-the-sea feeling, and although seafood preparations won't seem revelatory, taste and freshness are consistent. La Rustica is the kind of spot you visit when you want to take a break from being a foodie and just enjoy being a diner.

Lark

You'll be licking lots of small plates clean in a restaurant that will make you feel cool

www.larkseattle.com

Modern
Upmarket restaurant

Capitol Hill
926 12th Ave.
(206) 323-5275

Hours
Tue–Sun
5:00pm–10:30pm

Bar
Beer, wine, liquor

Credit cards
Visa, MC

Reservations
Accepted

Features
Date-friendly
Veg-friendly

Lark was once on the forefront of the small-plates and seasonal/local movement in Seattle. Because of this, and because it has turned out consistently high-quality food for six years, it is exempt from Small Plates Fatigue, with which we are so frequently afflicted.

Some dishes here are memorable in the truest sense—a black truffle rice pudding is stuck in one panelist's mind, like, well, dried rice pudding on a wall. Other dishes, like a bright carpaccio of yellowtail with preserved lemons and green olives, or a salty hearts-of-palm salad with vanilla-bean vinaigrette, are merely outstanding.

The menu does occasionally get a little precious—do we need to know that the snails are basil-fed?—but then you can always turn the page to charcuterie. The wine list is short, but tight, with some interesting producers you don't see every day.

Lark is in a old garage, but exposed beams and a pitched roof give the restaurant a rustic bistro feel. Curtains help provide privacy among the tables, which are pretty close together, as well as adding texture to a fairly standard set-up: a few booths and a tiny bar area ring a collection of café tables, some draped in white, others bare.

Le Gourmand

Where puppets watch you eat poulet

7.5	8.0
Food	Feel

$85	8.5
Price	Wine

www.legourmandrestaurant.com

Le Gourmand is one of those little neighborhood restaurants that you might drive by for years and wonder, "Who eats there?" But then one day, you try to make a reservation, and you're denied for the day of your request. That's when and you realize something must be going on inside.

Perhaps overshadowed by Sambar, which hipsters are hitting with great glee (the two share a kitchen), Le Gourmand is a Seattle institution that's recently been renovated. The new space is no longer stuck with décor from a century ago; it's now contemporary yet comfortable, unless you object to the eyes of the puppets that hover above you while you dine.

Chef Bruce Naftaly has been going at it for 25 years, but this is French fare still worth checking out. The meats may be simple, but Naftaly is a master of sauces, which adorn many of the menu items here. Simple, ingredient-focused preps work well, too. The "AQ" (as quoted) salad epitomizes the place: at our last visit, the locally foraged ingredients were fresh and the dressing delightful, but at quite a cost for a plate of mostly uncooked vegetables. If you're willing to open your wallet to such prices, we'd recommend the tasting menu with wines to match.

French
Upmarket restaurant

Ballard
425 NW Market St.
(206) 784-3463

Hours
Wed–Sat
5:30pm–10:00pm

Bar
Beer, wine, liquor, BYO

Credit cards
Visa, MC, AmEx

Reservations
Accepted

Features
Date-friendly

9.0	9.5
Food	Feel

$50	8.0
Price	Wine

Le Pichet

Quite simply the best French restaurant in Seattle—and it's just a simple bistro

www.lepichetseattle.com

French
Upmarket restaurant

Downtown
1933 1st Ave.
(206) 256-1499

Hours
Daily
7:00am–midnight

Bar
Beer, wine, liquor

Credit cards
Visa, MC

Reservations
Accepted

Features
Date-friendly
Live music
Outdoor dining

If there's a simulacrum of a Parisian cafe with a higher fidelity to the real thing, anywhere in the Pacific Northwest, we'd like to see it. Le Pichet is spot on in every way. The interior is a study in understated elegance, from the zinc-topped bar to the haughty waitresses with their Cuban seamed stockings.

This kitchen pulls off typical bistro plates exceptionally well. Nothing here misses a beat: breakfast, for instance, brings oeufs plats (two eggs and ham, covered in gruyère and broiled in a shallow baking dish). Dinner is similarly masterful; there's usually some kind of chicken or pork or veal sausage available, bursting from its casing and served atop choucroute (the Alsatian way) or, sometimes, white beans.

For dessert, chocolat chaud is the only way to go. It's not hot chocolate so much as a cauldron of melted chocolate, crowned with a fluffy halo of whipped cream, and it's so sweet it could soothe a broken heart. Le Pichet's French-focused wine list was one of the first in the city to offer multiple size options for many of their wines. It's well set up to match the food and the bistro vibe, and to encourage trying multiple glasses or "Pichet Pours" throughout the course of your meal.

The one caveat is that this is fairly simple bistro fare, so if you're particularly adept in the kitchen, then you might feel like you're paying a lot for something you could make at home. Even so, Le Pichet offers a full-fledged experience, which is worth a small surcharge, n'est-ce pas?

Lola

A solid after-work pan-Mediterranean spot
that brings out the best in Tom Douglas

7.5	8.0
Food	Feel

$60	7.0
Price	Wine

www.tomdouglas.com

It's not as good as Serious Pie or as classic as
Palace Kitchen, but Lola is one of the best
outposts of the Tom Douglas empire. Lola has a
fairly straightforward m.o., which helps: instead
of seafood fusion circa 1993, the kitchen turns
out reasonable interpretations of Mediterranean
and North African standards.

Tagines, done with traditional proteins like
lamb or goat, with flourishes like pine nuts or
Meyer lemon, are perfectly prepared, if a little
on the small side. Whole fishes (grape leaf-
wrapped trout, for instance) are moist and
flavorful. The kebabs are delicious, especially the
squid, octopus, and lamb varieties.

Lola suffers a bit from the '90s feel of many
of Douglas's restaurants, but it's much hipper
than Dahlia Lounge or Etta's. The huge oak cask
for aging wine is a great focal point behind the
bar (much better than the neon flame lights
hanging above it). It's a fun place to dine, in the
end, with lots of booths, a gorgeous curving
bar, great service, and good happy hour. This
could be the regular hangout for characters in a
prime-time drama about a plucky young law
firm—an aesthetic that blends in well with the
adjoining Hotel Ändra.

**Greek
Moroccan
Middle Eastern**
Casual restaurant

Belltown
2000 4th Ave.
(206) 441-1430

Hours
Mon–Fri
6:00am–midnight
Sat–Sun
7:00am–midnight

Bar
Beer, wine, liquor

Credit cards
Visa, MC, AmEx

Reservations
Accepted

Features
Date-friendly

Long Provincial

Less crowded than its Vietnamese sibling
Tamarind Tree, but less special, too

www.longprovincial.com

Vietnamese
Upmarket restaurant

Belltown
1901 2nd Ave.
(206) 443-6266

Hours
Sun–Thu
11:00am–midnight
Fri–Sat
11:00am–2:00am

Bar
Beer, wine, liquor

Credit cards
Visa, MC

Reservations
Accepted

Features
Veg-friendly

After playing around with an upscale vibe on a forgotten corner of the International District for a long time, the owners of the Tamarind Tree have entered the Belltown fray in full, nightclub-style force. Long borrows most of its menu from Tamarind Tree, but unlike its predecessor, it has fully realized the überlounge vision—most of the surfaces are black (except when they're red), bamboo screens obscure the outside world, and a jellyfish tank provides a few neon dots of color and entertainment. We know that a lot of downtowners eat lunch here, but we can't imagine stepping foot inside before 8pm.

The menu is stupidly long for a place where most revelers are sipping sparkling lychee foam. It's like they took every dish on the Tamarind Tree's gargantuan menu and then added a few more fusiony items to the mix. As at Tamarind Tree, you're best off favoring one extreme or another: order something simple like banh xeo (savory pancakes) or a rice dish loaded with lemongrass, or pick over the range of crossover appetizers like battered prawns served with hoisin-chili sauce and baguette slices.

The latter approach might be more satisfying: starters are usually interesting, and besides, eating pho in this type of environment just feels ridiculous.

Luc

The chef in the hat dons a second, cheaper one

www.thechefinthehat.com

7.0	6.5
Food	Feel

$45
Price

French
Casual restaurant

Capitol Hill
2800 E. Madison St.
(206) 328-6645

Hours
Daily
4:00pm–midnight

Bar
Beer, wine, liquor

Credit cards
Visa, MC, AmEx

Reservations
Accepted

Features
Date-friendly

Thierry Rautureau, the so-called "Chef in the Hat," opened this down-home café as a recession-friendly companion to tony Rover's. It is newer and cheaper, and there is definitely something lost in that translation.

Gone at Luc is the main strength of Rover's: the very focused (some might say bordering on sedate), thematically coherent menu. Some dishes at Luc are more flagrantly French than at Rover's—this is the place to try whole trout amandine, a dish that alone justifies a meal here—while some are bafflingly off-topic or unnecessary. Who wants a chef known for classic French cuisine to serve them a pizza or a mediocre, mayo-drenched burger?

That said, a bad day for Luc is a good day for some restaurants, and each weekday features a reasonably priced specialty dish for two (a whole roast chicken, perhaps, or a pork shoulder roast), which is a good, cheap way to see what all the behatted hype is about.

Luc has an updated look, but it's not nearly as cute or cool as reigning French cafés Le Pichet and Café Presse. But then, like Rover's, Luc caters to an older, wealthy Madrona crowd, for whom, perhaps, cute and cool have somewhat different meanings than they do for food-geek thirtysomethings like us.

7.0	4.0
Food	Feel

Lunchbox Laboratory

$20
Price

The most obscene burgers in the city, with a heap of toppings and a side of grunge

www.lunchboxlaboratory.com

American
Counter service

Ballard
7302 1/2 15th Ave. NW
(206) 706-3092

Hours
Tue
11:00am–3:00pm
Wed–Sat
11:00am–8:00pm
Sun
11:00am–5:00pm

Bar
None

Credit cards
Visa, MC, AmEx

Features
Kid-friendly
Outdoor dining

Lunchbox Laboratory makes burgers that resemble Popeye's burger-loving friend, Wimpy: the bun looks as silly and out-of-proportion on the burger as Wimpy's tiny derby looks on his misshapen body. It's a cliché, but this is food porn, no doubt about it.

The beef patties—there are also lamb, bison, chicken, and vegetarian falafel versions—are juicy and delicious, but they're all cooked the same way (no asking for rare here). But in the fully-cooked genre, these burgers excel. They're also not cheap.

The science experiments atop the patties range from reasonable/familiar (caramelized onions and gorgonzola) to ridiculous (duck, pork, salami, havarti, onions, shallots, and tomato sauce). Generally, the simpler the better (the duck/pork monstrosity does not work very well).

Lunchbox has survived a number of recent shakeups, including the loss of its main investor. The owners have made promises to rebound with a streamlined menu and special events. Let's hope they also use this second chance to clean up their act a little—literally. This place is inexplicably grungy, which is too bad because the vintage lunchboxes and Route 66-type road signs and pendants are cute and would look a lot better in a space that doesn't give germaphobes the heebie-jeebies.

Madison Park Café

French comfort food and souped-up homey
atmosphere for an older crowd

7.5 **6.5**
Food | Feel

$60
Price

Madison Park's dinner menu is really focused:
white bean cassoulet with duck leg confit, steak
frites, moules frites, and Muscovy duck with
simple seasonal vegetable sides. Desserts such
as warm chocolate tortes and fruit tarts with
Chantilly cream, are often highlights.

The brunch menu, on the other hand, is
studiously unfocused: you'll find everything
from ricotta pancakes to huevos rancheros to a
"New York-style" bagel sandwich. Brunch is
actually the more popular of the two meals—
maybe it has something to do with the
homemade scones and jams.

Madison Park Café is set in a converted
house, and is about as successful at making that
work as other upmarket restaurants—which is
to say, not very. The cobblestone patio is
adorable, with café tables covered in blue-
checked cloths, but inside, the white tablecloths
and oddly formal layout clash with the sunny
yellow walls and clichéd art.

Most of the city's French bistros attract a
good generational mix—even Café Presse's
tattooed, floppy-haired waiters don't deter the
older foodies—but Madison Park Café skews
old and white almost as much as Rover's.

It's probably the prices that deter the younger
crowd most, and not the food, which is
comforting and enjoyable without being too
heavy. The old and young might do well to
meet here for Mother's Day

French
Upmarket restaurant

Madison Park
1807 42nd Ave. E.
(206) 324-2626

Hours
Tue–Thu
5:00pm–9:00pm
Fri
5:00pm–10:00pm
Sat
8:00am–2:00pm
5:00pm–10:00pm
Sun
8:00am–2:00pm

Bar
Beer, wine, liquor

Credit cards
Visa, MC, AmEx

Reservations
Accepted

Features
Brunch
Date-friendly
Outdoor dining

6.5 Food | 6.0 Feel

$25 Price

Malay Satay Hut

A PacNW Malaysian chain that's heading a bit downhill, but is still reliable

www.malaysatayhut.com

Malaysian
Casual restaurant

Eastside
15230 24th St. NE
(425) 564-0888

International District
212 12th Ave. S.
(206) 324-4091

Hours
Mon–Fri
11:30am–2:30pm
5:00pm–10:00pm
Sat–Sun
noon–3:00pm
5:00pm–10:00pm

Bar
Beer, wine

Credit cards
Visa, MC, AmEx

Reservations
Not accepted

Features
Kid-friendly

There aren't many places that focus on Malaysian food, and this expanding Pacific Northwest chain is the real deal. The curries are delicious, and the menu has great variety that faithfully surveys the multitude of influences present in the cuisine, from sweet and spicy Chinese pork chops and black pepper crab to belachan string beans and prawns to mango tofu salad. A favorite appetizer is the roti canai, a fluffy bread served with potato.

Recent renovations have made the place a bit more attractive by adding some carved woodwork and tastefully ornate Malaysian knickknacks, but they've also made it more generic. The open kitchen that used to dominate the front of the house is gone, so you no longer get the privilege of watching "Auntie" making your roti canai. Gone, too, is one of the most exotic and exciting dishes: whole baby squid (they tell us they still serve them, but they never seem to have them available); squid "steaks" are now the boring, tentacle-less alternative. On a few recent visits, key ingredients were missing from several dishes, turning them one-dimensional, and the curry dipping sauce for roti canai has come out surprisingly granular.

Malay is still better than the average I.D. joint, but compared to what it once was, it's starting to go downhill. We hope the unevenness is temporary.

Maneki

A great I.D. standby for cooked Japanese
snacks that has withstood the test of time

7.5 Food

6.5 Feel

$30 Price

www.manekirestaurant.com

One of the oldest Japanese restaurants in the
city is still one of the best—especially when it
comes to cooked food rather than sushi. Maneki
excels at snacks like agedashi tofu, mozuku
(seaweed and cucumber salad in vinegary
sauce), and soups like the nabeyaki udon, with
noodles, egg, chicken, and assorted vegetables
are excellent. A must-try is the miso black cod
collar. Two must-avoids, on the other hand, are
the croquettes and the "octopus donuts."
(Nobody's perfect.)

Getting a seat in this place is a mystery to
many; it seems to be based on whether the
hostess—who can switch from grumpy to
cheery in a moment—likes you. (But once you're
seated, the service is top-notch.)

Layout and decoration also seem to follow no
rhyme or reason: the main appointments are
ceramic *maneki nekos* (good luck cats) and
some shoji screens. There's also a tiny sushi bar
purveying fresh and affordable fish; the
structure resembles a homemade basement bar
that you might find at a drunken uncle's house,
and the quirky '70s vibe is kind of cool in its
own right.

Japanese
Casual restaurant

**International
District**
304 6th Ave. S.
(206) 622-2631

Hours
Tue–Sun
5:30pm–10:30pm

Bar
Beer, wine, liquor

Credit cards
Visa, MC

Reservations
Accepted

Features
Veg-friendly

6.5 Food | 7.5 Feel

$5
Price

Marination Mobile

Overhyped but very inventive fusion tacos from a food cart

www.marinationmobile.com

**Korean
Hawaiian
Mexican**
Food cart

South Lake Union
Locations change daily;
check website for details
or Twitter
@curb_cuisine

Hours
Daily
11:00am–2:00pm

Bar
None

Credit cards
Visa, MC

Features
Outdoor dining

Korean and Hawaiian favorites treated like Mexican street snacks—Marination Mobile is mostly successful at a strange type of fusion.

The best offering is a quesadilla with zingy kimchi, salty, smoky pork, and cheese that holds two slightly crunchy tortillas together. There are a lot of textures in the mix, but it's not overloaded with too many strong flavors.

There are at least four varieties of cheapo tacos. Kalbi beef is the best one: the meat is tender and garlicky and topped with crispy sweet slaw. The worst is tofu, which fails to absorb enough of the vaunted marinade to taste like anything but tofu in a tortilla.

And for better or worse, there's a Spam slider, which tastes like, well, Spam. It's surprisingly good for what it is—nicely grilled, piled with kimchi and pulled pork, and encased in a sweet Hawaiian roll—and anyone hankering for a real island tradition will be happy.

The truck is in a different location daily, though it keeps a fairly regular schedule. Check out the website or Twitter feed (@curb_cuisine) for details.

Marjorie

An old, eclectic Belltown favorite, nicely
resurrected in Condoland

7.0	7.5
Food	Feel

$55
Price

www.marjorierestaurant.com

Developers have been steadily dragging
Belltown into Capitol Hill for years now, and
Marjorie has come along for the ride, relocating
in a new cookie-cutter condo building. If too
many developers interpret "mixed-use space" as
"characterless, cavernous box," then Marjorie
does the best it can to make its new home more
homey, with cobalt walls and cookbooks piled
willy-nilly on shelves above the partially open
kitchen. It reminds us of one of Seattle's mildly
mod library branches.

A seasonal small-plates menu that tosses a bit
of soul food into a Pacific Northwest m.o.
always has a few high points, like a pile of
plantain chips, expertly cooked cuttlefish with
andouille sausage, or pretty much any pan-fried
swimmer. Handmade pastas are more hit-or-
miss, and often not worth the money.

That brings us to our main complaint about
Marjorie: many of the plates are overpriced.
Plantains should never cost this much in Seattle;
we don't care if they're coated in powdered
unicorn horn.

Although there are vague themes running
through the menu, it oscillates a little too much
between generic modern Northwest conceits
and the brighter notes of the soul/island
offerings—we'd gladly trade the grass-fed rib
eye and pork belly for more of the stuff you
don't see elsewhere in town, like nairagi (striped
marlin) in a pomegranate-molasses sauce.

Modern
Upmarket restaurant

Capitol Hill
1412 E. Union St.
(206) 441-9842

Hours
Tue–Thu
5:00pm–10:00pm
Fri–Sat
5:00pm–11:00pm

Bar
Beer, wine, liquor

Credit cards
Visa, MC, AmEx

Reservations
Accepted

Features
Date-friendly
Outdoor dining

7.5 8.5
Food Feel

$35
Price

Marrakesh

Prix-fixe, belly-dancing, enormous-tagine-devouring madness

www.marrakeshseattle.com

Moroccan
Casual restaurant

Belltown
2334 2nd Ave.
(206) 956-0500

Hours
Daily
5:00pm–10:00pm

Bar
Beer, wine

Credit cards
Visa, MC, AmEx

Reservations
Accepted

Features
Live music
Veg-friendly

Marrakesh shoots for the pleasure-palace vibe, and it succeeds reasonably well, especially if you squint and pretend the belly dancer is not the same woman you've seen picking through overpriced organics at the co-op. It's super-cool inside Marrakesh: the low tables are surrounded by pillows, and gold billowy linen hangs from the ceiling.

You'll definitely want to bring along your entire harem, because the amount of food you get is truly gluttonous. Each meal starts with a spicy and creamy lentil soup, followed by another appetizer like ground chicken, nuts, and cinnamon wrapped in what seems like thousands of layers of phyllo dough and dusted with powdered sugar. Then you get a huge salad of diced cucumber, tomato, and carrot, with bread to scoop it up. After that, you can choose from a list of main courses: a tagine of chicken, lemon, and olives is salty and sour, while chicken, honey, and prunes version is syrupy-sweet. Braised hare tagine, perhaps our favorite, is succulent and spicy, while the "Brochette Marrakesh" is basically a lamb kebab, served over a giant pile of rice so fluffy you could stuff a pillow with it. The meal closes out with fruit salad and mint tea.

If you can deal with the extra bloat, try the Moroccan beers. They're nice, a light pilsners that pair well with the food.

Mashiko

Proving that sushi can survive the loss of bluefin tuna

8.0	6.5
Food	Feel

$50	7.0
Price	Wine

www.sushiwhore.com

Mashiko is Seattle's only sushi restaurant that declares itself to be "sustainable"; the chefs don't serve any wild fish that are on watch lists, and they purchase farmed species from low-impact operations that don't use antibiotics. What this means is many traditional favorites—bluefin, hamachi, and unagi—are missing from the menu.

Omakase is a gamble—one panelist has had a great experience, while another had no interaction with the chef and received what seemed like a hodge-podge of items off the regular menu. Considering the prices, this may not be a gamble worth taking. (If you're going to splurge, the 12-course kaiseki seems to be the better bet; advance reservations are required.)

Although serious sushi snobs don't often order rolls, Mashiko has a bit of fun with theirs: the "Idaho," for example, has tempura potato, dill, lemon, and trout. It's also worth noting that Mashiko can make even a flash-fried, Americanized roll taste reasonably complex. There are plenty of izakaya dishes, too, from albacore tataki to potstickers to clams steamed with butter and sake. Fried dishes tend to be a little greasy, but tasty nonetheless.

The restaurant is playful and a bit whimsical. Little Japanese toys line the sushi bar, and the menu includes Chef Hajime Sato's "rules," which, along with tipping and BYOB policies, include things like "Chopsticks are not drumsticks" and "Enjoy life."

Japanese
Casual restaurant

West Seattle
4725 California Ave. SW
(206) 935-4339

Hours
Mon–Thu
5:33pm–9:30pm
Fri
5:33pm–11:00pm
Sat
5:03pm–11:00pm
Sun
5:03pm–9:30pm

Bar
Beer, wine, BYO

Credit cards
Visa, MC

Reservations
Accepted

8.5	8.5
Food	Feel

$70	8.0
Price	Wine

Matt's in the Market

We're in love with the setting, but on strictly platonic terms with the food

www.mattsinthemarket.com

Modern
Upmarket restaurant

Downtown
94 Pike St.
(206) 467-7909

Hours
Mon–Sat
11:30am–2:30pm
5:30pm–10:00pm
Sun
11:30am–2:30pm

Bar
Beer, wine, liquor

Credit cards
Visa, MC

Reservations
Accepted

Features
Date-friendly

Matt's offers the quintessential Seattle experience, complete with Pike Place Market proximity. But unlike many restaurants in the belly of the downtown beast, Matt's doesn't feel corporate, contrived, or too frilly.

The space is great: the black-and-white checkered floor, retro leather barstools, and bare tables with simple bouquets of Market flowers create a French-café-meets-upscale-American-diner feel that's bright and bustling during lunch yet romantic by candlelight. Get a table by the arched windows, and you've got an unobstructed view of the Market's iconic neon sign plus glimpses of the Sound.

Matt's used to be a shoebox with a modest menu; now it's a slightly bigger restaurant with prices that are too high for what is fairly simple Northwest fare. The fun wine list has no geographical boundaries, simply pulling in what matches well with the menu. There are plenty of well-chosen glass pours to get you to experiment and mix and match.

The lunch menu harkens back to the good old days, with burgers, catfish po'boys, soups, and salads. We particularly love the lamb burger with goat cheese and bacon. At dinner, nothing's transcendent, but short ribs, luscious lamb shank, and roasted free-range chicken are all local and well prepared. A dish of grilled octopus, clams, and mussels with chorizo is also quite nice. Whole fish is so fresh you expect to see the Market's famous fish-throwers chucking them through the window. But, beware those "market prices."

Maximus/Minimus

Fine, but the least inspiring of Seattle's fleet of food carts

www.maximus-minimus.com

5.0 Food

6.5 Feel

$10 Price

The concept behind Maximus/Minimus seems simple. There are only three dishes: a pulled-pork sandwich, a vegetarian sandwich, and pork with pozole. Sides include slaw and chips. There are two beverages and two desserts.

But there's much more to the concept: each selection is available in either Maximus (hot and spicy) or Minimus (sweet and tangy) versions. For example, the Minimus sauce on the pork sandwich has molasses, tamarind, and honey and forgoes the hot peppers of the Maximus.

Some of this is fun. The drinks, for example, aren't what you'd normally find at a street cart—ginger lemonade (Maximus) and hibiscus nectar (Minimus)—and go well with their respective menu items. But ordering down one side of the menu or the other doesn't really create a cohesive, memorable experience. Partly this is because not all of the items pop on their own. The Minimus slaw is very good, but it's paired with the Maximus pork sandwich, which is a bit dry.

The truck is downtown most weekdays and makes the farmers' markets rounds on weekends; check the website for more information. The dining atmosphere varies depending on where it's parked, but you're eating pig from a truck that looks like a pig. Points for drawing bewildered looks from passersby.

Southern
Food cart

Downtown
2nd Ave. and Pike St.
(206) 601-5510

Hours
Mon–Fri
11:00am–2:00pm

Bar
None

Credit cards
Visa, MC, AmEx

Features
Veg-friendly

May Thai

Not your standard takeout Thai

www.maythaiseattle.com

Thai
Casual restaurant

Wallingford
1612 N. 45th St.
(206) 675-0037

Hours
Daily
11:00am–2:00am

Bar
Beer, wine, liquor

Credit cards
Visa, MC, AmEx

Reservations
Accepted

Features
Date-friendly
Live music
Outdoor dining
Veg-friendly

May serves many of the dishes you'll see on Thai menus all over town. But the setting and presentation here are far more sophisticated than at any of its peers. Lest this sound like code for fusion or other sorts of inauthenticity, that's not the case...well, not entirely: there certainly are those made-up dishes that cater to the American palate: "Babycorn Spicy Delight," asparagus with shiitake and tofu, pineapple fried rice. But there are also excellent versions of tom kha and tom yum soups, as well as crispy catfish with eggplant and curry paste. Even on the usual curries, more spice is built in and the individual flavors in Thai cooking are allowed to shine through—nice sour notes, no cloying sweetness. Even pad Thai, generally the ultimate Thai-American throwaway, is palatable here: instead of a glutinous mess, it's deconstructed with its components (sprouts, ground peanuts, and spices) served in separate banana leaves and mixed together at the table. In this dish and others, you'll also see some ingredients you won't find at most other Seattle Thai restaurants, like fried banana blossoms.

With an imported teak façade and walls, May looks as much like a temple plunked in Seattle as possible. The upstairs dining room is casually royal, with ornate utensils and serving dishes, and the downstairs bar follows suit, with red walls, gold fixtures, and Buddhist murals.

Mayuri

South Indian specialties plus all the usual suspects at dirt-cheap prices

7.5 Food

6.5 Feel

$25 Price

www.mayuriseattle.com

Mayuri is a favorite of Microsoft employees, who show up for the gut-busting lunch buffet, which is well stocked with both meat and vegetarian dishes, or the equally good-value dinner thali, which comes with a main, a vegetable curry, dal, naan, rice, soup, raita, and dessert.

Spicy and sizzling are the watchwords here. And buttery—the food here can only be considered healthy if you're on a 60 percent ghee diet. A section of the menu is devoted to South Indian cuisine, including dosai (crêpes made with mung-bean flour) stuffed with vegetable curries or more unusual (at least in these parts) combinations of cream of wheat and rice. Indeed, some of Mayuri's best dishes are southern creations, like the spicy chicken chetynadu. Otherwise, anything from the tandoor—including the unusual (and often disappointing) fish choice of tilapia—goes over well.

Although any place with a buffet can't be too elegant, Mayuri puts some effort into presentation. How many places with prices this low give you cloth napkins?

Indian
Casual restaurant

Bellevue
15400 NE 20th St.
(425) 533-2145

Hours
Sun–Thu
11:30am–2:30pm
5:00pm–9:30pm
Fri–Sat
11:30am–2:30pm
5:00pm–10:00pm

Bar
Beer, wine, BYO

Credit cards
Visa, MC, AmEx

Reservations
Accepted

Features
Kid-friendly
Veg-friendly

Meskel

When your taxi driver gives you a tip about tibs...

Ethiopian
Casual restaurant

Central District
2605 E. Cherry St.
(206) 860-1724

Hours
Tue–Sun
11:30am–10:30pm

Bar
Beer, wine

Credit cards
Visa, MC

Reservations
Accepted

Features
Kid-friendly
Veg-friendly

Looking for Ethiopian food in Seattle? Hail a cab, and chances are the driver can direct you to his favorite place for food from his homeland. And for most, Meskel is the choice.

The restaurant has a large terrace that's abandoned every drive-by, but the interior has some warmth from native art. And while the staff seems initially shy, if you express some interest in the food, they'll warm up quickly.

One of our panelists came to Meskel after learning that they offered the best kitfo (ground, raw meat in spiced butter) in the city, and he's now an addict. Don't forget to ask for it raw, though—that's not the default assumption, especially for non-Ethiopians. In addition to other meats like chicken and lamb (we recommend the yebeg tibs, or lamb sautéed with onions and chiles), Meskel also offers a number of vegetarian options such as red lentils and puréed chickpeas.

Mesob

A hovel, but one of the best Ethiopian eateries in the city

8.0 Food

4.0 Feel

$20 Price

The "speakeasies" in town should take a page from Mesob: no other place in town better hides its treasures. Go to the no man's land by Swedish Medical, get past the dumpsters outside the restaurant, and head to the back—to a Tiki-like bar room with several booths and about five small tables. This is where you'll find some of the best Ethiopian food in the city.

The best thing to order is the veggie combo platter, which arrives with plenty of injera (the spongy bread that you use to pick up the food), lentils, potato-cabbage-carrot salad, and, of course, the numerous unidentifiable concoctions that turn up on veggie platters.

Sambusas and tomato salad are the best starters. Mesob has a pretty good selection of beer—good Ethiopian representation plus one or two U.S. beers on tap—which really helps wash down some of the spicier dishes. All of this is particularly welcome in the wee hours, when Mesob turns into one of Seattle's late-night stars.

Ethiopian
Casual restaurant

Central District
1325 E. Jefferson St.
(206) 860-0403

Hours
Mon–Fri
1:00pm–midnight
Sat–Sun
4:00pm–2:00am

Bar
Beer, wine, liquor

Credit cards
Visa, MC

Reservations
Accepted

Features
Good beers
Kid-friendly
Veg-friendly

Metropolitan Grill

A flashy steakhouse with outdated décor
and a crowd that's, um, distinctive

www.themetropolitangrill.com

Steakhouse
Upmarket restaurant

Downtown
820 2nd Ave.
(206) 624-3287

Hours
Mon–Thu
11:00am–3:00pm
5:00pm–10:00pm

Fri
11:00am–3:00pm
5:00pm–10:30pm

Sat
4:00pm–11:00pm

Sun
4:00pm–9:00pm

Bar
Beer, wine, liquor, BYO

Credit cards
Visa, MC, AmEx

Reservations
Accepted

Features
Date-friendly
Good cocktails

Where do aging, paunchier frat boys and ex-sorority girls with over-processed blond highlights go to feel as if they're still reliving their glory days? You'll find a lot of them here—now perhaps stockbrokers, "interior designers who studied abroad," and PR minions—exchanging numbers at this downtown meat market.

Located in a historic 1903 building (set up with a 1980s-era interior), the Metropolitan Grill is one of the city's foremost steakhouses. The high-backed banquettes are comfy, although a horrific shade of olive green, and the brown swirly-patterned carpet looks like one you'd find at a retirement home.

While the décor is a little dated, the food is actually quite good. At happy hour, thick-cut onion rings with curried ketchup arrive in almost too-plentiful portions, while oyster shooters and beef sliders are available at rock-bottom prices.

On the list of quaffables, classic cocktails like Vespers and Old-Fashioneds abound. (Bonus: the bartenders aren't dressed in ridiculous Prohibition wear, either.) The wine list is spectacular, long, and covering all the bases. Come dinner, you'll find buttery prime steaks subtly perfumed by mesquite wood and fatty-licious sides like Yukon Gold potato cakes with crème fraiche and chives. Not a carnivore? There's your usual pesca-friendly picks like Alaskan King crab legs, or the prawn scampi with fettuccine alfredo. Now *there's* a throwback to the restaurant's 1981 birth year.

Mirak

Side-trip-worthy Korean that does almost everything well

8.5 Food

5.0 Feel

$25 Price

Korean
Casual restaurant

South Seattle
31260 Pacific Hwy. S.
(253) 839-6522

Hours
Daily
10:30am–10:00pm

Bar
Beer, wine

Credit cards
Visa, MC

Reservations
Accepted

Features
Kid-friendly

Increasingly, you have to travel farther and farther outside of Seattle for the best of the Asian and Southeast Asian cuisines. 20 minutes south of the city in the otherwise undistinguished suburb of Federal Way is one of our favorite Korean joints.

The marinated BBQ meats come ready to take on their beautiful char at tabletop grills, and there's a great variety of banchan. Other standouts are the delicious seafood pancake (not too greasy, although you should skip the overly chewy octopus version) and the grilled mackerel, which is oily and delicious, with that full-flavored (some might say "fishy") stank, its skin on and nicely crisped. The bulgogi and kalbi are also consistently good.

Mirak is another Asian restaurant with bare-bones décor, this time of the anemic pastel variety. The restaurant is divided in half: the tables on the right side are outfitted with grills, but the tables on left are not, so at least one section of the restaurant is relatively smoke-free. Service is usually pretty slow, which is problematic because the place is often very busy.

7.5 Food   7.5 Feel

$65 Price

Mistral Kitchen

A fun splurge that's strong on drinks and dessert

www.mistral-kitchen.com

Modern
Upmarket restaurant

Belltown
2020 Westlake Ave.
(206) 623-1922

Hours
Sun–Thu
11:00am–2:00pm
5:00pm–10:00pm
Fri–Sat
11:00am–2:00pm
5:00pm–midnight

Bar
Beer, wine, liquor

Credit cards
Visa, MC, AmEx

Reservations
Accepted

Features
Brunch
Date-friendly

Mistral has, in short order: a chef's table, a bar, a counter overlooking the dessert station, a tandoor, a wood-burning pizza oven, and an intimate fine dining room. It reminds us of a very dark, very fancy dining hall, only better, because you don't have to stand in eight different lines to try everything.

The space is pretty cool, but you have to be in the mood for it. Everything's very spare and angular—all black and stainless steel and dark woods—and it looks like a cross between a sexy library and a sexy holding cell.

The two major talents at Mistral are mixologist Andrew Bohrer and pastry chef Neil Robertson. Bohrer's cocktails are candy-colored and served in undignified stemware like a tiki mug or champagne flute, yet they're remarkably subtle. Robertson can work magic with ambitious desserts like rhubarb financier with fromage blanc, Szechuan peppercorn sorbet, and rhubarb soup—the clarity of flavor in the soup is laudable.

Dinner is more inconsistent: dishes are always cleanly presented, but fall flat too many times. Some nights the menu is just hard to fathom, jumping around from something as Northwest as butternut squash soup to foie gras mousse with pear and Riesling gelée to lemon-shiso cured salmon with a soy-ginger vinaigrette. The highlights are superb, but at this price point, we'd like to see more coherence and consistency in quality.

Molly Moon's

Boutique ice cream: gourmet ingredients, happy cows, and compostable utensils

www.mollymoonicecream.com

Molly Moon's is the Salumi of ice cream parlors. We've lost count of the restaurants that eagerly namecheck the establishment on their dessert menus, and Molly Moon Neitzel has become something of a celeb chef. Both branches have queues out the door nearly all the time, even in winter.

The contributing cows to this ice cream are hormone-free, and flavors change seasonally to make the most of the fruits, vegetables (there's a beet sorbet, for example), and seasonings of the Pacific Northwest and northern California. Flavors never get too crazy—honey lavender, cardamom, balsamic strawberry—but that's just fine. Molly Moon's strength is that flavors are generally pitch-perfect. Except in the too-sweet sorbets, the sugar content doesn't overpower those special ingredients: you can detect, for example, the slight chalkiness of Theo's premium dark chocolates. There is usually a seasonal coconut milk selection to placate vegans and the lactose intolerant. (In fact, the best thing we've had here was a coconut-milk ice cream lightly infused with espresso from local roaster Vivace.)

All that said, the fervent adoration that Molly Moon's inspires and sustains is a little puzzling. Perhaps people go not just for the ice cream, but also for the experience of standing in line with excited patrons, watching those awesome waffle cones come off the griddle while choosing flavors off a chalkboard.

Sweets
Ice Cream
Counter service

Capitol Hill
917 E. Pine St.
(206) 708-7947

Wallingford
1622 N. 45th St.
(206) 547-5105

Hours
Daily
noon–11:00pm
Hours vary by location

Bar
None

Credit cards
Visa, MC

Features
Kid-friendly

7.5 Food | 8.0 Feel

Monkey Bridge

The best full Vietnamese menu in the northern neighborhoods

$25 Price

www.themonkeybridge.com

Vietnamese
Casual restaurant

Ballard
1723 NW Market St.
(206) 297-6048

Hours
Daily
10:30am–9:30pm

Bar
Beer, wine

Credit cards
Visa, MC

Reservations
Not accepted

Features
Date-friendly
Veg-friendly

The most dressed-up Vietnamese place in Ballard, Monkey Bridge is a lesson in why one shouldn't judge a book by its cover—the food here is far better than it is at almost all the lovable grungy neighborhood joints. The quality of the pho is still up for debate—it has many fans, but can still be a bit too sweet for our tastes—and until Than Brothers completely declines in quality, you're probably better off slurping soup there.

But the rest of Monkey Bridge's menu has plenty of praiseworthy favorites like spring rolls bursting with fresh vegetables, banh xeo with prawns, seared bacon, and bean sprouts, and well-proportioned bun (rice noodle) dishes that don't skimp on the nicely marinated meats.

The place isn't going to win any major design awards, but it is proof that all you need to make an eatery even moderately pleasant is a little eggplant paint on the walls, a few boxy red lanterns, a cute bar area, and pop art that doesn't suck. This is one of the most date-night-worthy Vietnamese restaurants in the city whose menu still sticks closely to tradition.

Monsoon

Tricked-out Northwest Vietnamese for an upscale crowd

www.monsoonrestaurants.com

8.0	8.0
Food	Feel

$55	7.0
Price	Wine

Monsoon serves haute Vietnamese, and the Northwest pops up on the menu often—among the selection of lovely stir-fried greens are items like fiddlehead ferns. More ambitious crossovers occur in dishes like wok-cooked razor clams from the Washington coast served with asparagus and fermented black beans.

But most favorites, like drunken chicken, barbecued spare ribs with ginger-hoison sauce, and catfish claypot with coconut juice, have an older, if no longer straightforward, lineage. Dishes can come out over-seasoned, occasionally too sweet, but there's an underappreciated amount of talent here.

Brunch is among the best in the city: mix and match between traditional Vietnamese offerings like banh xeo (rice-flour crepes with pork belly and shrimp) or oxtail pho; a modest but excellent selection of dim sum; and "colony favorites" like Belgian waffles, pancakes, and baked eggs.

The interior is elegant enough to appease the wealthier crowd, but it's basically a fancy version of an I.D. joint: plain wooden tables and what looks like a designer's play on the padded black banquet chairs ubiquitous in Asian eateries. And the wine list is well-matched to the food, with plenty of aromatic wines to stand up to the Vietnamese fare.

A second location (out in Bellevue) called Monsoon East has accomplished the date night vibe with a more cohesive design, dimmer lighting, and gauzy white curtains cordoning off the main dining room.

Vietnamese
Upmarket restaurant

Bellevue
10245 Main St.
(425) 635-1112

Capitol Hill
615 19th Ave. E.
(206) 325-2111

Hours
Mon–Fri
11:30am–10:00pm
Sat–Sun
10:00am–10:00pm

Bar
Beer, wine

Credit cards
Visa, MC, AmEx

Reservations
Accepted

Features
Brunch
Date-friendly
Outdoor dining

Moshi Moshi

The rolls may not rock you, but the cocktails will

www.moshiseattle.com

Japanese
Upmarket restaurant

Ballard
5324 Ballard Ave.
(206) 971-7424

Hours
Sun–Thu
4:30pm–10:00pm
Fri–Sat
4:30pm–11:00pm

Bar
Beer, wine, liquor

Credit cards
Visa, MC

Reservations
Accepted

Features
Good cocktails

Most of the buzz surrounding Moshi Moshi is thanks to bartender Erik Carlson. The food is solid, the fish is fresh, and happy hour is great, but the only thing that makes this spot stand out from other good Seattle Japanese restaurants is the long menu of carefully balanced cocktails. The "Sweet Savage" (rye, aperol, maple, grapefruit) and the "Naughty Sven" (gin, aquavit, Cynar, amaro nonino, elderflower) are two highlights.

Moshi Moshi does a good job on snacks and cooked items (tempuras, short ribs, katsu); the kitchen also does oshizushi (sushi that is pressed together in a wooden box instead of wrapped in seaweed), which is something you don't see often. The long list of Japanese-American sushi rolls, on the other hand, can get a little fussy and lacking in subtlety; for example, rolls that include jalapeño (like the "Ginger-san," with avocado, hamachi, red jalapeño, cilantro, and ginger) always have too much of the pepper.

Except for a large artificial tree with LED cherry blossoms that looks like it's sprouting from the bar, the dining room is unmemorable, with white walls, light woods, and paper lanterns. Like so many Seattle restaurants, it makes some overtures toward being a special place, and then stops just short of fulfilling that goal—for example, that showcase tree has to compete for attention with a big-screen TV.

Mr. Gyros

Beautiful falafels cooked and served by
beautiful men

8.5	6.5
Food	Feel

$15
Price

www.mrgyroseattle.com

The local stroller brigade is obsessed with the young, strapping dark-haired men who run Mr. Gyros—and for good reason. The guys at this little Greenwood-area falafel joint are always ready with a charming smile and a quick quip with their regulars—and they cook up some delicious, inexpensive grub, too.

Seating is very limited—only a couple counter spots, and two sidewalk tables—and it's pretty dark and dim inside: the orangey-red walls (complete with Mr. Gyro T-shirts displayed for sale) contrast with the yellow awning outside. You order at the counter, off of the chalkboard menu.

The falafels at Mr. Gyros are fried light and airy, with a shatteringly crisp crust. Gyros are stuffed with slices of succulent chicken, lamb, or beef before being anointed with a tangy yogurt dressing.

They wrap it all up in a pita, and send you on your merry way back to the office with your portable meal in less than ten minutes. Have a bit more time? Savor your hummus plate—and the kitchen eye candy—at the lone sidewalk table. Seductive licking of baklava crumbs off your plate is entirely optional.

Middle Eastern
Counter service

Phinney Ridge
8411 Greenwood Ave.
N.
(206) 706-7472

Hours
Mon–Fri
11:30am–8:30pm
Sat
11:00am–3:00pm

Bar
None

Credit cards
Visa, MC

Features
Kid-friendly
Veg-friendly

Mulleady's

A surprisingly sophisticated gastro-menu
takes this Irish local to the next level

www.mulleadyspub.com

Irish
Casual restaurant

Queen Anne
3055 21st Ave. W.
(206) 283-8843

Hours
Mon–Fri
4:00pm–midnight
Sat–Sun
noon–midnight

Bar
Beer, wine, liquor

Credit cards
Visa, MC, AmEx

Reservations
Accepted

Features
Brunch
Kid-friendly
Outdoor dining

Mulleady's is an Irish pub with gastropub-like
aspirations. Sure, there are Irish favorites like
lamb stew, shepherd's pie, and Irish knockers
(those would-be Colcannon mashers with hard
cider beurre blanc). But, more interestingly, you
can also find specials like cider-braised pork
belly with apricot and cabbage tart.

Get past all the Irish offerings, and at the
bottom of the menu you'll find the Mulleady's
burger—the big reason why many dine here
regularly. It comes with a healthy portion of
fries, though note you can also get a separate
order of fries, complete with three sauces.
Service can be a tad slow, but simply another
reason to sit back, enjoy your beer, and
contemplate the next.

Decent food and decent drinks make this a
desirable neighborhood hangout. There's a
friendly feel with a cozy fireplace up front. Good
music reliably plays, sometimes live, and
Mulleady's also hosts trivia nights.

Oh…and might we mention that there's a
lounge-sized urinal in the men's bathroom?
Good information if you're a guy who's doing a
good amount of drinking.

Nettletown

Asian-tinged Swiss food that will charm you in a cute, woodsy lunch spot

7.5	7.0
Food	Feel

$20
Price

www.nettletown.com

If you're one of those gamines who wishes she lived inside the pages of a dreamy Anthropologie catalogue, you'll love Nettletown: the walls at this seven-table, robin's-egg-blue eatery are painted with a cutesy woodland-theme. A manly man with a predilection for extremely manly interiors might feel uncomfortable here whilst awaiting his elk meatball sandwich. (And he'll have to wait, too—the kitchen takes its slow, sweet time.) Those meatballs are subtly accented with lemongrass, freshened with a tangle of vegetables and garden herbs, and served on chewy Le Fournil baguette. It's seriously good. So good that Mr. Manly Man might just acquiesce to crossing his legs demurely and sipping tea after lunch.

Nettletown's charms don't end with the signature sandwich. The short Swiss- and Asian-inspired menu is a reflection of chef Christina Choi's heritage. There's knöpfle (Swiss spaetzle with cabbage and leeks), "Nettletown Noodles" with greens, seasoned wild mushrooms, tea eggs, and tofu, and a small selection of sweets like hazelnut tea cookies and cardamom huckleberry bread pudding. Generally, the food is great, if minimally seasoned. (Salt hounds like us make quick friends with the free and extensive Asian condiments bar.) If this all sounds swell, then grab your jauntiest chapeau, and daintily splish-splash your way down to Nettletown.

Modern
Casual restaurant

Eastlake
2238 Eastlake Ave. E.
(206) 588-3607

Hours
Tue–Thu
11:00am–3:00pm
Fri
11:00am–3:00pm
6:00pm–10:00pm
Sat
10:00am–3:00pm
6:00pm–10:00pm
Sun
10:00am–3:00pm

Bar
Beer, wine

Credit cards
Visa, MC

Reservations
Not accepted

Features
Brunch
Veg-friendly

Nishino

Save your omakase splurge, and skip the
competent but overrated Japanese fusion

www.nishinorestaurant.com

Japanese
Upmarket restaurant

Madison Park
3130 E. Madison St.
(206) 322-5800

Hours
Mon–Sat
5:30pm–10:00pm
Sun
5:00pm–9:30pm

Bar
Beer, wine, liquor

Credit cards
Visa, MC, AmEx

Reservations
Accepted

Nishino fills the dubious Nobu knock-off role
with a dated upscale vibe, service that favors
regulars to the exclusion of other diners, and a
pricey menu that is far too fusion-focused to
compete with the simpler sushi joints. We have
a hard time understanding why this place is
consistently rated tops for Japanese in some
publications.

It's not that the sushi here is bad—you won't
usually get a bad piece of fish, and one or two
dishes might knock your socks off. Amberjack,
yellowtail, mackerel, sardine, and eel tend to be
top-notch. It's just that the whole experience of
dining at Nishino is so uninspiring that there's
no reason to splash out here, at these prices,
when you can get far more satisfying meals at
places like Kisaku and Shiro's.

Nishino's omakase is dominated more by
fusion dishes (overcooked wild salmon, etc.)
than by sushi, and the sushi that does come
along may include something as banal as a
massive tamago-wrapped crab and shrimp roll.
Where's the interesting local fish, the
regionality, the uniqueness? In the words of
Stephen Malkmus, where is the danger?

It seems that here, "interesting" is something
meted out in respectable portions, like a tiny
dollop of wasabi. Hence the "daring" Fay Jones
paintings hanging in an otherwise sterile room
fit for a business lunch.

Noodle Boat

This authentic Thai is definitely worth the drive to Issaquah

9.0	7.0
Food	Feel

$25
Price

www.noodleboat.com

Issaquah may seem like an unnecessary schlep when within the city limits the ratio of Seattleites to Thai restaurants has to be about 5:1. But make no mistake: that extra 15 or 20 minutes in the car is the only reason Noodle Boat isn't on everyone's top-10 lists.

The food here is authentic: there's a grandma in the kitchen. Instead of settling on reasonable facsimiles of ingredients, the family makes a year's worth of chili paste during annual trips home to Thailand. The little details that fall by the wayside in high-turnover Thai joints are never overlooked; mieng kum, for instance—a must-order appetizer—comes with traditional cha plu leaves instead of the spinach leaves often substituted. On the spice scale, four stars might actually approximate "Thai spicy," and asking for anything above that will have you sweating like a BP shareholder.

Noodle Boat is nothing fancy, but it's hardly a hole in the wall. Presentations are beautiful and sometimes a little whimsical: pumpkin curry comes in a ceramic pumpkin, and the menus, in bound books with 3D elephants on the covers, make you feel like you're about to read a wonderful fairytale about a princess who has her mouth seared out by a sadistic Thai cook, and then falls into a wonderful food coma.

Thai
Casual restaurant

Eastside
700 NW Gilman Blvd.
(425) 391-8096

Hours
Mon–Thu
11:00am–2:30pm
5:00pm–8:45pm
Fri
11:00am–2:30pm
5:00pm–9:15pm
Sat
5:00pm–9:15pm
Sun
5:00pm–8:30pm

Bar
Beer, wine

Credit cards
Visa, MC

Reservations
Accepted

Features
Veg-friendly

6.0	8.5
Food	Feel

$30	6.0
Price	Wine

Ocho

They get the taverna part right, if not the actual tapas

www.ochoballard.com

Spanish
Casual restaurant

Ballard
2325 NW Market St.
(206) 784-0699

Hours
Mon–Fri
4:00pm–2:00am
Sat–Sun
noon–2:00am

Bar
Beer, wine, liquor

Credit cards
Visa, MC

Reservations
Not accepted

Ocho is the kind of fun, cozy corner bar at which you can lose all track of time. Gazing at the rectangular bar with its DIY wine racks, the small partially open kitchen, and the chalkboard of Spanish tapas, it's easy to forget that if you scooted your chair back too far, you'd end up on drab Market Street.

The tapas menu has so much potential, and although some standards like coca con jamón (similar to pan con tomate with Serrano ham) are perfectly satisfying, many of the selections fall short on authenticity. Patatas bravas, a favorite comfort food (potatoes drizzled in aïoli and a hot sauce that should ideally blend together seamlessly) come out more like fries slathered with competing tartar and tabasco sauces. Generally speaking, if you've eaten tapas in Spain, you'll be disappointed. But Ocho seems to appeal to a predominantly younger crowd that hasn't yet gotten snobbish about their post-grad year in *Barthelona*.

The beer list needs a few tweaks—especially on the domestic side. And the wine list is just lazy, way too short. But mixed drinks and sangría are good, and if you lower your expectations a bit on the food, this is a fine place to carouse the night away.

Oddfellows Café

Great as a glorified coffee shop or eclectic Capitol Hill watering hole

6.0 Food

9.0 Feel

$40 Price

www.oddfellowscafe.com

Oddfellows occupies a historic building in one of the coolest corners of the Hill, next to Elliott Bay Book Company and Easy Street Records. And the space, although maddeningly echoey and loud at times, has style in spades: rustic worn woods, exposed bulbs, and a few artifacts from the original hall.

Oddfellows undergoes constant transformation throughout the day. It starts as a sunny order-at-the-counter café. Later, the lights dim, the chatter gets louder, the bartenders stop pulling espresso shots, and the smell of cooking meat fills the air. The menu throughout the day is simple, seasonal, elevated pub grub—expect a lot of dishes to be served on rustic breads.

Over time, the quality and consistency of the food has slipped somewhat. Sometimes you'll still get something really great, like expertly prepared roast chicken or a nicely balanced charcuterie platter, but other times the formerly formidable pork sandwich might underwhelm. Either way, the food is overpriced ($9 for a butter lettuce salad with Goddess dressing?).

The best thing to do is not to take Oddfellows too seriously. Stick to the coffee and the pastry case (we go out of our way for the treats here). Or stick to the drinking: there's a great beer selection, with many Eastern European brews, giving you one more reason to spend time hanging out in this weird, wonderful environment.

American
Casual restaurant

Capitol Hill
1525 10th Ave.
(206) 325-0807

Hours
Mon–Thu
8:00am–11:00pm
Fri–Sat
8:00am–1:00am
Sun
8:00am–11:00pm

Bar
Beer, wine, liquor

Credit cards
Visa, MC, AmEx

Reservations
Accepted

Features
Good beers
Outdoor dining
Wi-Fi

8.5 Food | 9.5 Feel

$55 Price | 8.0 Wine

Olivar

Delicious French-inflected Spanish food served in an Art-Nouveau wonderland

www.olivarrestaurant.com

**Spanish
French**
Upmarket restaurant

Capitol Hill
806 E. Roy St.
(206) 322-0409

Hours
Tue–Thu
5:00pm–10:00pm
Fri–Sat
5:00pm–11:00pm
Sun
5:00pm–10:00pm

Bar
Beer, wine, liquor

Credit cards
Visa, MC

Reservations
Essential

Features
Brunch
Date-friendly
Veg-friendly

Harvest Vine's only serious competition in the arena of creative Spanish tapas, Olivar gains the slight advantage for consistency—and for providing a space that's actually pleasant to dine in.

Olivar is a beautiful restaurant. It's in the Loveless Building, a Tudor country manor in the midst of Capitol Hill. The interior is fairly simple but for one unique embellishment: dreamy Art Nouveau murals (remnants of a former restaurant that used to occupy the space) that depict a story by Alexander Pushkin.

Chef Philippe Thomelin spent as much time in Spain as he did in his home of France, and both countries are represented on a menu that is both creative and robust. For example, Serrano ham comes with Mahón gougères instead of Spanish cheese. Even dishes with the most basic of descriptions will likely be a complex blend of flavors; "Brussels sprouts" are halved, stuffed, roasted, and served with duck confit and a tomato-herb compote.

The restaurant isn't cheap, but in the spirit of the comfortable neighborhood restaurants in France and Spain that it's trying to imitate, Olivar has a very affordable wine list—not particularly deep, but with plenty of good pairings.

Osteria La Spiga

A pretty Italian restaurant that has been undershooting its Iron Chef expectations

7.0 Food

7.5 Feel

$50 Price

www.laspiga.com

It seems that La Spiga was the talk of the town when it opened in its current location, with patrons raving about the beautiful space. But just as quickly, people started complaining about poor service.

The chef got great recognition when she appeared as a contestant on Iron Chef America, and while that star quality flashes itself from time to time at La Spiga, it's of course harder to shine so brightly on a day-to-day basis, and perhaps almost impossible to live up to the expectations that television creates. Sometimes the food sparkles, as in insalata mista della casa, pastas with truffle butter sauce, and gnocchi al pomodoro. But small portions and poor service sometimes take the shine off.

The bar is a fine place for a friendly chat and an apéritif. We also like the courtyard area, especially if you can enjoy it at one of the restaurant's special events, such as its annual Ferragosto party. If immediate expectations can be a curse, they certainly do not prevent longevity and consistency from emerging over time, and we still have high hopes for the potential of this Italian kitchen.

Italian
Upmarket restaurant

Capitol Hill
1429 12th Ave.
(206) 323-8881

Hours
Sun–Thu
5:00pm–11:00pm
Fri–Sat
5:00pm–midnight

Bar
Beer, wine, liquor, BYO

Credit cards
Visa, MC, AmEx

Reservations
Accepted

Features
Date-friendly
Live music
Outdoor dining
Veg-friendly

Other Coast Café

A little bit of both coasts between bread in a simple, welcoming daytime deli

www.othercoastcafe.com

Sandwiches
Counter service

Ballard
5315 Ballard Ave. NW
(206) 789-0936

Hours
Daily
10:30am–6:00pm

Bar
None

Credit cards
None

Features
Kid-friendly

Somewhat ironically, the Other Coast Café—whose name is a comment on the East Coast's smug insistence that it's the only shoreline that matters—makes overstuffed East Coast-style deli sandwiches.

Most sandwiches here don't get any more complex than roast beef with horseradish, but there are a few standout signature creations, like the horribly named "Mantooth" (capicola, Swiss, and cherry peppers that are just spicy enough to make things interesting) and the controversial "Ragin' Cajun." The latter either gets rave reviews or derision—it's either the second coming or a turkey sandwich with gloopy chipotle mayo.

There are minor missteps here and there—the Italiano (roast beef, salami, and provolone) sometimes has so much balsamic vinegar that the grape-must vapors overwhelm the thing (and anyway, balsamic vinegar doesn't belong in a deli sandwich). But generally speaking, Other Coast is a reliable spot for a simple, tasty lunch.

Many of the delis are more pleasant places to eat at than Other Coast. The deli has a reasonably welcoming staff, although a few of them are cocky young kids who act like the customers are crashing their party—but when it gets busy and the line starts to wind its way through the place, things get miserable. During lunch rushes, call ahead, or you might be waiting in line until your kids graduate from college.

Pair

A romantic place to sip wine, eat cheese, and discuss the over-globalized menu

7.5	8.5
Food	Feel

$50	8.0
Price	Wine

www.pairseattle.com

Tucked away in residential Ravenna, this cozy French- and Mediterranean-inspired eatery is a good place for a quiet, romantic meal. The food isn't mind-blowing, but paired (sorry) with pleasant service and good wines, it's good enough—everything adds up to a perfectly lovely evening.

Sturdy bistro dishes are served as small plates, which is a little odd, if not unwelcome. The menu changes seasonally, but it's best when it sticks to simpler salads and French standards like steak frites. Otherwise, "European-inspired" can translate to "random": smoked wild salmon toasts, Moroccan lamb with minted yogurt, and gougères all on the same menu? Still, the execution is mostly there.

The wine list is very good, with Oregon, Washington, and France all well represented, but you'll definitely need your server's help in pairing wines with whatever dinner you end up constructing from this muddle.

Since the cheese plate is great—and generous—sticking to a few very light bites, a few glasses of wine, and maybe dessert, is probably the way to experience Pair.

Modern
Upmarket restaurant

Ravenna
5501 30th Ave. NE
(206) 526-7655

Hours
Tue–Sat
5:00pm–10:00pm

Bar
Beer, wine, liquor

Credit cards
Visa, MC

Reservations
Not accepted

Features
Date-friendly

8.0	8.5
Food	Feel
$55	6.5
Price	Wine

Palace Kitchen

The grande dame of an expanding empire who can still be counted on for innovation

www.tomdouglas.com

Modern
Upmarket restaurant

Belltown
2030 5th Ave.
(206) 448-2001

Hours
Daily
5:00pm–1:00am

Bar
Beer, wine, liquor

Credit cards
Visa, MC, AmEx

Reservations
Not accepted

Features
Date-friendly

As the flagship restaurant of the Tom Douglas empire, Palace Kitchen does show its age, but in a graceful way. The cool retro-looking neon sign and the huge U-shaped bar in the center of the dining room make it impossible to pass by the place without peeking inside. This is a tried-and-true Belltown watering hole, untouched by passing trends and seemingly without an agenda or niche.

A great bar deserves a good happy hour, and Palace Kitchen has theirs dialed in, with draft beers, sangría, and reliable small plates like barbecue pork short ribs and tarragon onion rings with rose-harissa mayo. (A great bar also deserves a wine list with more range, but at least there are some decent Northwest bottles.) You can do a modified happy hour off the dinner menu, too, since some of the favorites here—olive poppers, chicken wings, and Penn Cove clams—are starters.

An applewood-fired grill fills the restaurant with a sweet, soothing scent, and while the kitchen sometimes bumbles around with, say, goat cheese-and-lavender fondue or seasonal ravioli, it's comforting to know that you can always get something simple and good from the grillmasters. The inimitable restaurateur's signature coconut cream pie is always on the dessert menu, too, which means you don't have to suffer through an evening at Dahlia Lounge to try it.

Pan Africa

Ethiopian and more in a touristy but
comforting bistro setting

7.5	8.5
Food	Feel

$30
Price

www.panafricamarket.com

Pan Africa serves fancy versions of food we're
accustomed to eating with our hands. Indeed, it
can feel strange eating lentils and injera with
utensils sitting next to you, but Pan Africa isn't
the place to try if you want a hidden gem to
brag about.

Since it's the Pike Place Market crowd they're
feeding, prices are a tad higher than they are at
other restaurants serving similar dishes. But Pan
Africa is a really great way to sample Ethiopian
food (which dominates the menu), plus some of
the continent's other greatest hits, along with
some good South African wines. The menu
explains each of the dishes well.

Sambusas, lamb and groundnut stews, all
manner of meat and veg in piri piri sauce, and
plenty of vegetarian and vegan options make up
the core of the menu. Mango-pineapple curry is
one standout. Brunch items are bit more global,
but even frittatas and other standard brunch
items tend to have some African influences like
injera stuffing and berbere-chicken sausage.

During the day, the colorful space is a sight
for SAD eyes—this is a go-to spot for Seattleites
who need a little culinary comfort midwinter. At
night, candles and a blue-lit bar add a bit of
casual sophistication to the Market scene.

Pan-African
Casual restaurant

Downtown
1521 1st Ave.
(206) 652-2461

Hours
Tue–Fri
11:00am–3:00pm
5:00pm–9:00pm
Sat–Sun
10:00am–2:00pm
5:00pm–9:00pm

Bar
Beer, wine, liquor, BYO

Credit cards
Visa, MC

Reservations
Accepted

Features
Brunch
Outdoor dining
Veg-friendly

Paseo

The pork at this tin shack is the best thing between slices of bread in Seattle

www.paseoseattle.com

Sandwiches
Counter service

Fremont
4225 Fremont Ave. N.
(206) 545-7440

Ballard
6226 Seaview Ave. NW
(206) 789-3100

Hours
Tue–Fri
11:00am–9:00pm
Sat
11:00am–8:00pm

Bar
None

Credit cards
None

Features
Veg-friendly

Shove a huge pile of expertly grilled pork, thick-cut caramelized onions, jalapeños, and cilantro into a Macrina Bakery baguette slathered in garlicky mayo, and you've got the five-napkin enterprise that is Paseo's signature sandwich.

Most people order the original beast or Paseo's slight twist on a typical Cuban sandwich, but the menu includes everything from garlicky seared scallops or tofu to the "Onion Obsession," which is simply those melt-in-the-mouth caramelized onions with some tapenade and cilantro on a baguette. And the gluten-free needn't rend their garments: all of the sandwich fillings, plus a few other options (like black tiger prawns in a spicy red sauce), come as mains with vegetarian black beans, corn on the cob, and a salad topped with pickled beets and cabbage.

The Fremont location is a cross between a rehabbed shipping container and an opened sardine tin: the silver shack has barely enough room for the bustling kitchen and five tables. When the place is slammed, it's not a very relaxing place for a sit-down; patrons perch on curbs, eat in cars, or take their food down the street to the Buckaroo Tavern.

Pearl

Good, upscale Northwest food—surprising
for a place that feels more like a nightclub

7.0 Food

5.5 Feel

$60 Price

www.pearlbellevue.com

Oh goodness. The designers just didn't forget
anything. Cherry wood, biomorphic glass
sculptures, red banquettes, black gauzy curtains,
pendant lamps that look like smooth disco balls
or silver Christmas tree ornaments, white
tablecloths, frosted glass—they seem to have
torn a page from every dance club and hotel
lobby from New York to Moscow. Pearl is one
of the ugliest restaurants in Bellevue, but it
succeeds at creating that general swanky feel
needed to support a thriving bar scene, so fair
play to them.

With such eclectic décor, Pearl's
straightforward, steakhouse take on Northwest
classics is surprising—this is the type of place
where you might expect a menu riddled with
molecular gastronomy. Instead, the menu is
simple and well prepared, with occasional Asian
and Italian influences popping up now and
again. Starters are the usual upscale Northwest
hodge-podge of Penn Cove mussels, sliders, foie
gras, and salads. Mains are a mix of risotto and
pasta dishes, chops and ribs, though
occasionally things get Pan-Asian, as in the
excellent house specialty sablefish in a honey-
miso sauce with namya broth.

There are several different dining areas, with
a late-night happy hour keeping the lounge
packed on weekends. On the other end of the
spectrum, there's a chef's table for those who
would rather focus on the food than on
flirtation.

Modern
Upmarket restaurant

Bellevue
700 Bellevue Way NE,
Suite 50
(425) 455-0181

Hours
Mon–Tue
11:00am–2:30pm
4:00pm–9:00pm
Wed–Sat
11:00am–2:30pm
4:00pm–10:00pm
Sun
2:00pm–9:00pm

Bar
Beer, wine, liquor

Credit cards
Visa, MC, AmEx

Reservations
Accepted

Features
Date-friendly

<table>
<tr><td>8.0
Food</td><td>5.5
Feel</td></tr>
</table>

Pho Bac

Seattle's O.G. pho joint

$10
Price

Vietnamese
Casual restaurant

International District
1314 S. Jackson St.
(206) 323-4387

International District
415 7th Ave. S.
(206) 621-0532

Downtown
811 Stewart St.
(206) 621-8816

Beacon Hill
3300 Rainier Ave. S.
(206) 725-4418

Hours
Daily
8:00am–9:00pm
Hours vary by location

Bar
None

Credit cards
Visa, MC

Reservations
Not accepted

Features
Kid-friendly

Once upon a time, there were no pho shops in Seattle. When Pho Bac opened its purple doors decades ago, it drew in pioneering spirits who had never heard of the now-ubiquitous cheap lunch and cold remedy. Today Pho Bac could hardly have any more competition (unless it were a Thai restaurant, perhaps), and it's become its own mini-chain.

But the flagship shack is a piece of Seattle history, and the pho being served there is still way above average. Pho Bac's broth has some nice umami flavor, and the restaurant also seems to be a bit choosier than the other cheap spots about all the ingredients that go into the broth. Tendon, tripe, beef brisket, and meatballs are all tender, and you can get them all in one bowl.

The other branches serve the same menu in pleasantly nondescript digs—if the Jackson Street location skeeves you out, the nicest branch is the one on 7th in the heart of the I.D.

Pho Than Brothers

The Quiznos of downmarket pho chains,
going gently downhill but still serviceable

6.5 Food

4.0 Feel

$10 Price

www.thanbrothers.com

Eleven branches and counting—when we hear
"pho," Than Brothers is the first thing that
comes to mind, whether we like it or not. It's
more of a conglomeration than a chain; feel
varies greatly from shop to shop. The older
branches are marked by cracked vinyl booths,
iffy bathrooms, and a sense of despair, whereas
newer spots, like Ballard's, have that shiny
sterility we'd expect in a franchise: white
tablecloths still white; garish turquoise banquet
chairs still retaining their fresh-from-the-factory
puff.

The quality of the pho (about the only item
on the menu) varies, too. Aurora Avenue and U
District branches have better broth than, say,
Ballard. In some bizarre Dorian Gray trade-off,
both the broth and the noodles seem to have
shrunk in size with each new opening. But
when Than Brothers started, it was turning out
some fantastic pho, so declining quality
notwithstanding, this still remains a reliable—
not to mention convenient—choice. After all, no
matter where you are in the city, there has to be
one nearby.

Vietnamese
Casual restaurant

Ballard
2021 NW Market St.
(206) 782-5715

University District
4207 University Way NE
(206) 632-7272

Green Lake
7714 Aurora Ave. N.
(206) 527-5973

More locations
and features at
fearlesscritic.com

Hours
Daily
10:00am–9:00pm

Bar
None

Credit cards
Visa, MC

Reservations
Not accepted

Features
Kid-friendly

<table>
<tr><td>**7.5**
Food</td><td>**6.0**
Feel</td></tr>
</table>

Picnic

The antithesis of potato salad and Fresca

<table>
<tr><td>**$15**
Price</td><td>**7.0**
Wine</td></tr>
</table>

www.picnicseattle.com

Sandwiches
Café

Phinney Ridge
6801 Greenwood Ave.
N.
(206) 453-5867

Hours
Wed–Sat
11:00am–6:00pm
Sun
noon–5:00pm

Bar
Beer, wine

Credit cards
Visa, MC, AmEx

Features
Kid-friendly
Outdoor dining

Is there anything that shouts "urban privilege" more than a boutique deli predicated on the ideal picnic? Picnic's overly earnest mission statement to free charcuterie from the trappings of the traditional restaurant is a little hard to take, but kudos to the shop for putting everything in one place—you'd have a hard time constructing a more pretentious spread without having to stop at four or five different specialty stores.

Top-quality cured meats and artisan cheeses are available by the pound or in simple sandwiches like mortadella and Fontina, or house-made corned beef and Comté on rye. Quiche, seasonal salads (including an excellent and light chicken salad—no mayo), and soups can also be ordered for take-out. Everything emphasizes seasonal, and when possible, local ingredients. The boutique side of Picnic includes a good, but expensive, selection of wine.

Whether you take your lunch to an area park or just scarf it down at one of the few seats, you'll have a lot to tell your therapist later. If you've got blue-collar roots, then watching all the moms buzz around this cozy den of Euro-sleek, locally sourced smugness is bound to unearth feelings of rage regarding all the peanut butter and jelly sandwiches and Fritos you had to endure as a child during real family picnics. Be sure to take home some ragù or braised short ribs to comfort you later.

Pike Place Chowder

Not as touristy as it sounds, not as great as it claims

6.5	4.0
Food	Feel

$10
Price

www.pikeplacechowder.com

This shopping-mall-ish soup emporium claims to serve Seattle's best chowder, which, while not completely unfounded, is a bit of an overstatement. This is in fact tourist food. Exhibit A: bread bowls. Exhibit B: location, which depending on the branch is either next to the buskers populating Post Alley or in a food court at Pacific Place Mall. Exhibit C: prices.

Pike Place makes very creamy, New England-style chowder—basically stock, heavy cream, and salt, with clams or seasonal Northwest swimmers. It's an elemental flavor and texture mix that's hard to argue with, and if you try, you might find yourself just gulping it down rather than pointing out supposed flaws. (There's a vegan chowder, too, with vegetables and coconut milk, although it must be crushing to decline the bread bowl.) Seafood is also good in sandwich form—wild salmon, for example, is pan-fried crispy, sealing a nice softness within.

Obvious care goes into Pike Place's offerings—hot pepper sherry on the tables is a nice touch—but the place falters quite a bit. For example, the aforementioned salmon sandwich is paired with clumpy, too thick, and ill-distributed lemon-caper mayo. And the house salad is just boring—iceberg and romaine drowned in supermarket-caliber dressing.

The sampler of four five-ounce cups of chowder is your best bet, as it's enough food for two people and allows you to try the daily specials, indulge in the creamy New England clam chowder, and then chase it with something a little lighter.

Seafood
Counter service

Downtown
Pacific Place Mall, 600 Pine St.
(206) 838-5680

Downtown
1530 Post Alley
(206) 267-2537

Hours
Daily
11:00am–5:00pm

Bar
Beer, wine

Credit cards
Visa, MC, AmEx

Features
Kid-friendly
Outdoor dining

Pike Street Fish Fry

A great example of how to riff on comfort food without making a mockery of it

www.pikestreetfishfry.com

Seafood
Counter service

Capitol Hill
925 E. Pike St.
(206) 329-7453

Hours
Sun–Wed
11:30am–midnight
Thu–Sat
11:30am–2:30am

Bar
Beer, wine

Credit cards
Visa, MC

This cheerful caesura can fry the hell out of fish. Perhaps not the most stunning proclamation considering the eatery's name, but with the menu ever-expanding to include that which is not fried fish, we must warn you away from those other choices. Don't order the pulled-pork sandwich unless you like the idea of eating soggy, only vaguely porky, salt-and-vinegar potato chips. If you want Field Roast, head to Po Dog.

But halibut, cod, catfish, calamari, and anything on the daily specials board are all fresh and flavorful here. Coatings vary from beer batter to Panko bread crumbs to cornmeal, but Pike Street gets the ratios right each time— there's enough breading for a satisfying crunch, but not so much redundant batter and half-fried detritus that you're full before you hit the fish. The choice between a sandwich or a pile of crispy hand-cut fries is a tough one: rolls are from Macrina Bakery and are good vessels for the fish, tangy slaw, and aïoli. If you can handle even more fried stuff, the tempura-like fried vegetables are excellent.

It's clean and kind of cute inside, but it is also very small, sometimes a little warm, and often full of fryer fumes. (Some of us love that, though.) Also, if you belly up to the counter, you have watch hipster waifs smoke cigarettes while pretending to ignore the tour buses parked in front of Neumo's.

Pink Door

Good Italian food, even better entertainment

7.0	9.0
Food	Feel
$50	**8.0**
Price	Wine

www.thepinkdoor.net

The Pink Door is a Seattle institution. It's tucked into the chaos of the Pike Place Market area and offers Cirque-du-Soleil fun—an energetic, dreamlike experience punctuated with good food and drinks and happy people.

There are two good ways to experience the Pink Door. You can give into the spectacle and dine on one of the cabaret nights, or, if you don't like the idea of some flexible stranger sweating into your bassoon, come for lunch when you can sit at the bar or on the patio in peace. If it's wine you're after, the list here is nice, with the standard Seattle focus on Italy and the Pacific Northwest.

Not every dish at The Pink Door is great, but the kitchen does wonders with seafood and makes a consistently perfect lasagne. Pappardelle al ragù bolognese has delicate folds of wide egg noodles with just enough meat sauce clinging to them, plus curls of shaved reggiano. The risotto—recipes change often—can be a thing of beauty: for example, creamy yet distinct grains of rice floating in a supple butternut sauce with crisp ribbons of shaved fennel. But who cares about the risotto's texture when there's a stunningly attractive trapeze artist hanging upside down above your table?

Italian
Casual restaurant

Downtown
1919 Post Alley
(206) 443-3241

Hours
Mon–Thu
11:00am–10:00pm
Fri–Sat
11:30am–11:00pm
Sun
4:00pm–10:00pm

Bar
Beer, wine, liquor

Credit cards
Visa, MC, AmEx

Reservations
Accepted

Features
Date-friendly
Live music
Outdoor dining
Veg-friendly

Piroshky Piroshky

Happy stomach bombs served by sweet
Russian ladies

www.piroshkybakery.com

Russian
Counter service

Downtown
1908 Pike Pl.
(206) 441-6068

Hours
Daily
8:00am–6:30pm
Hours may vary
seasonally

Bar
None

Credit cards
Visa, MC

Features
Kid-friendly
Veg-friendly

Piroshky Piroshky will take years off of your life.
Not only are its delicious wares the things heart
attacks are made of—the easiest way to locate
this place is to follow the smell of butter—but
the cortisol your body releases while you're
braving the Pike Place Market crowds is bound
to take its toll as well.

But once you're inside this little shop (this
often involves waiting in a very long line), the
smells, sounds, and sights of those delightful
little pastries being patted and stacked will lull
you into a more meditative state. A popular
strategy is to choose one savory piroshky and
one sweet one. The simple ones—beef and
cheese, potato and cheese, or apple-
cinnamon—are best, but there are more
Northwesty options, too, like smoked salmon or
coffee-cinnamon.

If you suspect your piroshky has been sitting
out for a while, it's worth waiting for a new
batch to come out of the oven—when piroshky
aren't fresh, they turn into unyielding dough
balls.

Plum Bistro

Not as good as Sutra, but a sure step up for vegan cuisine

8.0	8.0
Food	Feel

$40	7.0
Price	Wine

www.plumbistroseattle.com

Plum serves vegan food with bold flavors—perhaps a few too many flavors. The chef's almost single-minded mission is to prove that vegan cuisine isn't bland. She accomplishes this admirably by focusing on Southern, Caribbean, Southwestern, and Latin influences.

Jalapeños do a lot of the heavy lifting (as in chili-crusted seitan, for example), as do citrusy notes, and at times both are overpowering. But given the history of vegan-only restaurants, it's nice to see someone err in this direction. There is tofu and tempeh and seitan in every conceivable form, but dishes tend to shine most when steering away from the processed-soy products: (huge) salads, seasonal soups, and sides like fried green tomatoes are usually excellent. Pastas fare well, too; eggplant linguini comes together beautifully with its jalapeño-vodka sauce. If you have non-vegans in tow, brunch is your best bet, as everyone can appreciate mofongo or banana pancakes.

People often describe Plum as upscale, and it is. It's contemporary and grownup, with concrete walls and candlelight, but the space still feels earthy and, at least during the day, shorts-and-sandals casual. In summer, the big garage doors roll up, which makes Plum a nice place for a glass of wine. The list here takes on the additional challenge of pairing wines with all vegan dishes, and mostly does a good job within those requirements; some surprising choices make for good matches. Prices are just a bit on the higher side, but not overwhelmingly so.

Vegefusion
Casual restaurant

Capitol Hill
1429 12th Ave.
(206) 838-5333

Hours
Mon–Fri
9:00am–10:30pm
Sat–Sun
10:00am–10:30pm

Bar
Beer, wine, liquor

Credit cards
Visa, MC, AmEx

Reservations
Accepted

Features
Brunch
Date-friendly
Veg-friendly
Wi-Fi

7.0 | 6.5 | Po Dog

Food | Feel

$10

Price

Fancy franks, for better or for worse

www.podogs.com

American
Counter service

Capitol Hill
1009 E. Union St.
(206) 325-6055

Hours
Mon–Thu
11:00am–midnight
Fri–Sat
11:00am–2:30am
Sun
11:00am–10:00pm

Bar
Beer

Credit cards
Visa, MC, AmEx

Features
Kid-friendly

There's no type of comfort food that Seattle chefs won't try to tart up. Po Dog's gourmet hot dogs are covered in more flair than a drag performer five minutes before curtain.

There's some fun stuff on the menu: an egg-roll-wrapped dog on a bed of red cabbage; a Field Roast dog that's arguably even better than the standard beef one; the "Morning Glory," which is basically a hot dog wrapped in breakfast; crispy and tasty McDonald's-style fries and even tastier (albeit greasier) house-made chips.

Most franks are served on a Macrina brioche bun, which is so soft and fluffy it's the bread equivalent of a Samoyed; however, the eggy, slightly sweet flavor can make some flavor combinations a little too rich. Also, although Po Dog has an excellent field roast wiener plus Uli's sausages on hand, their beef hot dogs are Hebrew National. So, if you've ever been to a barbecue, you can actually imagine exactly what each concoction tastes like.

Inside, we don't know how these folks settled on this particular version of industrial/hipster chic. It's what we imagine a hot dog joint in *A Clockwork Orange* would look like, except that instead of a bunch of mannequins decorating the place, there's a wall-sized photo of a pug licking its terrible little mouth.

Poppy

This Pacific Northwest take on nouvelle
Indian delivers on fun—and, usually, flavor

8.5	8.0
Food	Feel

$55	8.0
Price	Wine

www.poppyseattle.com

Obvious nods to Indian food (onion-poppy naan
and batata wada (potato fritters) share the table
with Pacific Northwest offerings (lavender duck
leg or stinging nettle soup), and it all adds up to
something that feels completely new. So does
the ordering system here, which is, to put it
charitably, a bit bewildering. A thali consists of
ten small plates; combined with an appetizer
and a dessert thali (which is a must), it's enough
food for two.

That said, many of us prefer the pared-down
happy-hour menus that focus on snacks like
virtually perfect eggplant fries drizzled with
honey and sprinkled with coarse salt, or
"naanwiches" stuffed with duck or beef cheeks.
But the thali is a big part of why Poppy works.
The chef can play around, customers can test-
drive new flavors, and none of this requires a
major financial or philosophical commitment. A
relatively small but creative wine list makes for
some great choices—you'll find yourself
wanting to select multiple wines to meet up
with all of the flavors of the food.

Poppy's design is controversial. None of us
can describe the bright oranges and blonde
wood without evoking IKEA. Fun and cute is an
appropriate vibe for this restaurant, but the big
round polka dots, the slashes of color, and the
simple squat furniture make us wonder if
crayons and a coloring-book place mat should
come with each thali. It's the constant buzz of
people, really, that keeps the atmosphere
feeling cool. And they come (and come back)
for good reason.

Modern Indian
Upmarket restaurant

Capitol Hill
622 Broadway E.
(206) 324-1108

Hours
Tue–Thu
5:00pm–11:00pm
Fri–Sat
5:00pm–midnight
Sun
5:00pm–10:00pm

Bar
Beer, wine, liquor

Credit cards
Visa, MC, AmEx

Reservations
Essential

Features
Date-friendly
Veg-friendly

Quinn's Pub

An amazing beer list to wash down
gastropub grub

www.quinnspubseattle.com

Modern
Casual restaurant

Capitol Hill
1001 E. Pike St.
(206) 325-7711

Hours
Mon–Thu
3:00pm–midnight
Fri–Sat
3:00pm–1:00am
Sun
5:00pm–10:30pm

Bar
Beer, wine, liquor

Credit cards
Visa, MC, AmEx

Reservations
Not accepted

Features
Good beers

Although it's always obnoxiously crowded and
the food seems to be on a continuous
downward spiral, Quinn's still holds a few of us
in its thrall, in part because of one of the best
draft beer lists in Seattle; the list is well thought
out, with plenty of international brews and local
faves, plus outstanding rotating IPAs and
Belgians. House-made pretzels with Welsh
rarebit and the house-made potato chips are
consummate beer food.

As far as the interior goes, Quinn's is the
perfect gastropub—a long wrap-around bar and
dark wood tables against huge windows on the
ground floor, and a cozier loft area close to the
exposed beams. Service is friendly, engaging,
and insightful—don't be shy about asking for
beer advice—and the place gets a nice cross-
section of Capitol Hill's evening revelers.

As far as the menu goes, Quinn's often
becomes a caricature of a gastropub, in which
novelty is substituted for good sense. The menu
has, at one point, included foie gras with funnel
cake—a combination that's definitely indulgent,
debatedly delicious. We also like the simple
meaty preps here. Brandade (whipped salt cod
with potato) is perhaps the most successful
amongst gastropub offerings, but a burger,
marrow bones, or wild boar sloppy joe are some
of the best.

Ray's Boathouse

4.0 Food
8.0 Feel

A popular tourist trap with a magnificient view that almost justifies the bad seafood

$65 Price

www.rays.com

If you live in Seattle long enough you'll hear rumors that Ray's used to be a real restaurant—the Canlis of Ballard, if you will—offering an upscale Northwest fare with incredible views. Either that was an urban legend, or boy, have times changed.

But let's start with the positives: the view of Shilshole Bay is gorgeous—an uninterrupted expanse of blue dotted with sailboats. Especially at sunset, the view nearly justifies putting up with the mediocre food and Midwestern tourists, although we feel compelled to mention that you get the same view down the road over a picnic basket at Golden Gardens Park. The casual deck of the cheaper upstairs café is our preferred perch; the more formal dining room, large windows be damned, is ugly and dated, and the service is cheesy. It's actually more difficult to get a table in the café than in the dining room.

Wherever you sit, expect overcooked grilled salmon (you can *try* ordering it "rare" if you want some dark-pink color within); underseasoned halibut; greasy, flavorless under-fried calamari and clams. The one dish that stands out on a thoroughly disappointing dinner menu is smoked sablefish. The fish is buttery and laid atop a tender tangle of sautéed spinach, and a slightly crisped ring of brandade. Sadly for those who come seeking Seattle seafood desserts, mostly old standards involving meringues and mousses, often turn out to be the best part of the meal.

Seafood
Upmarket restaurant

Ballard
6049 Seaview Ave. NW
(206) 789-3770

Hours
Daily
11:30am–9:00pm

Bar
Beer, wine, liquor

Credit cards
Visa, MC, AmEx

Reservations
Accepted

Features
Kid-friendly
Outdoor dining

7.0	6.5
Food	Feel

$50	7.5
Price	Wine

Red Fin

A hotel tries hand at sushi; and almost succeeds

www.redfinsushi.com

Pan-Asian
Japanese
Upmarket restaurant

Belltown
612 Stewart St.
(206) 441-4340

Hours
Mon–Fri
6:30am–2:30pm
4:00pm–11:00pm
Sat–Sun
8:00am–3:00pm
4:00pm–11:00pm

Bar
Beer, wine, liquor

Credit cards
Visa, MC, AmEx

Reservations
Accepted

Features
Brunch
Good beers
Outdoor dining

Red Fin is a hip-hotel-lounge-meets-diner with a Japanese fusion twist. It's connected to the Hotel Max, and like the hotel, it goes for the urban minimalist ultralounge vibe, with blocky lines and bright primary colors—in this case, red, red, and more red. This gives the place a rosy glow at night. The service follows the example of the Max, as well, by managing to be simultaneously snooty and efficient.

Presentation is sometimes stylized to the point of being childish—a spicy poke salad is served in a martini glass—but Red Fin is one super-hip fusion joint that impresses those who aren't sick of Pan-Asian fusion with its interesting flavor combinations: shiitake mushrooms in the miso, togarashi-seasoned fries with ginger ketchup, bits of Fuji apple in a spicy crab roll.

This is clearly not a place for purists—the menu of mains is particularly unfocused, with everything from an odd take on a "seafood pad Thai" to a standard burger with a few unnecessary twists (pineapple and star anise-pickled onions)—but ingredients are typically organic and well sourced, and everything tastes fresh. A good selection of sake and local and Japanese beers round out an excellent happy hour. The wine list is impressive for a sushi restaurant, but we could do without the bulk of the reds. Call us crazy, but we don't generally take our raw fish with Zinfandel.

Red Mill Burgers

Once the best burger in Seattle

7.5 Food **6.5** Feel

$10 Price

www.redmillburgers.com

Red Mill used to make the best burgers in town. They're still top contenders but with so many burger joints and every Pacific Northwest restaurant doing its own fancy beef slab, determining the best burger is about as easy as determining the best Thai joint.

Favorites are the simple "Red Mill Deluxe" with cheese, the "Verde Burger" with roasted Anaheim peppers and Jack cheese, and the boysenberry or Mandarin chocolate milkshake—how you manage to pair any of these is up to you. There are veggie burgers (definitely not the best in the city) and grilled chicken burgers, too, but the flame-broiled beef is where it's at. We like the fact that there are only about a dozen burgers—enough diversity for the pepper bacon, blue cheese, or onion jam aficionado, but not a build-your-own morass.

Red Mill is always hopping, and there's not enough room for the line, so it snakes out the door. Luckily for Seattle, there's no U.S. president to make the lines even longer in the wake of a visit, à la Ray's Hell Burger in Arlington, VA. Red Mill is a great family restaurant, and there are always lots of kids enjoying their burgers. Lines plus kids equals we usually grab our orders to-go. But if you happen to time it right, the place is actually fine for a sit-down, with its cute '50s checkered-floor and competing but not vomitous purple, red, and lime colors.

American
Counter service

Phinney Ridge
312 N. 67th St.
(206) 783-6362

Queen Anne
1613 W. Dravus St.
(206) 284-6363

Hours
Tue–Sat
11:00am–9:00pm
Sun
noon–8:00pm

Bar
None

Credit cards
None

Features
Kid-friendly
Outdoor dining

9.0	9.0
Food	Feel

$65	8.5
Price	Wine

Restaurant Zoë

A range of focused Northwest flavors that
have withstood the test of time

www.restaurantzoe.com

Modern
Upmarket restaurant

Belltown
2137 2nd Ave.
(206) 256-2060

Hours
Mon–Thu
5:00pm–9:45pm
Fri–Sat
5:00pm–10:45pm
Sun
5:00pm–9:15pm

Bar
Beer, wine, liquor

Credit cards
Visa, MC, AmEx

Reservations
Accepted

Features
Date-friendly
Veg-friendly

After 10 years and counting, Zoë is still an exemplar of seasonal Northwest cooking, and one of few restaurants in Belltown that feels neither like a trendy flash in the pan nor a tired over-the-hill tourist trap.

A big part of Zoë's appeal is its mastery of the swank yet understated vibe. They figured out how to make the place look modern without making it look like what science fiction writers in the 1950's thought 1990 would be. The result is that the room may feel a little too simple for those who look at the menu prices and expect something posh; Zoë's basically sports a collection of wood tables, chairs, and views out massive windows onto a reasonably non-sketchy corner of Belltown.

In some ways, however, Zoë is old-school, at least compared to the current trends in Northwest cooking. Instead of small plates full of disparate and deconstructed flavors that you must figure out how to mix together precisely lest the whole experiment blow up in your face, Zoë's dishes tend to have very focused flavors, with the whole dish working to promote one primary ingredient. For example, roasted wild mushrooms get some pine nuts and parmesan and are left well enough alone. The wine list is great, with a longer-than-usual selection of half-bottles. We heartily approve.

Ristorante Machiavelli

7.0	7.5
Food	Feel

Cheap, savory, old-school Italian

$40	7.0
Price	Wine

www.machiavellis.com

Machiavelli is always packed, and for good reason. While this is not the best or most creative Italian cooking in town, it's what a lot of customers want a lot of the time: the kinds of old-school Italian-American dishes, especially pastas (fettucine alfredo, for example), that you could order at the Olive Garden in similar portion sizes. But here, you know, they're actually good.

Fettucine carbonara, for example, is a thing of beauty at Machiavelli: it's creamy, cheesy, with a hint of spice and a soft glaze of scrambled egg. Little chips of crispy bacon peek out here and there. Veal saltimbocca, in a satiny Marsala sauce, has tender milky scallopine wrapped in crispy veils of prosciutto. In Rome, where it originated, the dish has no sweet, gloopy Marsala glaze—it's just veal, prosciutto, and sage—but hey, Americans like their sugar. Mains come with a side of lightly steamed vegetables and roasted potatoes, and while boring these are actually good, too.

It's cozy and homey inside Machiavelli, but the long wait for a table is a drag—if you don't get there either before 5 or after 9, we recommend that you not even bother showing up. The wine is cheap and plentiful, however, and the type of pastas Machiavelli makes tastes great when you're tanked.

Italian
Casual restaurant

Capitol Hill
1215 Pine St.
(206) 621-7941

Hours
Mon–Sat
5:00pm–11:00pm

Bar
Beer, wine, liquor

Credit cards
Visa, MC

Reservations
Not accepted

Features
Date-friendly
Veg-friendly

8.0 / 7.5

Food / **Feel**

$150 / 9.5

Price / **Wine**

Rover's

Beard-winning French

www.thechefinthehat.com

French
Upmarket restaurant

Madison Park
2808 E. Madison St.
(206) 325-7442

Hours
Tue–Thu
6:00pm–8:00pm
Fri
noon–1:30pm
6:00pm–9:00pm
Sat
6:00pm–9:00pm
Sun
5:00pm–8:00pm

Bar
Beer, wine, liquor

Credit cards
Visa, MC, AmEx

Reservations
Essential

Features
Date-friendly

The food at this conspicuous-consumption grande dame is not strictly classic French, but neither is it the work of a bunch of fiddlehead-fern Frankensteins. It's nouvelle cuisine, mostly, with some local touches. Roast quail is simply adorned with figs and duck prosciutto; scrambled eggs are both perked up and made richer with a lime crème fraîche and white sturgeon caviar; and simple foie gras preparations (seared or made into mousse) are paired with seasonal chutneys like rhubarb-beet or nectarine.

The wine list is a vast work of painstaking global research, including many older vintages, even, refreshingly, in half-bottle format. Although markups are reasonable by restaurant standards, there are few choices under $50. But Rover's is not without its flaws. It's in a converted house that feels like grandma's dining room dressed up for the holidays. The place seems to embody the tastes of a bygone generation of upper-class patrons, a caricatured version of old-time elegance that requires and sparks little imagination. The menu brashly advertises Panama-hat-wearing chef Thierry Rautureau's cult of personality, hawking his cookbook. It's all a bit off-putting. So are the prices; tasting menus run up to $135.

But even if the execution isn't always perfect, there is perhaps a time and place to dine this way, on occasion, with special ceremony, pomp and circumstance, and preposterous head-wear.

Saigon Deli

Cheap banh mi, rice balls, and neon-colored snacks

7.5 Food

5.0 Feel

$5 Price

Little Saigon's answer to the Uwajimaya food court, this deli has nearly every conceivable cheap Vietnamese lunch food portioned out under tight plastic wrap. Packages of ghostly spring rolls and rice dishes are stacked all over the place, nearly obscuring the hot food trays and the deli counter.

The latter is the real draw—made-to-order banh mi (Vietnamese baguette sandwiches). All the standard concoctions are here: pork, tofu, and three different types of salmon-tinged mystery meat known simply as "ham." There are plenty of fresh sweet snacks to end a meal with, too, like Vietnamese coffee with condensed milk, fried bananas, and sweet rice cakes.

When the place is busy, ordering can be kind of a free-for-all, so stand your ground and don't be shy about getting your order taken. Oh, and note that there are many Saigon Delis in town, none of them affiliated with the others. Trust your GPS, not any signage, to lead you to the right one.

Vietnamese Sandwiches
Counter service

International District
1237 S. Jackson St.
(206) 322-3700

Hours
Daily
7:00am–7:00pm

Bar
None

Credit cards
None

Features
Veg-friendly

7.5 Food | 9.0 Feel

$35 Price

The Saint

A tequila bar that turns out great cocktails, good small plates, and even better vibes

www.thesaintsocialclub.com

Mexican
Upmarket restaurant

Capitol Hill
1416 E. Olive Way
(206) 323-9922

Hours
Daily
5:00pm–2:00am

Bar
Beer, wine, liquor

Credit cards
Visa, MC, AmEx

Reservations
Accepted

Features
Good cocktails

Approaching this odd, narrow building is one of the pleasures of the Saint—the turquoise-and-white stucco facade could easily fit into to any centro histórico in Mexico. Inside, the Saint feels more rural Spain than D.F., with wood floors and white walls decorated with black-and-white portraits of famous bullfighters. The attractive bar keeps kitschy Mexicana to a minimum, too, settling on a steer's skull, white votive candles, and the extensive selection of premium tequilas for decoration.

There is a short dinner menu—puerco pibil and yuca fries with a spicy sauce are the best dishes—but this is mostly a place for happy hour, with discounted bites like carne asada tacos and ceviche. The food won't blow you away, but all of the ingredients are fresh and free-range, and dishes are well-balanced, light, and satisfying—definitely a step above chips-and-guac (though they have that too) fare.

Above all, the Saint is about its drink menu: sipping tequilas, good margaritas, and tequila cocktails (for example, the "Hacienda"—tequila, cherry liqueur, lemon, lime, and fresh cucumber) that are skillfully balanced. For the inner gringo in all of us, a few of the cocktails are served in Jarritos bottles, and there's a bucket of Coronitas on the limited beer menu.

Salty's on Alki Beach

The prices are insane for so-so seafood, but the view's unbeatable

6.0	8.5
Food	Feel

$70
Price

www.saltys.com

Forever walking the line between overpriced tourist trap and splurge-worthy Seattle institution, Salty's fares slightly better than its other similar restaurants. Location is a big draw here: there are terrific views of not only the sparkling sound, but also of Seattle's skyline. Plenty of tables inside enjoy this view, but the dining room is otherwise nondescript, and the deck is really the place to be when it's nice out.

Some people talk up the weekend brunch, but the buffet will not only make you feel like you're in Vegas or on a cruise ship, it will also likely feel like a rip-off no matter how much you eat—there are plenty of spots making excellent eggs Benedict or throwing a little crab into the mac and cheese for much less money. Lunch isn't much more of a deal, but there are a few "blue plate specials." Really, all you need is a cup of the signature seafood chowder, an intense and briny stew full of clams and scallops. At dinner, Dungeness crab rules, and shellfish samplers are popular. Fish fillets are sometimes overcooked, but the kitchen is reasonably competent with wild salmon and halibut.

The service is top-notch, and if you keep your eyes on the view while signing the check, the whole experience might almost be worth it.

Seafood
Upmarket restaurant

West Seattle
1936 Harbor Ave. SW
(206) 937-1600

Hours
Mon–Fri
11:00am–3:00pm
5:00pm–9:00pm
Sat
9:30am–1:00pm
4:00pm–9:30pm
Sun
8:45am–1:30pm
4:15pm–9:00pm
Winter hrs may be
slightly shorter

Bar
Beer, wine, liquor

Credit cards
Visa, MC, AmEx

Reservations
Accepted

Features
Brunch
Kid-friendly
Outdoor dining

8.5 Food | 7.5 Feel

$15
Price

Salumi

The kingdom of cured meats, ruled by the Batali family

www.salumicuredmeats.com

Italian Sandwiches
Counter service

Pioneer Square
309 Third Ave. S.
(206) 621-8772

Hours
Tue–Fri
11:00am–4:00pm

Bar
Beer, wine

Credit cards
Visa, MC

Salumi was started by Armandino Batali, father of the famous Mario. The former ran the place up until his recent retirement; it's still a family affair, with Armandino's daughter Gina Batali running the show now.

You'll see Salumi's meats on menus all over town—on charcuterie plates, in sandwiches, or tucked into pasta. For this reason, you don't actually have to visit Salumi to experience it, but the tiny storefront performs three important functions. First of all, it's a retail shop where you can purchase a full range of products, not all of which are available in gourmet markets. Secondly, it's a source for a hearty, salty sandwich. Lastly, it has a back room for private lunches (up to 10 people; about $45 per person).

A private, hours-long lunch with multiple courses, is a must if you want to experience Salumi beyond nibbling on the famous lamb sausage or mole salami (with cinnamon, chocolate, ancho, and chipotle). From pastas with shreds of the best cured meats; to old-fashioned dishes like bollito misto, these lunches aren't *like* hearty home-cooked meals—they *are* that.

The narrow main room has some communal seating, and jockeying for a spot to enjoy a sandwich or the awesome hot meat plate (meatballs, grilled lamb, peppers, porchetta) can be fun, as Salumi is the sort of place where people strike up conversations.

Sambar

Flights of fancy in cocktail and interior-decorating form, annexed to Le Gourmand

7.5 | **9.0**
Food | Feel

$40
Price

www.sambarseattle.com

Sambar is one of the coolest bars in Seattle. Much is made of its tiny size, and yes, you couldn't fit more than four or five hundred hamsters in here without it feeling a little tight. Come to think of it, a giant candy-colored Habitrail to accommodate said hamsters would fit right in with Sambar's, "eclectic" decor. With its uncomfortable minimalist furniture, panels of mirrors, and abstract murals, it looks like the brain of a '90s French club kid exploded. Yet somehow all of this feels totally natural and unerringly hip—you walk in and think: but of course.

Sambar serves good, seasonally inspired French bistro food: croque monsieur, soups, light salads, and soufflés, for instance, a nettle version with lemon-shallot béchamel and Comté cheese. There are also more substantial mains, like roast half-chicken with morels. The menu is short but necessary, as sampling masterful—and very potent—cocktails like the "Satiné" (rye whiskey, nocino, thyme syrup, cherry bitters) is a must. The employment of fresh fruits, local produce, and even flowers for color and flavor, is outstanding.

By the way, Sambar is attached to the pricey French restaurant Le Gourmand. If you have to use the bathroom, you'll get a good enough glimpse to conduct an interesting sociological inquiry. Who's having more fun: the finely dressed Francophiles at Le Gourmand, or the frite-snarfing hamsters at Sambar?

French
Bar

Ballard
425 NW Market St.
(206) 781-4883

Hours
Tue–Thu
5:30pm–midnight
Fri–Sat
5:30pm–2:00am

Bar
Beer, wine, liquor

Credit cards
Visa, MC, AmEx

Reservations
Not accepted

Features
Good cocktails
Live music
Outdoor dining

7.0 6.0
Food Feel

Samurai Noodle

Neither "top ramen" nor Top Ramen

$10
Price

Japanese
Counter service

International District
606 5th Ave. S.
(206) 624-9321

University District
4138 University Way NE
(206) 547-1774

Hours
Mon–Thu
10:00am–8:30pm
Fri–Sat
10:00am–9:30pm
Sun
10:00am–8:30pm

Bar
Beer, wine

Credit cards
Visa, MC, AmEx

Reservations
Not accepted

Features
Kid-friendly

This pleasant ramen shop next to Uwajimaya supermarket wouldn't stand out in Tokyo, but here, it's a reliable place for a little noodle slurping on a cold day. The best varieties are the tonkotsu ramen, whose long-simmered pork-bone broth might come decked out with sliced pork and wood ear mushrooms. Tofu ramen in a miso broth isn't bad either. The noodles could use a little improvement, but the rich broths compensate well enough for a lack of freshness. Beyond the ramen (there are chicken broth and fish broth varieties, too), the menu doesn't have much to offer beyond a pork teriyaki rice bowl.

Prices are a bit high for ramen, but Samurai isn't as much of a hole in the wall as most I.D. eateries. The red walls, low-slung wood tables, and samurai paraphernalia do impart a little bit of character, however worn they are, but the shop's small size and lunch lines sometimes make it hard to linger here.

Señor Moose

A crash course in regional Mexican specialties

www.senormoose.com

8.5	7.5
Food	Feel

$35
Price

Although the name conjures up images of Spring Breakers posing next to a visibly depressed donkey painted with a fake mustache, Señor Moose serves real Mexican food—that is, regional specialties that are neither immediately recognizable to most people nor covered in melted cheese.

Pork with manchamanteles (otherwise known as one of the other moles) from Oaxaca, seafood Veracruz-style (with tomatoes, onions, olives, and capers), higaditos de pollo (sautéed chicken livers with bacon, onions, and jalapeños) courtesy of Mexico City—from Chihuahua to Tampico, there's a taste of the comida típica from every major region of the country. Breakfast and brunch are the most popular meal here (waits are long), with hearty dishes ranging from simple tacos to the delicious huevos ahogados (poached eggs floating in a tomato broth seasoned with poblano chilis).

The interior perfectly captures the different influences suggested by the eatery's name. The main dining room looks like any small family restaurant in Mexico, while the counter and kitchen area look like a stuck-in-time greasy spoon you'd stumble onto while camping in the Cascades or on the Olympic Peninsula.

Mexican
Casual restaurant

Ballard
5242 NW Leary Ave.
NW
(206) 784-5568

Hours
Sun–Thu
8:00am–3:00pm
5:00pm–9:00pm
Fri–Sat
8:00am–3:00pm
5:00pm–10:00pm

Bar
Beer, wine, liquor

Credit cards
Visa, MC

Reservations
Not accepted

Features
Brunch
Kid-friendly

5.0	8.0
Food	Feel

$55	9.0
Price	Wine

Serafina

Middling Italian in a great location

www.serafinaseattle.com

Italian
Upmarket restaurant

Eastlake
2043 Eastlake Ave. E.
(206) 323-0807

Hours
Mon–Thu
11:30am–2:30pm
5:00pm–10:00pm
Fri
11:30am–2:30pm
5:00pm–11:00pm
Sat
5:00pm–11:00pm
Sun
10:00am–2:30pm
5:00pm–10:00pm

Bar
Beer, wine, liquor

Credit cards
Visa, MC, AmEx

Reservations
Accepted

Features
Brunch
Date-friendly
Live music
Outdoor dining
Veg-friendly

Serafina has a great spot in Eastlake. Park a few blocks away and watch the sun set over the hills and glisten on Lake Union while you walk to the restaurant—this might be the best part of your night.

At Serafina, disappointment snowballs: every person at the table will have some small complaint—the ravioli is ho-hum, the lamb is dry—that, when compiled, seem to add up to an irredeemably awful meal. Some of the food is more competent, but the complaints are numerous enough, and the prices high enough, that after a few tries, most of us aren't interested in going back.

So why bother, when Spinasse, Cantinetta, and Tavolàta beckon? There's the space, which despite a kind of fake Tuscan feel (lots of terra cotta accents), is comfortable and blandly sophisticated and includes a nice tree-filled patio. There's a good selection of Italian wines plus a decent beer list and good cocktails. There are also live music performances Friday through Sunday and on the occasional weekday, which can obliterate conversation. So if don't want cabaret-style jazz vocals or piano duos booming behind you while you eat, pick an off night for your visit.

Serious Pie

We're seriously surprised at how good this Tom Douglas pizzeria is

8.5	7.5
Food	Feel

$35	7.5
Price	Wine

www.tomdouglas.com

Serious Pie looks like an upscale brewpub, which we think is exactly what it should look like. The oblong pies in question, which are as serious as a heart attack (sorry, we couldn't resist), are baked in a stone oven that's fired by applewood. The crust is chewier and more reminiscent of rustic bread than what you'll find at other Italian-style pizza places around town, but it's also crispier, with less char. All in all, this is a very toothsome crust with more substance than you get from the competing limp-pie genre. Seasonal vegetables like chanterelles, Yukon gold potatoes, and squash provide some interesting toppings, but it's the pizzas that are consistently the best are guanciale; arugula and soft egg; and Penn Cove clams, pancetta, and lemon. The latter is like a terrific bowl of clam chowder, except that instead of some sad heel of bread, you have an entire pizza for dipping.

You can buy a bottle of wine or six pack with a to-go order, which is a nice touch and makes Serious Pie feel more like a neighborhood joint than just a Tom Douglas cash cow. Conversely, the ridiculous mark-ups on the wine list make you feel like you're in a big, overpriced restaurant.

Pizza
Casual restaurant

Belltown
316 Virginia St.
(206) 838-7388

Hours
Daily
11:00am–11:00pm

Bar
Beer, wine

Credit cards
Visa, MC, AmEx

Reservations
Not accepted

Features
Veg-friendly

Seven Stars Pepper

A tale of two Chinese restaurants

Chinese
Casual restaurant

International District
1207 S. Jackson St.
(206) 568-6446

Hours
Daily
11:00am–10:30am

Bar
None

Credit cards
Visa, MC

Reservations
Not accepted

Features
Veg-friendly

Ok boys and girls, here's a story for you: once upon a time, a little Szechuanese restaurant called Seven Stars Pepper opened up in the International District of Seattle. Foodies flocked, extolling the flakiness of their green onion pancakes, the savory, handmade dandan noodles. Then, the chef left. Some in-the-know foodies wrung their hands, but the departure was a quiet one. People continued to flock to a restaurant that sputtered along and coasted on its former reputation.

The problem was that classic ingredients like Chinese bacon were replaced with inferior ones like flabby Oscar Meyer-esque bacon, and pricier leeks were switched out for…celery. The hand-made noodles are still hand-made, a fact that has been seized upon by too much of the food media as a justification for undue reverence. Psst, here's the straight talk: the noodles are overcooked and swimming in a watery broth that looks as appetizing as, well, the after-effects of a meal at Seven Stars Pepper. And the inside is nothing special—just a bare-bones classic Chinese eatery with a whiteboard for specials written in Chinese and a tiled floor that's seen better days.

Steer clear. The princess did, and she ended up living happily ever after with Prince Charming, their 2.5 kids, a white picket fence, and a faithful droopy-eyed hound named Buster. The end.

Shiki

Great traditional sushi

8.5 Food
6.0 Feel
$45 Price

Japanese
Casual restaurant

Queen Anne
4 W. Roy St.
(206) 281-1352

Hours
Tue–Thu
11:00am–2:00pm
5:00pm–9:00pm
Fri
11:00am–2:00pm
5:30pm–10:00pm
Sat
5:30pm–10:00pm
Sun
5:00pm–9:00pm

Bar
Beer, wine

Credit cards
Visa, MC, AmEx

Reservations
Accepted

Shiki is the kind of sushi restaurant where you should only utter one word: omakase. Bait shrimp are pulled from the tank and served live, the tail still wriggling on your plate (while the head is in back being deep-fried). And chef Ken Yamamoto is one of only eight sushi chefs in the U.S. licensed to prepare fugu (the infamous puffer fish that if improperly sliced can kill you).

If you utter another word, it should be shabu shabu; the traditional Japanese hot pot is the best non-sushi option, with thinly sliced Wagyu beef, udon noodles, and vegetables, which you boil yourself in a simmering cauldron of stock.

Although omakase is a great value here, if you're on a budget, you won't be disappointed by the nigiri sushi: glassy crimson slabs of maguro, buttery supple salmon, and creamy albacore. The puffer fish, available December through April, is the opposite of value: $100+ gets you a fish with no more complexity than fluke plus a bowl of soup made from the fish's bones.

Shiki feels like a typical downmarket sushi restaurant: there are curtains everywhere, and Japanese calligraphy hangs from the walls. None of this is able to cover up the fact that Shiki is inside a typically dingy building in lower Queen Anne. But how could you hold that against them?

Shiro's

For texture, taste, and quality, one of the best sushi restaurants in Seattle

www.shiros.com

Japanese
Upmarket restaurant

Belltown
2401 2nd Ave.
(206) 443-9844

Hours
Daily
5:30pm–10:30pm

Bar
Beer, wine

Credit cards
Visa, MC, AmEx

Reservations
Accepted

Shiro's is Seattle's most iconic sushi restaurant. Chef Shiro Kashiba is a legend, and if you're a serious sushi eater, you must sit at the counter and order omakase—whether served by Shiro or one of his colleagues, it'll be good. Shiro's omakase isn't the most traditional; it stands out for its pairings. A raw piece of salmon may be accompanied by a fattier piece aburi-style (quickly seared with a blowtorch). A crunchy local clam may be paired with a silky scallop.

Away from the sushi bar, you'll miss salient advice like when to forgo soy sauce, but the standard menu is very strong. Shiro's has amazing unagi, and fried oysters with a sweet dipping sauce are also a must-order. Otoro is fatty and delicious, as expected, melting across your tongue. Amaebi, too, are divine, and they'll fry up the heads for you. Sweet, rich uni hits all the right notes. But don't miss out on the less commonly seen fishes that are sometimes available, like gizzard shad (a member of the herring family).

Although the restaurant occupies a prime Belltown corner, the space within is nothing special—it actually has a bit of a strip-mall sushi feel. But the service is great, and the vibe is largely driven by customer happiness.

Sichuanese Cuisine

Good if you're into hot pot, better if you speak Chinese

7.5	3.0
Food	Feel

$15
Price

www.sichuan.cwok.com

Chinese
Casual restaurant

International District
1048 S. Jackson St.
(206) 720-1690

Hours
Daily
11:00am–9:30pm

Bar
Beer

Credit cards
Visa, MC

Reservations
Accepted

Many Chinese restaurants are distrustful of Caucasians that assure the waitstaff they can handle the really spicy stuff. But Sichuanese Cuisine might be the I.D.'s most stubborn.

The specials board is only in Chinese, and if you ask the server for a suggestion, you'll get the safest dish on the menu. If you can't make your case in Chinese, or convince them that you were "last here with Chinese friends and liked their food more," the best you can hope for is that some of the strangers sharing the large, round communal tables will help you make sense of the specials—or at least won't mind if you point to their food.

The most reliable dishes here are the hot pots and the tasty, cheap dumplings. Sautéed green beans, or fresh Chinese greens stir-fried very simply, are good accompaniments. The amateur-hour dishes—Kung Pao chicken, for example—should be avoided. But when will these authentic Chinese restaurants open their minds to the possibility that white people might actually want to try their real food? The rise of a new food-blogging gastro-generation has created a huge opportunity for certain small, ethnic places to grow their audiences considerably, and encourage cultural intermingling while they're at it. By actively refusing requests for food that's spicy or authentic, they're missing a huge opportunity.

The place is a hole-in-the-wall, with cheap tables in a tiny space in the same sketchy parking lot that houses Tamarind Tree. Of course, sketchiness is a signal for authenticity.

Silence Heart Nest

Vegetarian and vegan fare under the gentle paternal gaze of Sri Chinmoy

www.silenceheartnest.com

Vegefusion
Casual restaurant

Fremont
3508 Fremont Pl. N.
(206) 633-5169

Hours
Mon, Wed–Fri
8:00am–2:30pm
Sat–Sun
8:00am–3:00pm

Bar
None

Credit cards
Visa, MC

Reservations
Not accepted

Features
Kid-friendly
Veg-friendly

Nobel Peace Prize nominee, teacher, advocate, musician, and poet of questionable talent Sri Chinmoy was the Kris Kristofferson of enlightenment. For reasons we don't need to fully understand, some of his school's meditation students are on a mission to make breakfast in Seattle a better thing.

Servers are mainly graying, sari-wrapped disciples, but beyond that and the woo-woo name, the café is fairly hip and nondenominational. It's cute, actually—white tables and blue walls with simple outlines of birds create a place of sincere peace and cheer that's mostly devoid of giggle-inducing details (well, except for an 8"x10" photo of Chinmoy in gym shorts deadlifting some improbable amount of weight).

Love is undoubtedly one of the main ingredients in the food. Fluffy omelettes, perfectly toasted fresh bread, zesty home fries of the chunky, real potato variety—these dishes are well crafted, and prove that you don't have to leave brunch in a grease coma. The soy bacon sucks, of course, but that's an universal fact of life we need to accept without emotion. Better is the signature dish: sweet potato biscuits with cashew gravy.

The lunch menu is too heavy on the fake meats, but the simpler dishes like salads, grilled cheese sandwiches on thick sourdough bread, and simple Indian curries and lentil soups, are winners. Service is friendly and prompt, if a bit glassy-eyed.

Sitka & Spruce

Seasonal ingredients, outstanding seafood
and game, and sprightly new digs

www.sitkaandspruce.com

9.0	9.5
Food	Feel
$50	8.5
Price	Wine

Before the Corson Building was hosting supper
clubs, chef Matt Dillon started out small with a
strip-mall space in Eastlake, and with this first
venture he has established himself as a master
of local-seasonal cooking.

The space in the Melrose Market building
feels like a greenhouse: sunlight streams in
through tall windows bouncing off white
accents, and mostly glass partitions separate the
restaurant from the rest of the open-air market.
They've kept the entire operation small, which
means getting a table of your own, or a seat at
the communal farm table, can be difficult. But
they've installed a counterbalance: Bar
Ferdinand, a bar/wine shop/waiting area across
the hall from the dining room. If you need to
wait, at least you can do it comfortably. The
wine list is lovely, with an Old-World focus—no
fruit bombs here.

This is a place to share plates. A typical meal
for two will require about four of them, which
makes Sitka a little pricey. Huge, plump mussels
might be topped with crispy fennel and served
on a bed of pickled cucumbers in an almost
meaty berry sauce. Or the kitchen might play it
straighter with house-smoked salmon lox—here,
crème fraiche and gooseberries stand in for
cream cheese and lemon juice.

Occasionally something won't come together,
but with ingredients this good, even the
disjointed parts of a pepper, peach, and crispy
pork salad are enjoyable on their own.

Modern
Casual restaurant

Capitol Hill
1531 Melrose Ave. E.
(206) 324-0662

Hours
Mon
11:30am–2:00pm
Tue–Fri
11:00am–2:30pm
5:30pm–11:00pm
Sat
10:00am–2:00pm
5:30pm–11:00pm
Sun
10:00am–2:00pm

Bar
Beer, wine, liquor

Credit cards
Visa, MC

Reservations
Accepted

Features
Brunch
Date-friendly
Veg-friendly

611 Supreme

Crêpes and French comfort food in a
supremely charming spot

www.611supreme.com

French
Casual restaurant

Capitol Hill
611 E. Pine St.
(206) 328-0292

Hours
Mon
5:00pm–11:00pm
Tue–Fri
11:00am–3:00pm
5:00pm–11:00pm
Sat–Sun
9:00am–3:00pm
5:00pm–11:00pm

Bar
Beer, wine, liquor

Credit cards
Visa, MC

Reservations
Not accepted

Features
Brunch
Good cocktails
Live music
Veg-friendly

You won't think you're in France or any such
nonsense, but 611 Supreme does a good job of
feeling just a little foreign. The exposed brick,
almond tables and accents, and low lighting
create the sort of universal unaffected urbanity
that classifies charming neighborhood cafés
from San Francisco to Paris. You can forget that
you're in Seattle, which is quite the feat in
Capitol Hill.

The dark lounge, with its vintage chandeliers,
art deco-esque metal bar stools, and low booths
with ottoman seating also straddles genres: part
lounge, part neighborhood bar. Possibly
because of this, 611 draws a much more diverse
crowd than you'd expect at a place across the
street from both a Stumptown Coffee and a
pawn shop that's a veritable warehouse of
shattered indie-rock dreams.

Savory and sweet crêpes get the inevitable
Seattle gourmet upsell—one of the best sweet
crêpes is the seasonal fruit version, which might
be Northwest berries, or mangoes and grapes,
depending on the bounty. This, in some cases, is
an improvement over "authenticity." Beyond
the crêpes, there are a few traditional French
bistro dishes (the gratin is very good).

The specialty cocktails are excellent, but
better sampled in the lounge after dinner—
alongside a crêpe, all the strong flavors tend to
compete with each other. The wine list is okay,
but could be more comprehensive.

Skillet Street Food

Airstream trailer. Seasonal street food.
Bacon jam.

www.skilletstreetfood.com

8.0
Food

5.0
Feel

$15
Price

American
Food cart

South Lake Union
Location changes daily;
check website or
@skilletstfood on
Twitter

Hours
Hours vary weekly.
Lunch served most
weekdays 11 to 2.

Bar
None

Credit cards
Visa, MC, AmEx

Skillet is exactly the type of street food that would flourish in a food-obsessed but not terribly adventurous city like Seattle: locavore bistro fare served up in a stylishly DIY manner. The shiny Airstream with the frying pan logo serves lunch in different locations each week and also caters special events both public and private; check the website or Twitter feed (@skilletstfood) to find out the when the truck will be in your neighborhood.

The menu of a half-dozen dishes changes weekly, but two are constant: rich poutine (hand-cut fries with gravy and cheddar), and a really good basic burger. The latter is dressed up with Skillet's signature bacon jam (a spreadable mixture of bacon, balsamic vinegar, onions, and spices), which adds some salty, tangy complexity to a hunk of grass-fed beef.

The Skillet team maxes out at three people, and although they have an efficient assembly system, if the line is long—as it is when they're at an event—you'll be in for a tense wait, punctuated by moments of disappointment when one of the skilleteers heads to the chalkboard to wipe off the names of dish as it runs out. Skillet seems to never run out of burgers, though, and standing around watching the excitement of passersby as they discover the Airstream is parked on their street is half the fun.

Smith

Northwest comfort food in a crumbling
Wild West Victorian drawing room

www.smithseattle.com

Modern
Casual restaurant

Capitol Hill
332 15th Ave. E.
(206) 709-1900

Hours
Mon–Fri
4:00pm–2:00am
Sat–Sun
10:00am–3:00pm
4:00pm–2:00am

Bar
Beer, wine, liquor, BYO

Credit cards
Visa, MC

Reservations
Not accepted

Features
Brunch
Date-friendly
Good cocktails
Kid-friendly

The hipster hunting-lodge vibe and the long list of beer, Bourbons, and other whiskies make this a solid drinking spot. The reasonably priced, high-quality, gut-busting vittles elevate Smith to neighborhood-favorite status.

Except for a few requisite salads, everything on the menu is rich and heavy. Smith occasionally mixes up the standard burger/mac-and-cheese menu with some interesting meats and game (rabbit and oxtail), but the go-to dishes are, in order: marrow bones; a hanger steak with seasonal vegetables; and fancy grilled-cheese sandwiches. Poutine is good, but poutine usually seems like a better idea than it is later in the evening. If it's a salty appetite destroyer you want, order the amazing house-made potato chips. One last note on salt: it's apparently the kitchen's favorite ingredient. Although most dishes come out fine, the burger, which actually has many loyal fans, could double as a salt lick.

The taxidermy-chic aesthetic isn't everyone's cup of tea, but Smith is not overbearingly ironic. The pheasants and naïve (read: ugly) portraiture of pioneers and former presidents are mounted high up enough that they're not too distracting—in candlelight, the nearly monochromatic dark woods and cozy booths along one wall actually make it a nice casual date place. And despite the efforts of fussy children, the place is comfortingly low-key at brunch.

Spiced

When the Chinese speak with their food dollars, we're all (spiced pigs') ears

www.spicedonline.com

8.0 Food

6.5 Feel

$20 Price

Chinese
Casual restaurant

Bellevue
1299 156th Ave. NE
(425) 644-8888

Hours
Mon–Thu
11:00am–3:00pm
5:00pm–9:00pm
Fri
11:00am–3:00pm
5:00pm–10:00pm
Sat
11:00am–10:00pm
Sun
11:00am–9:00pm

Bar
Beer

Credit cards
Visa, MC

Reservations
Accepted

Features
Veg-friendly

Szechuan is the hottest (in more ways than one) Chinese cuisine you'll find in Seattle, and every food snob worth his Szechuan peppercorn salt knows that the best examples of this genre reside on the Eastside. Unfortunately, Spiced had only been open for a few months when a failed health inspection closed the restaurant down for weeks. For some who like to live on the edge, its lengthy closure signaled authenticity. (Doesn't the best Chinese food come from the dirtiest hole-in-the-walls, after all?)

The closure didn't hurt Spiced's business—its largely Chinese clientele was ordering up the boiled fish in red chili oil the week after the restaurant re-opened. Spicy pigs' ears tossed in a numbing mix of garlicky Szechuan peppercorn oil, fried nuggets of golden Chongqing chicken with chiles, cold-sliced beef tendon, and amazing potstickers that (typically) come with a crisp lacy "skirt" of dough overtop are among the restaurant's best dishes. There are spicy, slightly gamey frogs' legs on the menu, too.

While Spiced is not the very best Szechuan restaurant in the area, it's certainly one of the better ones. It's a large restaurant, with round tables complete with Lazy Susans that will nicely bear the brunt of the 10 or so dishes you'll inevitably end up ordering. The atmosphere is casual, as it's mostly Chinese families eating.

9.0 Food	**9.5** Feel
$60 Price	**9.0** Wine

Spinasse

Outstanding pasta to go with the city's best visual interpretation of "rustic"

www.spinasse.com

Italian
Upmarket restaurant

Capitol Hill
1531 14th Ave. E.
(206) 251-7673

Hours
Mon, Wed–Thu
5:00pm–10:00pm
Fri–Sat
5:00pm–11:00pm

Bar
Beer, wine, liquor

Credit cards
Visa, MC, AmEx

Reservations
Accepted

Features
Date-friendly
Good cocktails
Veg-friendly

Spinasse does Northern Italian with serious soul and expertise. The pasta is the best in the city—it's tender and yolky and delicious every time. Wild boar ragù with fried sage leaves; squash ravioli with sage butter and crushed amaretti; and maltagliati with chickpeas and prosciutto are just a few of the preparations that have floored us.

Mains are equally good; whether venison, pork, rabbit, or quail, meat is coaxed to extreme tenderness here. And occasionally there's something that isn't cooking in every kitchen in town, like goat sausage. Spinasse has a very strong, well-chosen list of Italian wines, along with great aperitifs (Cynar and soda, etc) and digestifs. The only thing that doesn't shine is the dessert menu. Desserts are sometimes almost over-the-top in their simplicity, like half a nectarine filled with marscapone. Not that it matters much; if you make it through two or three courses you'll barely have room for a ladyfinger. The all-Italian wine list is carefully chosen, filled with old-school bottles.

Spinasse went for the Italian farmhouse feel—lace curtains, wood beams, and pottery throughout—and they nailed it. The place could only be more rustic if they threw dirt on the floors and let some donkeys live in the kitchen. If you sit at the bar at the early part of the evening, you can see the pasta teased into existence.

Spring Hill

A cutting-edge nose-to-tail showcase that's best for brunch and bivalves

8.0	7.0
Food	Feel

$60
Price

www.springhillnorthwest.com

Everything at Spring Hill has an artisan twist. The menu is littered with the macho gourmet ingredients of the 21st century, the sort of thing meant to separate the *No Reservations* crowd from Rachael Ray followers: plump scallops framed with curls of lardo; lamb tongue, duck ham, and veal sweetbreads; and foie gras terrine served with toasted brioche and tiny cubes of Lillet jelly. Even the simple roasted free-range chicken comes with mustard greens and a superfluous soft egg.

Spring Hill rocks the local shellfish: razor clams, geoduck clams, and mussels are outstanding. Kumamoto oysters are usually on the menu, and served with a cucumber vinegar that adds acid to bring out, but not overpower, their sweetness.

There are some dishes that look better than they taste. But it's worth the risk. Brunch is always a reliable choice; Spring Hill has the best cheese grits and fancy corned beef hash in the city. The former is made with Beecher's cheese and a soft-poached egg on top, with a ham steak added for good measure. The latter uses top-notch Oregon beef and comes with two poached eggs.

Spring Hill sounds like a place where flowers bloom and bunnies frolic, but instead, the restaurant boldly chose "spare and forbidding" as a design scheme. It's status-quo chic, with the familiar concrete floors, lack of artwork, and plywood booths.

Modern
Upmarket restaurant

West Seattle
4437 California Ave. SW
(206) 935-1075

Hours
Mon–Fri
5:45pm–10:00pm
Sat
10:00am–2:00pm
5:45pm–10:00pm
Sun
10:00am–2:00pm

Bar
Beer, wine, liquor

Credit cards
Visa, MC, AmEx

Reservations
Accepted

Features
Brunch

8.5	8.0
Food	Feel

Spur Gastropub

Seasonal small plates with a dollop of molecular gastronomy

$55
Price

www.spurseattle.com

Modern
Upmarket restaurant

Belltown
113 Blanchard St.
(206) 728-6706

Hours
Daily
5:00pm–11:00pm

Bar
Beer, wine, liquor

Credit cards
Visa, MC, AmEx

Reservations
Accepted

Features
Date-friendly

It-boys Dana Tough and Brian McCracken have gotten a lot of attention for doing things like deep-frying béarnaise, folding foie gras into ice cream, and perpetuating the trend of turning anything from hard cheeses to oyster mushrooms into foams. Anyone looking for a tiny, affordable, and fairly restrained taste of molecular gastronomy should give Spur a shot.

Even if eating an egg laid by chickens is more appealing to you than eating an "egg" made of cauliflower and squash, Spur will deliver. Most of the menu consists of items that are wholly recognizable. Pork belly sliders are plopped onto toasted mini-brioche buns and served with a touch of a sweet Bourbon sauce. The grass-fed beef burger is just that, although it's sometimes accompanied by pork belly. Usually, when Spur gets cute, it's in a way that's in touch with its customers, like offering a haute breakfast at happy hour in the form of a "chicken-fried egg" (now there's a new spin on the old philosophical dilemma) served with bacon and gravy.

The intimate space has a subdued Western theme—a large screen that sometimes plays silent black-and-white cowboy movies, a tavern-like setting, a bar focused on whiskey and Bourbon—but also all the qualities of Belltown hot spots. Expect a pretty crowd of late-night revelers.

St. Cloud's

A perfect neighborhood hangout

7.5	8.0
Food	Feel

$45
Price

www.stclouds.com

St. Cloud's has all its bases covered. The menu is divided into "Home for Dinner" (unadulterated comfort food like ribs, roast chicken, and burgers) and "Out for Dinner" (slightly more adventurous fare, like an appetizer of grilled bread with goat cheese and caramelized onions). The best of the comfort-food mains is the garlic fried chicken with mashed potatoes; the best of the "out" is the tender, Parmesan-crusted pork tenderloin over pasta—so '80s, but so good. A simple fudge sundae, made with coconut ice cream and homemade fudge sauce, is the best way to end a meal.

Brunch is even simpler, though also divided up into "Standards" like eggs, waffles, and pancakes, and "Not So Standards" like chicken-fried steak and the "Imperial Mix Up," a favorite egg scramble with rice, scallions, ginger, and either marinated tempeh or Portuguese sausage.

St. Cloud's is a popular neighborhood spot: the menu is short and straightforward, and the space is family-friendly. On most nights there's live music: jazz, soul/funk, or singer/songwriter sessions. Although the skill levels of performances vary, the whole package is more inviting than the similar but pricier experience offered at Serafina. And if you're live-music-averse, the piano bar area is nicely separated from the main dining room.

American
Casual restaurant

Madrona
1131 34th Ave.
(206) 726-1522

Hours
Mon–Thu
5:00pm–11:00pm
Fri
5:00pm–midnight
Sat
9:00am–2:00pm
5:00pm–midnight
Sun
9:00am–2:00pm
5:00pm–11:00pm

Bar
Beer, wine, liquor

Credit cards
Visa, MC, AmEx

Reservations
Accepted

Features
Brunch
Kid-friendly
Live music
Outdoor dining

Steelhead Diner

Pike-Place-Market–fresh, upscale comfort
food in throwback diner surroundings

www.steelheaddiner.com

Modern
Upmarket restaurant

Downtown
95 Pine St.
(206) 625-0129

Hours
Daily
11:00am–10:00pm

Bar
Beer, wine, liquor

Credit cards
Visa, MC, AmEx

Reservations
Accepted

Features
Outdoor dining

Steelhead is an incredibly literal interpretation of an upscale diner, right down to the sea-foam-colored booths and the old-school vinyl-and-chrome stools. There are concrete floors instead of linoleum, a long bar backlit by the Seattle skyline, and a red accent wall with a 3D art installation celebrating the beauty of fly fishing.

The mix is well executed, and the place feels warm and laid-back. However, sometimes (okay, whenever the place is overrun with the cruise ship crowd) Steelhead feels less date-night special and more Tuesday night in New Jersey—pop music playing, placemat-size menus, poor service from uninformed servers. The wine list, however, is surprisingly sophisticated, with quite a few Washington State bottles.

Steelhead's menu skips around the globe—catfish tacos may have a Veracruz-style salsa, while black cod gets the Pan-Asian treatment, and fish and chips stick to tradition with a good ale-based batter. The best dishes play off of our favorite fast foods: fried chicken, the "Rich Boy" (a sausage po'boy), and fried Beecher's cheese curds. Proteins are often cloaked in too many ingredients: salmon may not only have a red-wine reduction, but also farro, and kale, and a glaze, and then some more stuff that winds up masking the primary properties of the fish. Desserts, on the other hand, are delicious, and a few indulge some nostalgia of favorites long out of style: if you thought crème brûlée was dead, come here.

Stumbling Goat Bistro

A farm-to-table pioneer that still gets it right

8.0 Food

8.0 Feel

$50 Price

www.stumblinggoat.com

Nearly ten years ago, the Stumbling Goat Bistro was on the forefront of the farm-to-table movement. Today, even after a recent change in ownership, the introduction of a new chef, and a "green" facelift that installed an attractive new bar made of salvaged materials, the restaurant hasn't wavered from its original mission a bit.

Stumbling Goat gets the farm-to-table idea right: when you focus so meticulously on ingredients, you'd better stand back and let them shine through. That doesn't mean a lack of attention to preps; it means ingredient pile-ons. A starter might be steamed clams with house-made chorizo or a simple soup like apple or sorrel and tarragon. Hanger steak, served with a morel mushroom demi-glace is some of the kitchen's best work, but the New York steak is equally good, served with a simple side like sautéed kale.

Feel-wise, the Goat is just a slightly more upscale version of a neighborhood café. There are a few votives made from old wine bottles, a red accent wall or two, and that lovely new bar, which begins and ends at exposed brick, but otherwise the space is simple and quaint. One thing we like about the dining room is that the tables are well-spaced; you need not know anything about your neighbor's love life or work troubles. This is a nice counterpoint to communal dining trends and increasingly packed houses.

Modern
Upmarket restaurant

Phinney Ridge
6722 Greenwood Ave. N.
(206) 784-3535

Hours
Tue–Thu
5:00pm–9:00pm
Fri–Sat
5:00pm–10:00pm
Sun
5:00pm–9:00pm

Bar
Beer, wine, liquor

Credit cards
Visa, MC, AmEx

Reservations
Accepted

Features
Date-friendly
Outdoor dining

Sutra

One of the best herbivore haunts in town, and quite a deal for the supper clubbers

www.sutraseattle.com

Vegefusion
Upmarket restaurant

Wallingford
1605 N. 45th St.
(206) 547-1348

Hours
Sun
6:30pm–6:45pm
6:30pm–6:45pm
Wed–Thu
7:00pm–7:15pm
Fri–Sat
6:30pm–6:45pm
7:00pm–7:15pm

Bar
Beer, wine

Credit cards
Visa, MC, AmEx

Reservations
Essential

Features
Date-friendly
Veg-friendly

Sutra is a supper club for vegetarians and vegans, and carnivores too will enjoy what is essentially a clinic on creating upscale veggie fare that doesn't rely on gimmicks or fake meats.

Sutra follows the standard supper-club playbook: one seating per night (Wednesday and Thursday at 7pm; Friday and Saturday at 6:30pm and 9pm; Sunday at 6:30pm) for a four-course meal of local, seasonal food, preceded by a few words from the chef. The meal starts light—an asparagus-thyme bisque or roasted sunchoke and tarragon soup, for instance—but portions are large; even salads are given some extra heft with elements like breaded fiddlehead ferns. By the time you hit the main dish, you might be too full to finish it. That would be a shame, because it might be a nicely textured risotto cake piled with seasonal veggies; vegan lasagne; or perhaps a curried potato or squash dish. Desserts are excellent, often using premium dark chocolate from local factory Theo. There's a decent selection of organic wines and beers.

The tiny room, painted spring green, is modern but still has a yoga-retreat feel. Dining is communal, and most seats at the two L-shaped tables have a view of the prep area. Service is very personal and the set-up precludes any sort of privacy, so this is best for a medium-sized group or an extremely casual date.

Szechuan Chef

"Can you really eat that?"

www.szechuanchefbellevue.com

6.5 Food

7.5 Feel

$20 Price

It's easy to argue that all the good Chinese food in the area is on the Eastside. Szechuan Chef (in this case, Cheng Biao Yang) is instructional in that argument.

Despite its foreboding strip mall location, this is far from the typical overly fluorescent lit, drab Chinese restaurant. Colorful walls, touches of greenery, and faux-bamboo dividers give the place an almost-elegant appeal. An extensive menu and quality at price point make this worth the trek from Seattle.

At press time, Yang had moved on to open Spicy Talk in Redmond, so it will be interesting to see how Szechuan Chef survives his absence. This "upscale" (for Chinese) restaurant packs 'em in, even on weeknights, with predominantly Asian diners, many chewing intestines from hot pots while chatting well into the night.

Forego Honey Walnut "Anything" and opt instead for more fiery selections, denoted by chili pepper ratings (1-5) on the menu. Favorites include the aforementioned hot pots (from mixed mushrooms to pork intestines), dry-cooked fish fillet with hot pepper, and dan dan noodles.

If you're a Caucasian diner, expect strange looks and surprised reactions if you order anything like intestines. (Your server will likely ask, "Can you really eat that?") But while the restaurant does a decent job with a few of the more "mainstream" dishes, it's the more exotic fare where Szechuan Chef is at its finest. Insist on authenticity, but know full well that when this restaurant uses Szechuan in its name, you can expect true Szechuan spiciness as a result.

Chinese
Casual restaurant

Bellevue
15015 Main St.
(425) 746-9008

Hours
Sun–Thu
11:00am–9:00pm
Fri–Sat
11:00am–9:30pm

Bar
Beer, wine

Credit cards
Visa, MC

Reservations
Accepted

Features
Kid-friendly
Veg-friendly

7.0 Food | 6.5 Feel

$40
Price

Table 219

There's a standout brunch here; they can keep the rest

www.table219.com

American
Upmarket restaurant

Capitol Hill
219 Broadway Ave. E.
(206) 328-4604

Hours
Tue–Thu
4:00pm–10:00pm
Fri–Sat
9:00am–10:00pm
Sun
9:00am–3:00pm

Bar
Beer, wine, liquor, BYO

Credit cards
Visa, MC

Reservations
Accepted

Features
Brunch

Most of Table 219's dinner menu is inspired by the type of generally regrettable American recipes that monied Gen-Xers would feel the need to "reimagine": sloppy Joe sliders, "nachos" with duck confit, corn dogs made with chicken andouille sausage, a gourmet version of a ding dong.

None of the above is meant to imply that this is a bad restaurant. Some of this stuff is actually pretty delicious, and if Table 219 had had the garlic-bacon deviled huevos to stick with their gimmick till the end of the menu, we could certainly join in on the fun.

But tonally, this restaurant is all over the place. The other half of the menu is very un-ironic, with ambitious Pacific Northwest preps like Coho salmon with pea vine purée. The drink menu actually employs the word "pometini." And the space is entirely too earnest and corporate-looking for corn dogs, no matter how beautifully they're plated.

All of that said, the brunch here rocks. French toast is soaked overnight before being griddled, and Table 219's version of the Denny's Grand Slam (the "Seattle Slam") is just right: pancakes are fluffy, eggs are done the way you like, the bacon is carefully cooked to temperature. This dish is the only one with a funny callback; the rest of the menu is a mix of traditional favorites, like a great eggs Benedict, and dressed-up omelettes (chorizo, potato, and Manchego, for example). Simple, savory, and delicious. Now, was that so hard?

Taco Gringos

A very focused business model: late-night fancy tacos for drunks

6.5 Food

3.0 Feel

$10 Price

Mexican
Counter service

Capitol Hill
1510 E. Olive Way

Hours
Tue–Sat
8:00pm–2:30am

Bar
Beer

Credit cards
None

You're not reading the hours wrong: Taco Gringos exists only to sober up your drunk self (or to provide a foundation before you start really making the rounds). This place does much of its business after people are already sufficiently inebriated.

A lot of people complain that Gringos' tacos are too small for the price, but then again, a lot of people who eat here have voluntarily impaired their own judgment of anything related to taste, portion size, appetite, their general whereabouts, wisdom of sending an "I miss you so much" SMS to their ex while stumbling out the front door of a bar, ambulated by two bouncers and one friend distractedly attempting to display concern.

The menu here always offers three options: one vegetarian, one standard meat, and one slightly more adventurous meat. Past offerings have included sweet potato, spicy chicken, and rabbit. Each taco is wrapped in one tortilla instead of the standard taco-truck two, which for some people is a deal-breaker. Hot sauces are available, but aren't necessarily needed, as the tacos are on the spicier side.

There are definitely gringos behind the grill here: although there's not much of an interior (i.e., nowhere to sit), they did manage to hang a Nite Brite open sign. Good, if unsmiling (can you blame them?), service moves the line along quickly. It's a good thing, because impatience can reign at 2am, and this is the best late-night snack on the western edge of the Hill.

Tacos El Asadero

All aboard the taco bus for cheap street food 101

Mexican
Food cart

South Seattle
7300 Martin Luther King
Jr. Way S.
(206) 760-9903

Hours
Daily
10:00am–10:00pm

Bar
None

Credit cards
Visa, MC

Features
Outdoor dining

Despite Seattle's lame restrictions on food vendors, the city's fleet of taco trucks is growing. Although you'll get better tacos by sitting down at places like La Carta de Oaxaca and El Mestizo, you can't beat this popular tacomobile for value. Among taco trucks, you can't beat it for convenience; it's right off the Othello light rail stop—no serendipity or driving around needed.

Don't look for a traditional walk-up truck, though. There is one of those a bit north on Rainier Avenue South, but this here is the taco bus. An old-school bus painted white and outfitted with stainless steel counters and bar stools, a small kitchen, a TV blaring Univision, and a cooler full of Jarritos.

Among the many meats waiting to be stuffed into fresh tortillas, we like the carne asada (beef), carnitas, and tender lengua the best. Tacos El Asadero also carries all the usual sopecitos, burritos, mulitas (meat stuffed between two tortillas and grilled), and tortas.

Tagla Café

One of the affordable anchors of Columbia City's Ethiopian culinary nerve center

7.5	**7.0**
Food	Feel

$20
Price

www.taglacafe.com

Of the many restaurants that cater to Columbia City's large Ethiopian population, Tagla is our favorite. This is an injera emporium—they make the injera that you'll see in local markets and in other restaurants.

This place purveys huge platters of flavorful spicy food, with either falling-off-the-bone meat (or simply uncooked—an downright delicious—meat, as in the case of kitfo) or fantastic vegetables and beans, like shero-wot with chickpea flour or miser-wot with lentils. A limited breakfast menu has Western-style egg sandwiches and Ethiopian standards like foul medammas (a dish of fava beans, tomato, onion, cheese, and pepper) and buttered injera. A take-out menu includes injera sandwiches and sambusas.

Tagla is staffed by some of the friendliest people in town. They treat this place like it's their home. It's not the classiest place, and the loud TV is kind of distracting, but the vibe is still just so darn welcoming. And the large windows let in a lot of light, helping the place feel even roomier and happier. The prices will make you happy, too.

Ethiopian
Casual restaurant

Columbia City
4423 Rainier Ave. S.
(206) 721-3355

Hours
Mon–Thu
10:00am–9:00pm
Fri–Sat
10:00am–11:00pm

Bar
Beer, wine

Credit cards
Visa, MC

Reservations
Not accepted

Features
Kid-friendly
Veg-friendly

Tamarind Tree

A worthy stop in the I.D., if not totally deserving of its long waits

www.tamarindtreerestaurant.com

Vietnamese
Casual restaurant

International District
1036 S. Jackson St.
(206) 860-1404

Hours
Sun–Thu
10:00am–10:00pm
Fri–Sat
10:00am–midnight

Bar
Beer, wine, liquor

Credit cards
Visa, MC

Reservations
Accepted

Features
Kid-friendly
Outdoor dining
Veg-friendly

Tamarind Tree suffers from a bit of an identity crisis. The so-called "provincial Vietnamese restaurant" actually serves slightly modernized (though not egregiously fusion-y) food. Artsy flourishes like an exterior waterfall (next to which you can dine, weather permitting) and cubic light fixtures that glow green and orange are awfully flamboyant for a restaurant stuck in the back corner of a dingy strip mall that adjoins…another strip mall. Well, never mind. Tamarind Tree's efforts to create a bamboo-fringed world within a shabby corner of Little Saigon are appreciated, even if they are a bit overblown.

The menu is huge, and even though it will affect your chances of securing a table quickly, it's best to bring a group here to share a bunch of dishes. Pho and satays are pretty standard—not the best in the city—but the salads are typically good, and the green mango salad is a must-order. The less traditional dishes are more memorable: steamed prawns on a coconut rice cake, the "Tamarind Tree Roll" (fresh herb-filled goodness with coconut, peanut, jicama, and tofu), and vegetarian crêpes all rate high.

Tamarind Tree does have some unique pleasures—the waterfall and green tea vodka are two. Plus, its service has improved from miserable to, well, serviceable—even friendly, if you're persistent.

Tango

It takes two...to eat an El Diablo

www.tangorestaurant.com

Date night with an El Diablo dessert. Tango wants to be more than that, but for many, that's the best it can be.

Oh, it's a charming place where you can sit with a loved (or you're-hoping-will-soon-be-loved) one, staring into each other's eyes as you await your chance to share a paella for two, which might be too oily or too dry, depending on the night. And the place holds a lot of promise with a menu of cold and hot tapas, Spanish soups, salads, seafood, and more. But most of the food lacks oomph, even if the date-night atmosphere lives up, with low lighting and warm, dark colors.

That said, Tango's been doing its dance for ten years now. Our recommendation: try a drink while nibbling on some small plates, some cheese, and maybe the "Cheap Dates" (Medjool dates wrapped in bacon, grilled eggplant, and red onion).

And if your date wants to try the famed El Diablo, get one to share. It's beautiful to behold, but far too sweet for one person to finish. Besides, you're probably trying to save some appetite for sweet nibbles of another kind.

Spanish
Upmarket restaurant

Capitol Hill
1100 Pike St.
(206) 583-0382

Hours
Sun–Thu
5:00pm–10:30pm
Fri–Sat
5:00pm–midnight

Bar
Beer, wine, liquor, BYO

Credit cards
Visa, MC, AmEx

Reservations
Accepted

Features
Date-friendly

8.0 Food

7.5 Feel

$55 Price

TASTE

Redefining the museum meal as one you'd actually like to have

www.tastesam.com

Modern
Upmarket restaurant

Downtown
1300 1st Ave.
(206) 903-5291

Hours
Wed–Sat
11:00am–10:00pm
Sun
9:00am–8:00pm

Bar
Beer, wine, liquor, BYO

Credit cards
Visa, MC, AmEx

Reservations
Accepted

Features
Brunch
Date-friendly
Veg-friendly

Located in the Seattle Art museum, TASTE is a sleek, bright white eatery that dares to be different, with spurts of success. Large floor-to-ceiling windows look out onto a busy downtown street, which makes for great people-watching. The menu is essentially fancy versions of traditional comfort food—the Stokesberry fried chicken and waffles, served with zippily dressed collard greens, is an excellent brunch dish. Some would argue that the main drawback at happy hour or dinner is the prices—slightly higher than you'd expect, with Karen Carpenter portions. (The skimpy patty on the happy hour burger is just a tease, and we wish there were a little more smoked salmon on the tasty flatbread.) A perk, though, for green-minded folks: TASTE's menu is almost completely locally sourced.

The highlights at TASTE are the whimsical desserts, heavily geared to bringing back any warm-fuzzy childhood feelings. The warm cookie plate is an assortment of mini classics, all hot and gooey from the oven, with a shot of milk. "Grandma's Caramel Rolls" are sticky and cinnamony-sweet with a lovely pool of caramel sauce for dipping. And need we mention there's a peanut-butter-and-jelly ice-cream sandwich to be had? We wish these were available back in the day for after-school noshing. Jem and the Holograms would've dubbed them truly outrageous.

Taste of India

Indian that gets the basics right, even if it doesn't blow your socks off

www.tasteofindiaseattle.com

8.0	6.0
Food	Feel

$30
Price

Expatriated Microsoft engineers drive from the Eastside to this cute little house in the heart of the U District for a taste of home. It's always packed, as it's also a favorite of UW students and professors. The rooms are kind of tight—or at least feel that way thanks to low ceilings—and sporadically decorated with houseplants and batik tapestries. The staff is attentive to a fault (it'd be nice to set down a water glass without three servers pouncing on it).

Quirks aside, Taste of India is tough to beat when it comes to the basics. There's not much creativity in the kitchen or arcane house specialties, just meats and fish from the tandoor, coconut curries, and plenty of vegetarian masalas. The fun part is the rogan josh and vindaloo dishes.

And they're the real thing, done really well. (Taste of India has a small selection of dishes like falafel and shish kebab, but those are overpriced and not as good as the Indian food.) The dessert menu is fairly long and includes treats like traditional condensed milk ice cream and kheer (rice pudding with cardamom and nuts).

Indian
Casual restaurant

University District
5517 Roosevelt Way NE
(206) 528-1575

Hours
Mon–Sat
11:30am–10:00pm
Sun
11:00am–9:00pm

Bar
None

Credit cards
Visa, MC, AmEx

Reservations
Accepted

Features
Kid-friendly
Veg-friendly

7.5 | 6.0
Food | Feel

$15
Price

Tat's Delicatessen

Decidedly nonfancy sandwiches, but still nothing special in their own right

www.tatsdeli.com

Sandwiches
Counter service

Pioneer Square
159 Yesler Way
(206) 264-8287

Hours
Mon–Fri
8:00am–7:00pm
Sat–Sun
11:00am–7:00pm

Bar
Beer, wine

Credit cards
Visa, MC

Features
Kid-friendly
Outdoor dining

Another East Coast deli—this one Philly-style—Tat's is a middle finger in the face of the fancy sandwich spots popping up all over town. You can get a cheesesteak with Cheez Whiz, which is possibly the polar opposite of local, seasonal, and artisanal—and, also, in its own way, awesomely delicious.

Tat's makes big sandwiches, sometimes with (genuinely) funny names—the "Tatstrami" (a pastrami cheesesteak with Swiss cheese and Russian dressing) has a very loyal following, although we think the basic cheesesteak (whiz wit') is better. There are hoagies and grinders on Italian rolls, and meatball or chicken parms. This is very basic deli fare, but sandwiches have the balance and structural integrity lacking in many more pedigreed snacks. Speaking of snacks, if any misguided East Coaster is missing Tastykakes, you can find them here.

Tat's does most of its business during lunch and before and after Sounders and Seahawks games (they even shift their hours around to accommodate the games). Service is brusque; you'd better be ready to order when your turn is up. But at midday or after the game, what more do you need than a soft Italian roll absorbing griddle grease and lovely meat juices, fats, onions and sucs, and oozes of Whiz? The pleasure centers of the brain are powerful motivators, and the lines at Tat's are often longer than the ones at Salumi.

Tavern Law

Another Prohibition Era–obsessed cocktail bar, but one with great nibbles, too

8.0	8.0
Food	Feel

$50
Price

www.tavernlaw.com

Tavern Law is up to its ears in its own B.S. This is the kind of place where there's a long-winded explanation for every detail and drink, where dapper dudes in vests and ties serve up Old Fashioneds, Sidecars, and Rob Roys.

The interior is dark and attractively done up in a modern yet stately library motif, save for the incongruous and irritating presence of a TV over the bar. There's a "secret" upstairs, which can either be reserved in advance or accessed by picking up an old-timey telephone and asking the waitress if there's room for your party. The 21 Club it's not.

The drink menu is encyclopedic. Some experiments work better than others (booze with Earl Grey tea is not our favorite combo) but Tavern Law's seasonal flights of fancy and twists on classics are typically outstanding. Actually, the best thing to do is just tell the bartender what type of liquor you want and let him take his inspiration from the moment and ingredients on hand.

Tavern Law is another installment from the people behind Spur Gastropub, so there are tasty haute small plates to match the fancy cocktails—foie gras terrine and crispy pork belly are two that make frequent appearances and never disappoint. Fried oysters are another winner, as is a lovely burger.

Modern
Bar

Capitol Hill
1406 12th Ave.
(206) 322-9734

Hours
Daily
5:00pm–midnight

Bar
Beer, wine, liquor

Credit cards
Visa, MC, AmEx

Reservations
Not accepted

Features
Date-friendly
Good cocktails
Outdoor dining

8.5	8.5
Food	Feel

$50	8.5
Price	Wine

Tavolàta

Some of the best pasta in Seattle at a Belltown trendsetter—surprised?

www.ethanstowellrestaurants.com

Italian
Upmarket restaurant

Belltown
2323 2nd Ave.
(206) 838-8008

Hours
Sun–Thu
5:00pm–11:00pm
Fri–Sat
5:00pm–midnight

Bar
Beer, wine, liquor

Credit cards
Visa, MC, AmEx

Reservations
Accepted

Features
Date-friendly
Good cocktails
Veg-friendly

Our favorite of Ethan Stowell's restaurants is also the most Italian, with a focus on careful, delicious homemade pastas, with the occasional Northwest flourish: showstopping spaghetti with anchovies and chili; sweet and sublime agnolotti with ricotta, brown butter, and sage; or campanelle (pasta shaped like bells) with mussels, preserved lemon, squash, and pesto. Protein mains are sometimes less memorable, but still well thought out—a pork chop with Medjool dates and hazelnuts, roasted leg of lamb with a mint salsa verde.

A long series of tables is flanked by wooden banquettes on one side and booths on the other. It's not our favorite layout—lots of people are always facing the wall. The design is spare—a collection of mirrors mounted on exposed concrete over the bar is one of few embellishments—and the place feels like an industrial-chic dining hall, loud and social. Getting a seat at the bar isn't a consolation prize: the mixology is particularly good here, and the bar itself feels like a natural extension of the übercool dinner party happening around it. The wine list is more of a bright spot—even if prices start to stray a bit high.

We have an obscure but closely observed Fearless Critic policy that a half-point in feel rating shall be deducted from any establishment whose name includes a made-up accent just to make the word seem more foreign. (See e.g. Crú in Austin; Amazón Grill in Houston; Vicenté's Pizza in Portland; Maté in Washington, DC.) So Tavolata=9; Tavolàta=8.5. Sorry guys.

Thai Curry Simple

Doing a lot with a shockingly cheap menu

5.0 Food

7.5 Feel

$10 Price

www.thaicurrysimple.com

**Pan-Asian
Coffee**
Casual restaurant

**International
District**
406 5th Ave. S.
(206) 327-4838

Hours
Mon–Sat
9:00am–4:00pm

Bar
None

Credit cards
None

Reservations
Not accepted

"Real Thai food: no kidding."

That's the introductory phrase on the Thai Curry Simple website. Leading off the menu? "No fish sauce."

Come again?

Let us get this straight: a restaurant that builds its reputation around the notion of *real* Thai food, then *advertises* that its disdain for the defining flavor element of Thai cuisine is so intense that it refuses to use it—*ever*.

There is the occasional appearance of an interesting Chinese-Thai dish on the special menu, like roast pork with egg or fish-ball noodles or khao man gai (steamed chicken) that bears some decent resemblance to Bangkok street food...but read that menu, and you might start to think that Thai Curry Simple does harbor some desire to make authentic Thai food. But then you notice that the garlic-black bean dipping sauce is more Chinese-American than anything else. Milk teas, tapioca pearls...wait a minute...is this place even Thai?

Move away from that label, and consider this as Seattle pan-Asian-American food, and then you start to get it more; it's actually, in fact, a cute coffeehouse of sorts. It's also a grocery store, and a dessert and breakfast place—Seattle through and through. Breakfast consists of sweet roti—pan-fried flatbread topped with condensed milk and banana, chocolate, or eggs.

Yes, there may be certain curries that come "Thai spicy" if you ask, and hot sauce made with "bird's eye chili." But our bird's-eye view of Thai Curry Simple: it's simply not Thai.

Thai Tom

Just ask the college kids—this is where you go for cheap Thai-American food in a hurry

Thai
Casual restaurant

University District
4543 University Way NE
(206) 548-9548

Hours
Mon–Sat
11:30am–9:00pm
Sun
noon–9:00pm

Bar
None

Credit cards
None

Reservations
Not accepted

Thai Tom is a bright spot in the midst of all the Ave's schlock, yet it's still kind of a gross and crowded hole in the wall. But the open kitchen here is awesome: sit at the bar next to the frightening flames and watch the unbelievable mess that the tiny kitchen becomes.

Thai Tom's menu doesn't look any different from the other eight million Thai joints in town, but the cooks here turn up the heat more than most, even in banal dishes like pad Thai and the ill-inspired "Swimming Rama" (chicken, spinach, bean sprouts, peanut sauce)—a two or three will be spicier than most places' fives. But that doesn't mean this food is authentic. It's still mostly Americanized recipes (bean sprouts? sweet peanut sauce?) without the tang or subtlety of authentic Thai cuisine, even if the searing chili is there. This is cursory food, made to order, yes, but without the obsessive care that yields the great balance of Thai food. Still, it's a notch above your average Thai-American slop.

If you can't snag a seat at the counter, just get takeout. Thai Tom gets packed with UW students, and the waits aren't worth a sit-down in this hot and loud place. Take-out also minimizes your time with the waitstaff, who have a reputation for being surly.

13 Coins

Mixed metaphors and mediocre food at this otherwordly disappointment

3.0 Food

8.5 Feel

$55 Price

www.13coins.com

The Rat Pack. Alice in Wonderland. What do the two possibly have in common? They have an equal hand in the carnival that is 13 Coins. Like Alice, white knee socks flashing in the reflection of perpetually rained-on concrete, you run through the no-man's-land of South Lake Union, following an equally inebriated muse to the only 24-hour restaurant that isn't a complete dump.

Once inside, you're swallowed by an outsized dark-leather padded booth for the Mad Hatter's Sadomasochistic Tea Party. Characters come and go: society ladies with opera afterglow, bros and brosefs, prematurely aged doyennes who will tell you how great Belltown was when it was "all artists," and South Seattle thugs. The bartenders trade barbs with the kitchen staff in seemingly authentic New York patois. Sinatra croons, you pick up a fork sturdy enough to kill a crocodile, and slip deliriously into the next allegory.

And that's when extortion of mafia-like proportions begins. 13 Coins charges black-market prices for everything, even veal piccata that's a rubbery medallion cloaked in thick breading and drizzled in a gloopy sour lemon and caper sauce, or a "Philadelphia steak sandwich" that would hopefully be rewarded with a punch in the throat in the real Philly (red wine? mozzarella?). Ah, fuggedaboutit.

American
Upmarket restaurant

South Lake Union
125 Boren Ave. N.
(206) 682–2513

South Seattle
18000 International Blvd.
(206) 243-9500

Hours
24 hours
Hours vary by location

Bar
Beer, wine, liquor

Credit cards
Visa, MC, AmEx

Reservations
Accepted

Features
Date-friendly
Live music

35th Street Bistro

If Goldilocks' porridge were a French-inspired locavore bistro

www.35bistro.com

French
Upmarket restaurant

Fremont
709 N. 35th St.
(206) 547-9850

Hours
Tue–Thu
11:00am–9:00pm
Fri–Sat
11:00am–10:00pm
Sun
11:00am–9:00pm

Bar
Beer, wine, liquor

Credit cards
Visa, MC, AmEx

Reservations
Accepted

Features
Brunch
Outdoor dining

After going through more changes than the quickly morphing neighborhood around it, the 35th Street Bistro may finally have settled into its "just right" phase. The space, which includes a lovely lighted tree in the middle of the room and a cozy corner bar, is neither too fancy nor too casual—the staff is friendly, but if you try to stroll in underdressed at dinner, you might be told that the empty room before you is completely booked.

The fare, as the moneyed Fremont faction would demand, focuses on local, organic and artisanal ingredients. In summer, for example, everything is well garnished by the berry harvests. One of our favorite dishes is a simple roast free-range chicken, accompanied by some sort of seasonal side dish like a root vegetable purée.

The local focus doesn't work as well on the drink menu. The wine list is serviceable, but its predominantly Northwest and domestic wines seem to contradict the Mediterranean-French message the bistro tries so hard to push. There are lots of fancy, hoppy selections on the beer list, but it would be nice to have more pale, refreshing options available, especially since this place serves lunch and brunch.

Thoa's

Don't let the burgers blind you—there's some good Vietnamese food here

6.5 Food
7.0 Feel

$40 Price

www.thoaseattle.com

Vietnamese Sandwiches
Casual restaurant

Downtown
96 Union St.
(206) 344-8088

Hours
Mon–Thu
11:30am–3:00pm
4:00pm–9:30pm
Fri
11:00am–3:00pm
4:00pm–10:00pm
Sat
noon–3:00pm
4:00pm–10:00pm
Sun
noon–3:00pm
4:00pm–9:30pm

Bar
Beer, wine, liquor, BYO

Credit cards
Visa, MC, AmEx

Reservations
Accepted

Features
Outdoor dining

Thoa's made a nearly seamless transition from an upscale Hawaiian restaurant to an upscale Vietnamese restaurant. (You can't say that about many places.) It was almost a little too seamless, maybe, as many patrons have yet to wean themselves off the teriyaki burgers that are still offered at happy hour.

That's a shame, because Thoa's modern take on Vietnamese includes some lesser-known dishes and some great fusion dishes, like the Vietnamese version of steak frites, with steak, onions, bell peppers, and fries happily co-mingling.

If you can avoid Thoa's experiments, like "summer rolls" laced with mango or chile-lime dipping sauce, you can find some more focused food here: lemongrass Penn Cove clams, very competent banh mi, green papaya salad, and pho, although even these things can sometimes sport unfamiliar herbs like flat chives or Vietnamese coriander (all helpfully defined in the menu's glossary).

The restaurant still has a vague islander theme, sort of upscale tiki with a few Vietnamese cues thrown in. Too bad it just barely misses out on a great water view. It's a pleasant place to dine, but be aware that the bar area, which fills up for happy hour, can feel a bit too young and raucous for an evening meal.

<table>
<tr><td>**7.0**
Food</td><td>**7.5**
Feel</td></tr>
<tr><td>**$40**
Price</td><td>**7.0**
Wine</td></tr>
</table>

Tidbit

Mediterranean nibbles and a great neighborhood vibe

www.tidbitbistro.com

Spanish Italian
Casual restaurant

Capitol Hill
1401 Broadway
(206) 323-0840

Hours
Mon
11:00am–4:00pm
5:00pm–9:00pm

Tue–Thu
11:00am–4:00pm
5:00pm–9:30pm

Fri
11:00am–4:00pm
5:00pm–10:00pm

Sat
5:00pm–10:00pm

Sun
5:00pm–9:00pm

Bar
Beer, wine, liquor

Credit cards
Visa, MC, AmEx

Reservations
Accepted

Features
Date-friendly
Veg-friendly

True to its name, Tidbit is best for tapas or happy-hour sampling. The Italian and Spanish dishes, which are refreshingly simple and free of fusion flourishes, are skillfully made but ultimately more satisfying in small portions over a few glasses of something or other (there are grappa and sambuca flights, but we can't imagine pairing them with food). The wine list here is short, but tight, and there are numerous by-the-glass and happy hour options.

Tapas survey the hits from both countries, from marinated white anchovies to gnocchi with gorgonzola cream sauce. We recommend saffron-infused fried risotto cakes and rosemary-dusted sweet potato fries. Mains are serviceable but pasta-heavy; there's better pasta to be found on the Hill.

Tidbit deserves a pat on the back for is its vegan menu—it's pretty short, relying on unsurprising choices like eggplant fries, but to put any thought into vegan dining and gluten-free pasta options demonstrates an understanding of the needs of Capitol Hill's residents.

But boy, do they have their work cut out for them in their new space. The interior with dark woods and sherbet-orange curtains is pleasant enough and perfect for a boisterous happy hour crowd, but it's a strange space that's part of a QFC/Bartell's complex—an overlooked corner of the Hill next to a Great Clips.

Tilikum Place Café

Great pasta, great brunch, great space—this place deserves more accolades

8.5 Food
9.0 Feel

$50 Price

www.tilikumplacecafe.com

It's amazing that Tilikum Place has remained under the radar for more than two years—maybe it's because it reminds Seattleites of Tillicum Village, a touristy Native American "village" reached via Argosy Cruises. But Tilikum Place isn't peddling salmon bakes; it's serving satiny house-made pastas, baked beans with pliant pieces of smoky ham hock and maple sweetness, and inspired seafood mains like crisp-skinned halibut piled with chanterelles frizzled in butter and served with "Farrotto" (farro cooked risotto style) in a moat of orange-carrot sauce. Tilikum also serves one of the best brunches in the city; a must-try is the "Dutch Baby," stuffed with treats like pulled duck and sour cherries.

The designer must be in possession of a bag of magic fairy dust, because someone here actually got the sophisticated-yet-unassuming, vaguely-European-bistro feel just right. A few wooden tables and some banquette seating, a bar that's basically a big bookcase crammed with bottles, and vintage postcards creating an eye-level wallpaper border on white walls—Tilikum is a simple but supremely enticing space.

Modern
Casual restaurant

Queen Anne
407 Cedar St.
(206) 282-4830

Hours
Mon, Wed–Fri
11:00am–3:00pm
4:00pm–10:00pm
Sat–Sun
8:00am–3:00pm
4:00pm–10:00pm

Bar
Beer, wine, liquor

Credit cards
Visa, MC, AmEx

Reservations
Accepted

Features
Brunch
Date-friendly
Veg-friendly
Wi-Fi

Tilth

A trendsetter that's fallen behind its
copycats; inconsistency rules supreme here

www.tilthrestaurant.com

Modern
Upmarket restaurant

Wallingford
1411 N. 45th St.
(206) 633-0801

Hours
Mon–Thu
5:00pm–10:00pm
Fri
5:00pm–10:30pm
Sat
10:00am–2:00pm
5:00pm–10:30pm
Sun
10:00am–2:00pm
5:00pm–10:00pm

Bar
Beer, wine, liquor

Credit cards
Visa, MC, AmEx

Reservations
Accepted

Features
Brunch
Date-friendly
Outdoor dining
Veg-friendly

We can't quite understand the amount of hype
this place has received. With so many
restaurants at the same price point adhering to
the local, seasonal mantra, Tilth fails to
differentiate itself in the most important way—
what actually makes it onto the plate.

Tilth is old enough to have worked out the
kinks, yet the food is still hit-or-miss. The
miniature duck burgers are sometimes a
highlight, sometimes overcooked and dry,
sometimes haphazardly seasonal. On the other
hand, something as simple as a carrot risotto
may, on a particular visit, be jaw-droppingly
good. Pork preparations are usually strong (Tilth
helped set in motion the pork-belly craze), and
vegetarians will be happy, as salads and
seasonal vegetable dishes are appropriately
fresh and flavorful. Tasting menus show off
Tilth's talent at picking good wine pairings.

In context of the overall dining scene, Tilth is
still doing a lot right. When directly compared to
some of its newer peers, however, it just doesn't
seem like that big of a deal. One thing it does
still have going for it is a very charming space,
on the bottom floor of a scallion-green cottage.
The acoustics are terrible, so the restaurant can
be very noisy when full, but otherwise it's the
epitome of dining in someone's sunny dream
home.

The Tin Table

Not a destination restaurant, but a fun, old-school place for drinks and small plates

7.0	8.0
Food	Feel

$50	8.0
Price	Wine

www.thetintable.com

The Tin Table is owned by Century Ballroom. The doors to Century are always wide open, so when class is in session or a dance night is in full swing, the landing between the ballroom and restaurant is a type of limbo—the swirling cacophony of dancers to the left, the low-key swank of the lounge to the right.

The Tin Table has kept the details of the historic Odd Fellows building intact—dark wood bars and tables let the exposed brick, wood floors, and beamed ceiling be the focal points. It's the kind of nondescript swank that attracts a nice mix of age groups.

This is not the place to find the most up-to-date haute cuisine or to fawn over signature dishes, but the kitchen doesn't seem to have an off night. We recommend nibbling, sharing, and having a few cocktails rather than ordering a bigger plate of steak frites or pan-seared halibut. The fries and fish tacos are recommended, as are the burger and any of the seasonal vegetable plates.

Drinking is a must here: solid wine list, great bubbly (including a Willamette Valley sparkling wine flight), and excellent specialty cocktails of simple, often citrusy concoctions like the Moscow Mule (vodka, lime juice and ginger beer). And in contravention of the thesis of this paragraph, they'll also make creative mocktails for teetotalers.

Modern
Upmarket restaurant

Capitol Hill
915 E. Pine St.
(206) 320-8458

Hours
Tue–Thu
4:00pm–1:00am
Fri–Sun
3:00pm–1:00am

Bar
Beer, wine, liquor

Credit cards
Visa, MC

Reservations
Accepted

Features
Good cocktails
Veg-friendly

7.5 | 6.0
Food | Feel

$10
Price

Ton Kiang

Some of the best barbecued duck in the I.D., with delicious chicken and pork belly, too

Chinese
Casual restaurant

International District
668 S. Weller St.
(206) 622-3388

Hours
Daily
9:00am–9:00pm

Bar
None

Credit cards
Visa, MC

If the barbecued duck here isn't the closest thing to what you'd find in Hong Kong, it's at the very least about the closest thing to the best Chinese fast-food joints of British Columbia—a comparable compliment.

This is the type of tiny hole in the wall where, after you order your whole duck (or half or quarter portions), you can watch as the chef unhooks a bird from the window display and chops it up.

If you bother to read the white boards after ordering the duck, the best dishes are the poached free-range chicken (be sure to specify free-range, as there two types of chicken) with spicy ginger-scallion oil and the barbecued roast pork belly.

The couple that runs Ton Kiang is very sweet, and will even steer you toward the better offerings of the day so that you get something a little more nuanced than a pound of pork belly.

Toulouse Petit

A bit contrived, but Creole food this serious
is worth the suspension of disbelief

8.0	8.0
Food	Feel

$50	8.0
Price	Wine

www.toulousepetit.com

Toulouse Petit creates as much of a French
Quarter vibe as is possible in Queen Anne. The
large, modern loft space has great floor-to-
ceiling windows, plush booths, some ridiculous
number of glass and ceramic tiles, and gorgeous
custom-built wood tables, but it still feels a little
like a movie set.

The food is much more inspired. The Creole
menu ranges from light and springy to
sumptuous. Oysters Rockefeller are prepared
using Pacific oysters, spinach purée, cheese,
cream, and lots of bacon chunks—they're rich,
elegant and better than the version you can get
at Antoine's in New Orleans, where the dish
was invented. There's also a wonderful version
of "Crab Maison," with blue crab with
tarragon-chive ravigote on top of scrumptious
fried green tomatoes. Jambalaya and crawfish
étouffée are equally well executed, and there's a
fun section of "Curiosities," like fried gator and
Helix snails. In fact, the only Louisiana standard
Toulouse Petit doesn't do well is beignets. The
solid wine list has lots of good food-friendly
choices, but not many bottles that one would
want to have by without a meal.

The menu is really too big, and the drawbacks
of the bloated menu are evidenced by servers
who don't seem very knowledgeable and
courses that are not well timed—they're just
delivered whenever the kitchen manages to get
them through the line. That said, the little-bit-
of-everything approach is always welcome at
the fabulous breakfast, which is one of the best
deals in town.

Southern
Upmarket restaurant

Queen Anne
601 Queen Anne Ave.
N.
(206) 432-9069

Hours
Daily
9:00am–3:00pm
5:30pm–1:00am

Bar
Beer, wine, liquor

Credit cards
Visa, MC, AmEx

Reservations
Accepted

Travelers Tea Company

Kitsch, authenticity, veg-friendliness, and value all in one darling spot

www.travelersteaco.com

Indian
Café

Capitol Hill
501 E. Pine St.
(206) 329-6260

Hours
Tue–Thu
11:30am–3:00pm
Fri–Sat
11:30am–3:00pm
5:00pm–8:00pm
Sun
noon–3:00pm
5:00pm–8:00pm

Bar
None

Credit cards
Visa, MC, AmEx

Features
Veg-friendly

Unless you're the type of person who carries your yoga mat everywhere and works the words "transcendent" and "Nepal" into every conversation, you probably wouldn't know that there's a very good café crammed into Travelers Tea Company, a shop that sells East Asian goods as envisioned by someone whose most prized possessions are a dog-eared Lonely Planet guide and a copy of *Monsoon Wedding*. Go past the Bollywood posters, the essential oils, and the figurines of Hindu gods, and you'll find a few café tables adjacent to the windows.

Travelers has some of the best (vegetarian) Indian food in the city and offers one of the best cheap lunches on the Hill. The rice bowl is our favorite; it changes daily but is normally topped with chutney and curried vegetables or beans. They also serve thalis that include dal and raita, two veggie dishes (for example, green spinach-potato dumplings in red curry), another side salad, basmati rice, and chutney. If you're a vegan, they will adjust most dishes for you with no fuss, with the exception perhaps of the one crossover dish: naan pizza (garlic naan topped with green chutney, Monterey Jack, tomatoes, and red onions). Chai here is cheaper than at any of the neighborhood's coffeeshops, and there's a long list of sweets to go with it.

Trellis

This is how you do farm-to-table—hotel or no hotel

9.0 Food
8.0 Feel

$60 Price

www.heathmankirkland.com/html/trellis-restaurant.asp

Trellis is as farm-to-table as it gets: Chef Brian Scheehser's menu is dictated by what he harvests from his own farm, which is just a few miles from the restaurant. What his own farm doesn't provide, Scheehser gets from other local purveyors.

The chef has a light hand even with typically heavy dishes: veal osso buco is brightened by charred tomatoes. The lobster jus accompanying a piece of seared sea bass is delicate enough to be sipped like soup. Lamb carpaccio is a must to start out the meal, and any simple salad is likely to have been picked only a few hours before it ended up on your plate; its presentation is beautiful, with vibrant vegetables giving dishes the color usually provided by squirts of superfluous neon-colored sauces—we've never seen grilled onions look so good on their own.

Trellis's location in the Heathman is a tad regrettable. Yes, it means you have the option of retiring to a comfy room when you're done feasting. But no matter how hard they try, hotel restaurants can't fully rid themselves of the hotel taint. Although Trellis does a good job of evoking thoughts of the European countryside with its different colored and textured woods and rustic bouquets, it still has a blandly upscale patina, which seems out of place next to food that's so deeply connected to the earth.

Modern
Upmarket restaurant

Eastside
220 Kirkland Ave.
(425) 284-5900

Hours
Mon–Thu
6:00am–2:00pm
5:00pm–9:00pm
Fri–Sat
6:00am–2:00pm
5:00pm–10:00pm
Sun
6:00am–2:00pm
4:00pm–9:00pm

Bar
Beer, wine, liquor

Credit cards
Visa, MC, AmEx

Reservations
Accepted

Features
Brunch
Date-friendly
Outdoor dining

Trophy Cupcakes

Probably the best cupcakes in Seattle

www.trophycupcakes.com

Sweets
Counter service

Wallingford
1815 N. 45th St.
(206) 632-7020

University District
2612 NE Village Ln.
(206) 395-2255

Bellevue
The Bravern, 700 110
Ave. NE
(206) 632-7020

Hours
Mon–Fri
8:00am–8:00pm
Sat
8:30am–8:00pm
Sun
8:30am–5:00pm
Hours vary by location

Bar
None

Credit cards
Visa, MC, AmEx

Features
Kid-friendly
Outdoor dining

With its old-timey candy store motif, all turquoise accents, and brown-candy-striped awnings, Trophy hits you with the adorable right away and doesn't let up. These are picture-perfect cupcakes, often with cute names (like the "Hummingbird") and concepts (like varieties that recreate a PB&J sandwich, snickerdoodles, or Girl Scout Samoas).

Rich concoctions like lemon cake with coconut butter cream topped with coconut shavings or carrot-walnut cake with cream cheese frosting can require two sittings to finish—unless you're into immediate post-meal waves of shame and nausea. Although frostings generally have some nice stiffness that saves them from being too gooey or syrupy, they're still pretty heavy and sweet—the peanut butter frosting, though delicious, has the kind of consistency that painfully adheres itself to our cavities. Clearly, Trophy knows its way around the arty cupcake, and the chai cardamom variety has no equal in the city.

Tsukushinbo

Ramen Friday: the reason to visit this place
that's a bit snazzier than its I.D. cousins

8.0 Food

6.0 Feel

$25 Price

Japanese
Casual restaurant

International District
515 S. Main St.
(206) 467-4004

Hours
Mon
6:00pm–10:00pm
Tue–Fri
11:45am–2:00pm
6:00pm–10:00pm
Sat
6:00pm–10:00pm

Bar
Beer, wine

Credit cards
Visa, MC, AmEx

Reservations
Not accepted

Tsukushinbo is a gem no matter what—
especially in light of the steady disappearance of
Japanese restaurants in the I.D.—but the main
reason to come here is Ramen Friday.

Once a week, Tsukushinbo makes the shoyu
(soy sauce-based) broth for ramen, and the
limited number of bowls go quickly as soon as
the place opens for lunch. This is one of very
few places that serves this type of broth (versus
the more popular pork-bone variety); the
noodles are also exceptional, similar to what
you'd find in Japan.

On other days of the week, you can expect
decent sushi (ask if they're doing anything
aburi-style), good tempura, udon, and donburi.
Tsukushinbo offers great value at both lunch
and dinner—the ramen comes with rice and
gyoza.

Although this might be the worst looking of
the remaining Japanese restaurants in the I.D.,
lining up some pretty sake bottles on a shelf can
only do so much for a space. Yet somehow, it's
still a pleasant and inviting place for a meal, and
when you're jousting for a table on Ramen
Fridays, at least you know you're in on
something special.

<table>
<tr><td>8.0
Food</td><td>6.5
Feel</td></tr>
</table>

Tutta Bella

Highly acclaimed pizza that sometimes justifies the hype

$35	7.0
Price	Wine

www.tuttabellapizza.com

Pizza
Casual restaurant

Columbia City
4918 Rainier Ave. S.
(206) 721-3501

Eastside
715 NW Gilman Blvd.
(425) 391-6838

South Lake Union
2200 Westlake Ave.
(206) 624-4422

Wallingford
4411 Stone Way N.
(206) 633-3800

Hours
Sun–Thu
11:00am–10:00pm
Fri–Sat
11:00am–11:00pm

Bar
Beer, wine, liquor, BYO

Credit cards
Visa, MC, AmEx

Reservations
Accepted

Features
Kid-friendly
Live music
Outdoor dining
Veg-friendly

What a coup for local pizza chain Tutta Bella. It was recently named "2010 Independent Pizzeria of the Year" by *Pizza Today* magazine. (We must have lost that issue amidst our piles of *Teriyaki Tomorrow* and *Pho-rever Young* magazines.) And immediately afterward, Tutta Bella's founder was summoned to meet Barack Obama during his visit to Seattle. So is the pizza truly of presidential quality?

We want to say yes, especially as the Tutta Bella empire grows in the area. Pizzas range from a cheese-less Napoletana and the classic "Regina Margherita" (translation: margherita) to pies with goat cheese, fig, and other fresh toppings. But while Tutta Bella has its devoted fans, some of our panelists have had forgettable pizzas, complaining of consistently soggy crusts, while others have had more luck. Keep in mind that the cracker-thin crust some associate with Naples is in fact a more Roman style of pizza; the real Naples crust is thicker, to some people's surprise, and, to a certain degree, soggier. The basic margherita has shown to be best at defeating sogginess, as it has fewer ingredients to weigh it down with moisture.

This is a place that takes pride in protecting the DOC certification granted to it by the Associazione Verace Pizza Napoletana, so make sure to behold the wood ovens amidst the hustle and bustle of these shops.

If this pizza is your style, you can enjoy one with a salad and a beer, followed by some gelato, an Attibassi espresso, and finally a selection from the extensive grappa list.

Umi Sake House

Hopping happy hour sake stop where the focus is on the libations, not the fish

www.umisakehouse.com

6.0 Food | **8.0** Feel

$50 Price

Japanese
Upmarket restaurant

Belltown
2230 1st Ave.
(206) 374-8717

Hours
Daily
4:00pm–midnight

Bar
Beer, wine, liquor

Credit cards
Visa, MC, AmEx

Reservations
Accepted

Of all the decorating hijinks perpetrated in Belltown, Umi's take on an upscale Japanese sake house is the best realized. It's a maze of rooms: a front bar, a main dining room with the sushi bar in the center, an atrium filled with real trees, and a few tatami rooms. There's a dizzying variety of seating options, including booths, sofas, and bar-height stools. The zen touches are neither hokey nor too prolific; the restaurant is Belltown sexy in a few spots, but simple and comfortable enough to attract diners in comfortable shoes.

Happy hour is a terrific value and the best way to try Umi if you're not into fancy rolls. Unlike at most sushi happy hours, the dishes here are the standard sizes, and there's a good selection of simple rolls and sashimi plates (which, on the regular menu, are a bit overpriced).

It's hard to get behind a menu that includes such sushi-roll abominations as the "Tropical Paradise" (salmon, strawberry, avocado, tobiko, and cucumber wrapped in tuna and mango, and served with blueberry sauce). Umi also serves more traditional snacks like yakisoba, garlic short ribs, and a spicy crab soup that's an incredible cold remedy. Purists probably stopped reading at "Tropical Paradise," but there's something for everyone here, and in its better moments, Umi is great fun, especially for large groups.

Ventana

With platings like these, the Spanish word for "mishmash" is a more fitting moniker

www.ventanaseattle.com

Modern
Upmarket restaurant

Belltown
323 1st Ave.
(206) 441-4789

Hours
Daily
4:30pm–midnight

Bar
Beer, wine, liquor

Credit cards
Visa, MC, AmEx

Reservations
Accepted

Features
Date-friendly

Ventana bears two trusted hallmarks of mediocre Seattle dining—views of Elliott Bay and/or Puget Sound and a small plates menu with no provenance—and does nothing to disprove that these elements tend to damn downtown restaurants.

The large space is innocuously contemporary, with dark brown leather banquettes, glass-topped wood tables, and silver pendant light fixtures, but it's also a little too big and sparse. The big ventanas (windows) do frame a nice view, but unless it's the middle of summer, if you show up here late enough to actually be in the company of other patrons, it's going to be too dark to enjoy it anyway.

There are often too many elements on each plate coming out of this kitchen, making a mess of what could be simple Northwest fusion comfort food. The "Ventana Burger" is not only stuffed with a chili relleno and cheese and draped with bacon and escarole, but it also comes with a goat cheese dressing. Occasionally, one or two plates really come together—if you see duck on the menu, it's probably a safe bet—but the food is simply too inconsistent (and at times, not particularly carefully cooked) for this spot to rise above average.

On a positive note, this is a fine place for a happy hour cocktail, or a wine from the plonk-free list, and the three-course set meal is a good way to hedge your bets.

Veraci Pizza

Neapolitan slices from applewood-fired ovens—nothing wrong with that

www.veracipizza.com

7.5 Food

6.0 Feel

$25 Price

Veraci offers a rarity: Neapolitan-style pizza by the slice. (Most Seattle pizza joints pick one side of the fence or the other: full Neapolitan pies or sloppy standard slices.)

The crust is ultra-thin, perhaps thinner than the real Naples style, with minimum char but a nice smoky flavor. The classic three-cheese and margherita pizzas really let the crust and slightly spicy sauce shine, but Veraci also offers some solid toppings. Seasonal vegetables (zucchini, yellow squash, and spinach, for example) often find their way into the mix, as do piles of cured meats and sausages from CasCoppio Brothers, a local Ballard company.

The space used to be occupied by a Domino's Pizza, so the folks at Veraci didn't have a good starting point as far as décor or ambience. Still, they've managed to make the family-friendly space comfortable, if a bit small. We prefer take-out, or checking the website to track down Veraci at local farmers' markets, where they bust out a wood-fired oven on wheels.

Pizza
Counter service

Ballard
500 NW Market St.
(206) 525-1813

Hours
Wed–Mon
11:00am–9:00pm

Bar
Beer, wine

Credit cards
Visa, MC

Reservations
Not accepted

Features
Kid-friendly
Veg-friendly

Via Tribunali

Real DOC pizza that's boosted further by
solid appetizers

www.viatribunali.net

Pizza
Casual restaurant

Capitol Hill
913 E. Pike St.
(206) 322-9234

Belltown
2200 2nd Ave.
(206) 441-4618

Fremont
4303 Fremont Ave. N.
(206) 547-2144

More locations
and features at
fearlesscritic.com

Hours
Mon–Fri
5:00pm–midnight
Sat–Sun
5:00pm–1:00am
Hours vary by location

Bar
Beer, wine, liquor

Credit cards
Visa, MC, AmEx

Reservations
Not accepted

Features
Veg-friendly

Via Tribunali's wood-fired pizzas are not for
everyone. The vaunted Margherita DOC pizza,
for all its fanfare and EU certifications, has a
floppy crust, thin tomato sauce, and huge
rubbery pools of melted buffalo mozzarella.
Now, some defend this style—buffalo
mozzarella naturally has a lot of moisture that
can sog out a crust—while some deride it,
claiming that only fior di latte (cow's milk
mozzarella) should be used. They've got that
here, too, so you can compare and contrast. The
lasagne pizza, with chunks of ham and tangy
ricotta, is a little more complex, but such
creations still seem to fall flat compared to what
Serious Pie and others are turning out.
Fortunately, happy hour offers discounted pizze,
so you can give Via Tribunali's pies a taste while
saving room for the stuff they do well.

Salads are pretty standard in construction, but
good, especially the "Tricolore." The starter of
acciughe marinate is outstanding—it's an entire
bowl full of white anchovies in olive oil and
lemon juice. There are a few calzones, too, but
they're nothing special.

The wine list—all Italian—is excellent, and
more importantly, the light style of many of the
wines is particularly well matched to pizza
(which really matches best with beers). Most Via
Tribunali branches are dark and moody, though
definitely not elegant or spiffy. The Capitol Hill
location is goth-ish inside, with ominous heavy
chandeliers, stained glass, and marble—nothing
(the crowd, space, cuisine) seems to match up
here. The other locations are a little homier.

Viengthong

Food from Laos that's neither Laos-y nor overly adulterated for the American palate

8.5 Food
4.0 Feel

$25 Price

In a city saturated with Thai restaurants, here's one with a twist. A bit off the beaten path close to where MLK hits Rainier, Viengthong offers a mixed menu of Thai and Laotian fare.

Sure, you can get pad Thai here, but you shouldn't. This is a place to sample some specialties from Laos. We especially recommend the perfect trio: barbecued chicken and som tam (green papaya salad), which are the perfect accompaniments to the white sticky rice which comes in cute little bamboo baskets. Regional specialties from Northern Thailand are also stars here. Make sure to try any of the larb—salads of ground meat with fish sauce, chili, and mint.

Despite some token colorful decorations, Viengthong is a bit dingy. The workers, who seem somewhat reluctant to be there, add to the dark mood. One of our panelists has made it a mission to try to get the waitress with the floor-length hair to smile. Mission unaccomplished. But the food will make *you* smile—especially if you come with an open mind to spice, sourness, fermented shrimp paste, and even crab shells (if you don't know what we mean, try to get your hands on some authentic tam mak hoong with crab).

Thai
Laotian
Casual restaurant

Beacon Hill
2820 Martin Luther King
Jr. Way S.
(206) 725-3864

Hours
Tue–Thu
11:00am–8:00pm
Fri–Sat
11:00am–9:00pm
Sun
11:00am–8:00pm
Fri
5:00pm–10:00pm

Bar
Beer

Credit cards
None

Reservations
Not accepted

Vietnam Restaurant

Go-to pho in the northern neighborhoods, but where ambience is non-existent

www.phovietnams.com

Vietnamese
Casual restaurant

Ballard
7040 15th Ave. NW
(206) 783-4310

University District
4235 University Way NE
(260) 547-1709

Hours
Daily
10:00am–8:30pm

Bar
None

Credit cards
Visa, MC, AmEx

Reservations
Not accepted

If the I.D.'s outside your door, Vietnam Restaurant may not be worth a side trip. But above the Lake Washington ship canal, this minichain is one of the best options for pho. Vietnam is demonstrably better than Than Brothers—in fact, it reminds us of what Than Brothers used to be, and that's saying something.

The broth is rich and redolent of anise and the noodles are pliable but not mushy. Beef in its various forms is, of course, the way to go; try the pho tai, or the "everything" varieties. Naturally, the chicken pho is nothing great, but the vegetable-and-tofu version is surprisingly good for a place that otherwise relies so heavily on beefy goodness to give weight to the soup. Freshly made spring rolls and complimentary cream puffs help to round out a meal, and there are also bubble teas (not great) and Vietnamese coffee (better).

As far as feel goes…it's just a mom-and-pop pho joint. If the table's clean, that's about as much as you can ask. Maybe wait until you get home to go to the bathroom.

Vios

No-frills Greek that's neither gyros nor diner
nor unnecessarily Northwested

7.5	**7.0**
Food	Feel

$35	**8.5**
Price	Wine

www.vioscafe.com

The lamb slider craze has to end eventually, at
which time this easily mishandled meat will go
back into the faithful hands of places like Vios.
Both the lamb souvlaki and the lamb burger are
excellent. You'll also find all the undiluted
classics here: great Greek salads, grilled meats, a
thorough selection of dips and tapenades like
taramosalata (salmon caviar spread), and more
elaborate braised meat mains, market fish
specials, and so on. The to-go menu is
extensive, and you can order hummus or tzatziki
by the pound. The branch at Third Place Books
in Ravenna serves a weekend brunch that is a
mix of standards (waffles, eggs and bacon on a
baguette) and Modern, vaguely Med-inspired
dishes (harissa pork hash; lemon-ricotta
pancakes).

The cafés are pretty basic, with sturdy
wooden tables and cheerful but unobtrusive
colors, but they manage that nice neighborhood
feel—the one where being surrounded by
families is endearing. This is thanks in part to
each café having a designated, well-cordoned-
off play area for kids.

Vios can easily become a regular spot to duck
in for a bite and a beer or glass of wine. Mad
props for the all-Greek wine list—it's vast by the
Greek-wine standards of the Pacific Northwest,
and its prices are eminently reasonable (few
bottles over $40 and many interesting choices
hovering around $30). The world's oldest wine
region deserves this kind of respect.

Greek
Casual restaurant

Capitol Hill
903 19th Ave. E.
(206) 329-3236

Ravenna
Third Place Books, 6504
20th Ave. NE
(206) 525-5701

Hours
Tue–Sat
11:00am–9:00pm
Hours vary by location

Bar
Beer, wine

Credit cards
Visa, MC

Reservations
Accepted

Features
Brunch
Kid-friendly
Veg-friendly

7.0 Food ## 7.5 Feel

$55 Price ## 8.0 Wine

Volterra

Outshone by newer places, but still doing fine with Northwesty Italian cuisine

www.volterrarestaurant.com

Italian
Upmarket restaurant

Ballard
5411 Ballard Ave. NW
(206) 789-5100

Hours
Mon–Thu
5:00pm–10:00pm
Fri
5:00pm–11:00pm
Sat
9:00am–2:00pm
5:00pm–11:00pm
Sun
9:00am–2:00pm
5:00pm–9:00pm

Bar
Beer, wine, liquor

Credit cards
Visa, MC, AmEx

Reservations
Accepted

Features
Brunch
Date-friendly
Outdoor dining
Veg-friendly

Volterra's allure is very site-specific. The owners got married in the eponymous hillside Tuscan village (you can see some of the photos of the blessed union on the walls), some of the fixtures were designed by artisans in Volterra, and the first appetizer is called "Bruschetta Volterrana."

The menu, however, is not quite as faithful to its provenance. A lot of complaints come from people lured into this restaurant with the promise of authentic Italian cooking. But any place at a certain price point with a picture of the chef on its homepage is likely to be engaged in some American meddling in the kitchen. Better pastas can be found around town, but the polenta with Fontina and wild mushrooms is delicious, and Volterra has some succulent meat and poultry dishes, like wild boar in gorgonzola sauce.

Another misconception about Volterra is that it's a great place for romance. If you try to propose in this place on a busy night, your partner may not hear you, but all of the people sitting two inches away from you will. The wine list has plenty of high-acid wines that will stand up well to hearty tomato-based Italian fare. Volterra's red walls and banquette seating make the place classy enough for a special occasion, but more like an old-friend-in-from-out-of-town occasion. The patio is actually our favorite spot, and the preferred spot for brunch (which is solid but not very Italian; think challah French toast. Not that there's anything wrong with that.

Volunteer Park Café

A great breakfast spot if you can get
around the strollers

www.alwaysfreshgoodness.com

7.0	8.0
Food	Feel

$50	9.0
Price	Wine

It's unfortunate that dinner here isn't as
consistent or good as breakfast or lunch,
because the evening is the only time this place is
bearable. Earlier, especially on weekends, the
place is overrun with North Capitol Hill
families—you'll be tripping over strollers,
squeezing past yoga moms, and you won't be
able to find a seat once you're inside. But when
it's calmer, this place is quite sweet, with its
checkered curtains and communal farm table—
it feels like it should be serving sweet tea in a
Southern state.

Baked goods are decadent and delicious.
Panini—particularly bacon and egg with gruyère
or apple brie with lavender honey—are also very
good, though you should opt for croissants, as
the baguettes are sometimes a bit too chewy.
The quiches are fine, though not particularly rich
or complex. The wine list digs deep to feature
some interesting producers.

At lunch, the standouts are the beef brisket
sloppy Joe and the chicken salad sandwich with
apple slices. Dinner mains are simple, too, some
embracing the rustic (beef brisket with fontina
polenta or English pea risotto), some taking an
index card from grandma's recipe box (pork and
beans, mini chicken pot pie).

Modern American Breads
Casual restaurant

Capitol Hill
1501 17th Ave. E.
(206) 328-3155

Hours
Tue–Fri
7:00am–9:00pm
Sat
8:00am–9:00pm
Sun
8:00am–4:30pm

Bar
Beer, wine

Credit cards
Visa, MC

Reservations
Accepted

Features
Kid-friendly
Outdoor dining

6.5 | 6.5
Food | Feel

$45
Price

Wabi Sabi

Pricey, sleek, ambitious, and the 'hood's best choice, for now, in a so-so lineup

www.wabisabicolumbiacity.com

Japanese
Casual restaurant

Beacon Hill
4909 Rainier Ave. S.
(206) 721-0212

Hours
Mon
4:30pm–9:30pm
Tue–Thu
noon–2:30pm
4:30pm–9:30pm
Fri–Sat
noon–2:30pm
4:30pm–11:00pm
Sun
4:30pm–9:00pm

Bar
Beer, wine, liquor, BYO

Credit cards
Visa, MC, AmEx

Reservations
Not accepted

Wabi Sabi is the poster child for Columbia City's growing pains. Before light rail connected it to downtown, Columbia City was difficult to reach, so it had a few good restaurants to serve its residents but nothing striving to be a dining destination. Wabi Sabi is part of the second wave: a restaurant with ambition, coming in to fill a gap in a rapidly growing and gentrifying area. So far, its reception has been lukewarm at best.

For less than a plate of edamame, you can take the light rail to one of the city's best sushi restaurants, so Wabi Sabi had better be careful with the pricing. The menu is split between safe—California rolls, agedashi tofu, and Bento boxes—and more innovative, like the "Five Spice Tuna Tataki."

Here, simple is best. The best thing to do here is to sit at the counter, tell the chef exactly how much you're willing to spend, and let him put together a sort of poor man's omakase. If you do instead order off the menu, try the Kumamoto oysters with ponzu sauce, standbys like hamachi or scallops, or the fresh catch of the day.

The draw at Wabi Sabi is the sleek layout of the room, with funky killer fish artwork on the walls, blond wooden booths against exposed brick, and a wraparound bar built in anticipation of future swillers of sake and ginger-lime mojitos.

Waterfront Grill

You'll pay a lot for this view, in both dollar
and opportunity-cost-of-seafood terms

6.0	8.0
Food	Feel

$85	9.0
Price	Wine

www.waterfrontpier70.com

Waterfront is beautifully situated on Pier 70,
capitalizing on the belief that being eye-level
with the Puget Sound will make any seafood
dish taste better. But we've had mixed
experiences here. At times, Waterfront is among
the best seafood restaurants in the city,
featuring over-the-top feasts like the "Seafood
Bacchanalia," a tower for two of wild salmon,
lobster tail, sea scallops, wild prawns, and red
king crab legs. At other times, even that notable
offering is boring: pasty shellfish, watery and
flavorless flesh.

With Waterfront's kitchen being so
inconsistent, it's hard to justify the heavyweight
hit to the pocketbook (a "Thai-style" seafood
stew's price tag is just laughable, and lobster
tails or crab legs will put you way back). But
keep things simple—the more ingredients in a
dish, the shakier the results.

The place is huge and properly fancy for those
who like to throw money around, but it feels a
bit corporate and rather cold, as if a hotelier or
someone with an ice heart designed it—all
those white tablecloths and lavishly upholstered
booths are less impressive when they hover
above the sort of industrial carpeting you'd find
in a movie theater. The wine list has plenty of
lovely white bottles that will pair magnificently
with seafood. Do yourself a favor and save this
spot for warm weather when you can sit on the
patio and enjoy the water view without the
dining room to spoil it.

Seafood
Upmarket restaurant

Downtown
2801 Alaskan Way, Pier
70
(206) 956-9171

Hours
Daily
5:00pm–11:00pm

Bar
Beer, wine, liquor

Credit cards
Visa, MC, AmEx

Reservations
Accepted

Features
Date-friendly
Live music
Outdoor dining

Wild Ginger

Dated pan-Asian in a space of enduring
beauty and a wine list for the ages

www.wildginger.net

Pan-Asian
Upmarket restaurant

Bellevue
11020 NE 6th St.
(425) 495-8889

Downtown
1401 3rd Ave.
(206) 623-4450

Hours
Mon–Thu
11:30am–3:00pm
5:00pm–11:00pm
Fri
11:30am–3:00pm
5:00pm–midnight
Sat
11:00am–3:00pm
4:30pm–midnight
Sun
4:00pm–9:00pm
Hours vary by location

Bar
Beer, wine, liquor

Credit cards
Visa, MC, AmEx

Reservations
Accepted

Features
Brunch
Date-friendly

There was a time when Wild Ginger was one of
the most exciting restaurants in Seattle. But
those days are long gone, and it's now in its last
days of downtown disco—literally; the location
also cooks for Triple Door, the music club next
door. The restaurant itself, even today, is
impressive in its design: it's huge, with booths,
tables, lounge areas for happy-hour drinks, and
multiple bars on the ground floor, plus a cool
catwalk-like loft holding a few more tables. And
this remains one of few supremely busy places
in town that doesn't feel understaffed; service is
professional and efficient.

But the food feels as dated as its logo's
Orientalist font. Wild Ginger seems to have
textural dyslexia: kebabs are too dry, noodles
too wet and pasty. Curry sauces can be watery,
and dumplings gummy. The menu travels all
over the world in a seemingly endless series of
airport layovers—kung pao chicken, pad Thai,
dim sum, potstickers, satays. Points are awarded
for the attempt to add some "hawker
specialties" to the brunch dim sum menu, but
the dreaded pad Thai shows up there, too, so
they're not delving too far into the rich and
complex world of Asian street food.

Specialty cocktails are sweetly mediocre, but
then, just as you're about to write Wild Ginger
off totally, you open the wine list. It is a work of
profound beauty, elegance, and deep obsession,
with dazzling verticals of Alsatian and German
Rieslings that go well into the 1970s, yet are
priced lower than wine-store levels. This is more
than a wine list: it is a gift to the city.

The Zig Zag Café

Cocktails for the ages, and we forget the rest

6.0 Food | **9.0** Feel

$35 Price

www.zigzagseattle.com

What used to be a hidden gem on the Hill Climb (a set of stairs behind Pike Place Market) is now a perennial award-winner; most recently, Zig Zag nabbed the #1 spot on GQ's "25 Best Cocktail Bars in America."

It's the bar where everyone knows the bartender's name: Murray Stenson is a Seattle legend (his co-workers are pretty talented, too). The Zig Zag has a long list of specialty drinks with humorous names like "Satan's Soulpatch" (Bourbon, sweet and dry vermouth, Grand Marnier, and orange bitters) and the "Drink Without a Name" (vodka, Cointreau, green Chartreuse), but regulars know the best thing to do is let Murray and crew whip up something based on whatever you're craving. Whether the base is Bourbon or Lillet, you'll get a subtle drink free of the seasonal fruit juices and house-infused liquors so often abused by younger mixologists.

There's nothing gimmicky about the Zig Zag. It's not a speakeasy or an ultralounge. The room, though comfortable, isn't anything special: a few wooden bar stools, a few curved booths, chandeliers, and amber mood lighting. It attracts a diverse crowd: office workers, hipsters, Belltown clubgoers, firemen.

The short menu has bar snacks like olives, flatbread pizzas, sandwiches, and a few daily seafood specials. The food's satisfying if you need something to soak up the alcohol, and the kitchen sources from Pike Place, so everything is very fresh-tasting. But the best things here come in cocktail glasses, not on plates.

Modern
Bar

Downtown
1501 Western Ave.
(206) 625-1146

Hours
Daily
5:00pm–1:00am

Bar
Beer, wine, liquor

Credit cards
Visa, MC

Reservations
Accepted

Features
Date-friendly
Good cocktails
Outdoor dining

Zoka

Coffee and the sweet and savory things that so nicely accompany it

www.zokacoffee.com

Coffee
Sweets
Café

Green Lake
2200 N. 56th St.
(206) 545-4277

University District
2901 NE Blakeley St.
(206) 527-0990

Eastside
129 Central Way
(425) 284-1830

Hours
Daily
6:00am–10:00pm
Hours vary by location

Bar
None

Credit cards
Visa, MC

Features
Kid-friendly
Outdoor dining
Wi-Fi

Sinking into one of the oversized leather chairs, pushing the newspapers littered on the table for the appropriate section, and making sure your purse isn't being continuously rammed by an over-zealous stroller mom is part of the Zoka experience. It's a big, somewhat messy, totally comfortable coffeeshop—kind of like an extension of your living room.

The coffee here is reliably good; signature blends run the gamut of fruity and slightly acidic to full-bodied with tobacco and brown-sugar notes. Although the quiche, sandwich, and sweets selections have dwindled over the past couple years, you'll still find more choices here than your average Seattle brewhouse.

At lunch, the caprese sandwich is popular, as are the oversized cookies (try the chocolate truffle), massive wedges of banana cream pie, and "Zoka Bars" (essentially deliciously retro seven-layer bars). A few vegan selections, like the oat-y Jam Dots and vegan chocolate chip cookies, ensure happy eating and caffeinating for all.

Fearless Critic Index

Index